"*The Buddha and the Borderline* is a strikingly cai [illegible] account of the author's personal experiences of the effects of borderline personality disorder spanning more than two decades. Van Gelder is a very well informed, engaging, and talented writer. She reveals the multiple and complex symptoms of borderline disorder as manifested in her life with great honesty, revealing the devastating pain with moving and insightful vignettes that are tempered on occasion with a finely tuned sense of humor. This is a must-read for people with this disorder, their families and loved ones, and mental health professionals."

—Robert O. Friedel, MD, author of *Borderline Personality Disorder Demystified*

"*The Buddha and the Borderline* is a masterpiece. Kiera shares her road to recovery in a captivating way that brings a unique understanding to a confusing, challenging, and controversial disorder. Having the privilege to personally know Kiera, I applaud her on so many levels, least of all this must-read book. She is an inspiration to all who strive and hope for recovery from borderline personality disorder."

—Perry D. Hoffman Ph.D., president of the National Education Alliance for Borderline Personality Disorder (NEA-BPD)

"Kiera's book is destined to become a classic in the growing literature on borderline personality disorder. I expected to get a somber account of a transformation from suffering to enlightenment, but the book I read was not only entirely entertaining and revealing, but also had me up way past my bedtime in stitches. *The Buddha and the Borderline* is seriously funny, authentic, and sublime in its wisdom. The book embodies the Four Noble Truths of Buddhism and integrates the world of core unrelenting suffering with the world of freedom from suffering. Transcendent stuff."

—Blaise Aguirre, MD, medical director of the Adolescent Dialectical Behavior Therapy Residential Program at McLean Hospital in Belmont, MA

"Kiera creates a window into the soul of one coming to grips with severe mental illness. Fully exposed, she shows us the pain, pleasure, and finally, the redemption of the borderline experience. Her gripping story sheds new light upon one of the most misunderstood and stigmatized of all human conditions, and for that, I am deeply grateful. Her words will quite possibly be shocking to some, but will validate and comfort those with the disorder and those who are trying to understand them. Welcome to our world: the pain, shame, and pleasure, and then, finally, the insight and skill-building that leads to healing, love, and happiness. Kiera captures the experience brilliantly."

—Tami Green, internationally recognized speaker, life coach and advocate for those in recovery from mental illness.

"*The Buddha and the Borderline* is a gripping, authentic, and ultimately inspiring portrayal of one woman's triumph over borderline personality disorder. An intriguing, riveting, and compelling read, the depth and complexity of both character and story are to be savored. Kiera Van Gelder has shared the private depths of her heart and soul and, in doing so, has bestowed upon the reader a great and sacred gift."

—Roy Krawitz, author of *Borderline Personality Disorder: The Facts*

"A very educational and insightful look into the inner world of borderline personality disorder and its treatment. Kiera Van Gelder's witty tone and engaging journey brilliantly chronicles the dialectic of profound suffering and how that suffering can be transformed into a life worth living."

—A. J. Mahari, author of *Life Coach* and *Mental Health Coach*

"*The Buddha and the Borderline* by Kiera Van Gelder is captivating, literary, and insightful. Van Gelder's use of metaphor enhances the haunting nature of her journey through life. As I read the book, I recognized her pain, and cheered her on. Her insights led me to a better understanding of myself and the nature of borderline personality disorder."

—Lisa Dietz, owner of www.DBTSelfHelp.com

"Out of a profoundly painful experience, Kiera Van Gelder has written a brave and hopeful book exploring her recovery from borderline personality disorder. Kiera's story will undoubtedly touch countless lives and be a source of inspiration to those who have been diagnosed with borderline personality disorder, their families, and the mental health professionals who play a crucial role in the complex nexus of education, treatment, and support. *The Buddha and the Borderline* is a compelling and invaluable narrative for anyone wanting to learn more about the difficult, yet ultimately rewarding, process of recovery."

> —Amanda L. Smith, Florida Borderline Personality
> Disorder Association

"*The Buddha and the Borderline* is a cross between *Girl, Interrupted* and *Bridget Jones's Diary*. While reading it, I found myself admiring Kiera's talent for vividly describing borderline hopelessness and pain while keeping me laughing with her tales of life as a 'lonely and increasingly horny receptionist.' While this book has something for everyone, Kiera's detailed account of how she recovered from this deadly disorder will be enormously inspiring to people with borderline personality disorder and their family members."

> —Randi Kreger, author of *Stop Walking on Eggshells* and
> *The Stop Walking on Eggshells Workbook*

"Kiera Van Gelder's *The Buddha and the Borderline* is a remarkably clear, coherent, and candid description of the author's turbulent internal world and chaotic life, as well as a mental health system that can be inconsistent and contradictory. As she searches for a path to recovery, she finds that the way has not been well established and shares her journey of building the very road that she wishes to travel. This groundbreaking book provides a much-needed and highly personal example of how recovery can occur, making it a very generous and significant contribution to the field."

> —Seth R. Axelrod, Ph.D., associate professor in the department
> of psychiatry at Yale University School of Medicine

the buddha &
the borderline

my recovery from
borderline personality
disorder through
dialectical behavior
therapy, buddhism
& online dating

Kiera Van Gelder

New Harbinger Publications, Inc.

Publisher's Note

Distributed in Canada by Raincoast Books

Copyright © 2010 by Kiera Van Gelder
New Harbinger Publications, Inc.
5674 Shattuck Avenue
Oakland, CA 94609
www.newharbinger.com

Acquired by Catharine Sutker
Cover design by Amy Shoup
Edited by Jasmine Star

Library of Congress Cataloging-in-Publication Data

Van Gelder, Kiera.
The Buddha and the borderline : my recovery from borderline personality disorder through dialectical behavior therapy, Buddhism, and online dating / Kiera Van Gelder.
    p. cm.
Includes bibliographical references.
ISBN 978-1-57224-710-9
1. Borderline personality disorder. 2. Dialectical behavior therapy. 3. Meditation--Therapeutic use. I. Title.
RC569.5.B67V36 2010
616.85'852--dc22
                         2010011984

12 11 10   10 9 8 7 6 5 4 3 2 1   First printing

FSC
Mixed Sources
Product group from well-managed forests, controlled sources and recycled wood or fiber
Cert no. SW-COC-000952
www.fsc.org
© 1996 Forest Stewardship Council

This book is printed with soy ink.

To Raymond Hartman, Renee Rushnawitz, and Saul Rosenthal—
the other Three Jewels.

Contents

Part 2
Last Resort

Part 3
Shifts in Light

Part 4
Emergence

Part 5
Transformation of Suffering

Prologue (1985)

I am fifteen when I meet a boy named Jimmy at the summer arts program. We smoke hash in the graveyard at the far end of the Bennington campus. We dare each other to order margaritas at the local Mexican restaurant, and when we are actually served, share salty kisses over plates of rice and beans. I give him a blow job in the back of a class-room, and he says he has feelings for me but he doesn't know what they are. Jimmy is pale and wears eyeliner and is as close to a boyfriend as I've ever gotten. When he confesses he has a "real" girlfriend back in New York, I spend a long evening sniffing liquid paper out of a plastic bag. Passing out and waking up to the exploding lights in my head, I finally throw up my dinner.

I consider cutting off my pinkie finger and giving it to him. I'd go to the art studio where they have those paper cutters with three-foot blades. Lop it off, wrap it up. *Here. Look what you've done to me. You're leaving me, and taking me with you.* But I like my fingers. Even the some-what useless pinkies.

So instead I make myself bleed, as I've learned to do. The instru-ment can't be too sharp, or it will go too deep and sever important bits. It can't be so blunt as to be useless. I like the thin, flexible razor blades that can be taken off a disposable plastic shaver—ubiquitous and easy to remove from the plastic casing. I enjoy the slide of metal into giving skin. Each line eases the rage and sharpens the colors of the room. Regular cutting means you have to rotate the areas, so as not to overtax the skin too much: forearm, then wrist, then upper arm, then back to the forearm. After the razor passes over, there's a moment before the blood when the faintest film of clear liquid rises, as though the flesh itself is weeping for you. Then garnet beads of blood rise and elongate into the thin tracks you've laid between pain and release.

I wipe and blot the wounds with the calm patience that always follows the bloodletting and think, *I could paint with this. I could write with this.* I must have cut a lot—enough blood to fill five notebook pages with finger-painted words: "Please." "Don't leave me." "I need you." I put the wet pages on the floor to dry. In the morning, the large words are maroon and waxy, with my fingerprints captured at the beginning and end of each letter's stroke. The pages go into an envelope with Jimmy's name, and the letter is placed on his bed in the neighboring dorm. I have known him two weeks.

After lunch, I am pulled from poetry class by the counselor. In a degree-paneled office, the stack of papers sits on the desk like a thesis I must now defend. The counselor asks me why I'd do such a thing. I cannot explain it. I have no words. "Frantic efforts to avoid real or imagined abandonment" does not readily come to mind. And if this counselor sees borderline personality disorder, he doesn't say it.

He calls my mother. She drives to the campus and they talk. Then she goes back home.

I remain at the program but must agree to check in with the counselor during the last two weeks. He gives me back the blood letter, perhaps to remind me that it holds a part of myself that I am always inflicting on others, a part of myself I am always throwing away.

Years later I ask my mother, "What were you thinking when you drove away?"

She says, "Adolescence is always difficult; I thought maybe it was just a phase." She says, "I didn't know what to do; the whole thing was overwhelming." She says, "The counselor told me you would be okay."

The truth is, I have borderline personality disorder. But it will take many therapists, many diagnoses, many medications, and many treatments before a name is put to this suffering and I can start down the path to recovery.

This is the story of how it happened.

Borderline Personality Disorder:

A pervasive pattern of instability of interpersonal relationships, self-image, and affects, and marked impulsivity beginning by early adulthood and present in a variety of contexts, as indicated by five (or more) of the following:

1. Frantic efforts to avoid real or imagined abandonment;

2. A pattern of unstable and intense interpersonal relationships characterized by alternating between extremes of idealization and devaluation;

3. Identity disturbance: markedly and persistently unstable self-image or sense of self;

4. Impulsivity in at least two areas that are potentially self-damaging (e.g., spending, sex, substance abuse, reckless driving, binge eating);

5. Recurrent suicidal behavior, gestures, or threats, or self-mutilating behavior;

6. Affective instability due to a marked reactivity of mood (e.g., intense episodic dysphoria, irritability, or anxiety usually lasting a few hours and only rarely more than a few days);

7. Chronic feelings of emptiness;

8. Inappropriate, intense anger or difficulty controlling anger (e.g., frequent displays of temper, constant anger, recurrent physical fights);

9. Transient, stress-related paranoid ideation or severe dissociative symptoms.

Diagnostic and Statistical Manual of Mental Disorders (DSM-IV-TR; American Psychiatric Association 2000)

PART 1

Love Bird

1

Mentally Ill, Suicidal Drug Addict

Beginnings have never been too hard for me: to shape the words of a first line or to chose the right outfit—to pull off a good first act. For me, it's always after the entrance that things deteriorate, especially in relationships. Fifteen years after the episode with Jimmy, I've pulled myself together somewhat. No more drinking until I puke in men's laps. No more taking bottles of pills and being hospitalized. If you met me, you'd never suspect the suicide attempts, hospitalizations, and diagnoses. But if you saw me in a relationship, you'd know something isn't quite right. I'm always good in the beginning, but after that first flush of romance, my lipstick will be smeared like a clown's and I'll revert to the dismay of a child lost in the department store, curled up and wailing on the floor.

It's no different with Bennet, who I meet when I'm thirty. He's a musician and a carpenter, with a lanky body habitually clothed in jeans and T-shirts, his pointy hipster sideburns and flop of brown hair making him seem boyish, even though he's almost a decade older than I am. When we meet, I'm wearing a corset, a latex skirt, and black platform boots, which would be appropriate for a night club, but not the Narcotics Anonymous (NA) convention dance we're both attending. Bennet, however, isn't fazed—not by my outfit, and not when I say to him, "You know I'm fucked-up."

"We both are," he grins. "Who here *isn't* a mentally ill, suicidal drug addict?" He gestures around the auditorium. We leave the dance, walk through the parking lot, and end up on a small plot of grass with a single tree. We hold each other for an hour and kiss, and since we've discovered each other at NA, where it's often easy to mistake honesty for sanity, having sex seems like a reasonable thing to do.

It's a familiar bondage. As soon as he touches me, Bennet becomes my universal reference point. His body grounds me, and his voice brings me back from the various ledges I perch on. He seems okay with my need, but there is one serious complication, one fatal flaw that will eventually cause me so much pain I'll scream until I lose my voice: Alexis. Bennet's ex-girlfriend.

Alexis's name makes me think of electricity and axes and Greek goddesses. A heavy-lidded beauty, strongly opinionated, and smart, with a degree in film studies from art school, she plays the bass and wears combat boots, and, more to the point, not only was she Bennet's girlfriend for ten years, now that she's his ex, she *still lives with him*. Their apartment is in Lowell, an old Massachusetts mill town struggling to revive itself. Their place is filled with guitars, amplifiers, and art. Together, Alexis and Bennet own Bancha, a plump, colorful lovebird who lives in a wire cage suspended from the kitchen ceiling. Often, after the three of us eat dinner, Bennet or Alexis will open the cage and let Bancha frolic under a drizzling water faucet. She flies awkwardly around the kitchen and, landing on their shoulders, makes joyful little noises while she nuzzles their ears as though she has a wet nose instead of a razor-sharp beak. The beak, she reserves for me.

"Just stick out your finger and she'll climb onto it," Bennet advises more than once. Every time I try, Bancha sinks her beak into my finger, like a fishing hook catching a fat worm.

"Ooh, just look at how feisty she is," Bennet croons as I'm being skewered. I don't know what threatens me more—Alexis the Ex or Bancha the Bird. When I witness the three of them bonding in the kitchen, I want to throw knives. Instead, I let Bancha bite me, over and over. It takes the edge off the whole situation.

In my life, relationships are like rubber bands. They stretch and snap back so many times, but eventually something breaks and there's no way to repair the damage. I know that to keep Bennet, I have to control myself—not let my insecurity and pain stretch us too far. I really adore Bennet: his tenderness, his hardness. I stare at him with the doped eyes of desire and make him pull over on the side of the highway so we can have sex before he drops me off at an NA friend's house where I'm staying until I can find a job and a place of my own.

Bennet doesn't think it's odd that I don't have a place to live or a job. But to put things into perspective, we're both recovering addicts, steeped in a world of 12-step meetings, living "one day at a time" away from the liquids, pills, and powders that nearly killed us. Perks like homes and jobs, much less 401(k) plans, aren't the highest priority in our crowd. Staying alive is. This suits me fine, because despite being clean and sober for almost a decade, I'm still a mess. Something deeper than drugs, depression, or anxiety keeps destroying my life. By the time I meet Bennet, I've quit two teaching jobs, spent over six months in mental hospitals, been on a dozen medications, and seen even more therapists. I dropped out of high school, then out of college. I'm like a cat with nine lives: prep, punk, goth, hippie, hipster... My periodic breakdowns somehow coincide with shifts in musical taste, and they generally lead to more diagnoses: depression, anxiety, post-traumatic stress disorder (PTSD), alcoholism, and drug addiction.

Right now I call myself a recovering drug addict and alcoholic. I attend meetings almost every day. In 12-step communities, you're told that sanity comes from admitting that you're powerless over your addiction. You share the story of your downfall and honestly admit your faults, and they say you're only as sick as your secrets. And my dirty little secret? I am always on the verge of drowning, no matter how hard I work to keep myself afloat. And the only way I know to stay afloat— to survive—is to find a savior. Bennet, as it turns out, has a bit of a savior complex.

But then there's Alexis. I can barely say her name. Since I know how deeply insecure I am and what jealousy does to me, I must do my best to control it. From the start, Bennet insists that there's nothing but a strong friendship between him and Alexis anymore, and I try to believe him, but what proof do I have? Jealousy is an emotion that entirely consumes me, leaving only cinders of regret and shame. All summer, I douse it with reason and avoid mentally feeding the flames, but when I take a job early in the fall that requires traveling five days a week as an addictions educator, the dam finally breaks. Each night after lecturing to classrooms about the perils of drugs and alcohol, I retreat to my hotel room and dial Bennet's number, desperate to hear his voice. But of course, whenever I call, *she's* home. I know this because, inevitably, I hear her.

"Hey, Bennet," she shouts from the living room as I'm trying to get my boyfriend fix. "Where's my briefcase?"

He sighs like a tired husband. "Where you left it."

"Yeah, but *where?*" Bennet always apologizes when she interjects and pulls him away, but it's hardwired between them, this inevitable interchange. He can't say no when she says his name. Even if she's silent while Bennet and I talk, I envision the two of them all cozy at home together: having dinner, playing with Bancha. These images propel me into a ball on the bed, curled around my useless suffering and heaving with sobs. I believe Bennet is more devoted to Alexis than he is to me, and no amount of reasoning makes this go away.

Although Bennet does try reasoning with me, this only leads to fights. I'm the very image of self-possession at work, whether lecturing to an auditorium or running a workshop, but as soon as Bennet and I get on the phone or I drive over to see him, the smallest things trigger me: a glance between him and Alexis, the mention of a shared supermarket errand. I swallow my anger, but as soon as we we're alone with the door closed, it rises up in my throat like a burning coal I have to spit out. The words, once let loose, travel furiously: "You fucking bastard, you don't understand! You fucking bastard!" In an instant, I shift from a woman to a wild-haired girl kicking furniture to a balled-up weeping child on the bed, begging for a touch.

"This isn't about me and Alexis," Bennet insists. "You don't feel like you belong *anywhere.* You'd have the same kind of problem with me even if I lived alone."

When he says things like this, I get twisted up with confusion. My unshakable belief is that if he could prove he's more committed to me than he is to Alexis, I'd finally be okay. But I also know that Bennet is right. I've never felt like I belong—anywhere. Ever since I was a young girl, I've shaped myself into personas and ideals designed to entice others to love me. Now it's happening again with Bennet. I've ditched the fetish clothes and the nipple rings, painfully inserted a couple of months earlier at a tattoo parlor in New Hampshire, along with my tongue ring because he says they're gross. Now I wear jeans and T-shirts and Bennet's leather jacket. It feels like my life hangs in the balance of his affection—as though his heartbeat and skin, his voice and eyes, bring me back to myself. As though I don't exist without him.

The cycle, once started, is unstoppable. My jealousy and insecurity begin to devastate the relationship like a wrecking ball as I helplessly watch the slow-motion collapse of the building. The more upset I am, the more Bennet withdraws. And his retreat in the face of my desire spurs me to greater and greater levels of panic and fear. Yet the more I try to capture his attention, the less of him there is, so the cycle continues, with his absence propelling me back toward him with a force that borders on violence. We've been together only four months, and already he's stopped caressing me. The sex is a cement that will not dry and set. Sometimes I feel genuine hate for him, even as my need for him consumes me.

Late November is never a good time for me. My sense of being unmoored amplifies in the dark afternoons, and I long for bed no matter what hour of day it is. My job is grueling, with so much travel and public speaking every day. I've grown tired of telling my story about addiction over and over again. And my body is rebelling: tremors, profuse sweating, a racing heart, and a dry mouth every time I'm in front of a crowd—all signs that my "anxiety disorder" is full throttle. I call my doctor and he switches me to a newer antidepressant said to help with anxiety, but it's no match against my biology. In fact, every day I feel like I'm getting worse. Then, one night a group of students harasses me during a workshop on the dangers of marijuana, and I burst into tears in front of fifty high school seniors. I drive back to Lowell bawling and suicidal and quit the job the next day.

Three days later I'm still crying, and I'm also afraid to leave the house. "I don't know what's wrong with me," I tell Bennet. I know it was a horrible workshop, but something more is going on. I can feel it resurfacing, that thing at the core of me that I'm always trying to control. Given enough stress and heartache, it always comes back and breaks through my façade. I'm so good at beginnings, but in the end I always seem to destroy everything, including myself.

"You should probably go to a meeting," Bennet says. Instead, I retreat into his bed. For a week I don't get out except to eat or use the bathroom. I curl up with the covers tucked under me on all sides while Bennet dresses for work. When he leaves, I feel relief. When Alexis leaves, I'm doubly relieved. But then I feel worse—achy with rage and helpless, but too exhausted to do anything about it. At the end of that week, I somehow drag myself to my therapy appointment. Anna, my counselor, specializes in drug and alcohol addiction. I've been seeing her for almost three years. Although she's saddened that I quit my job, she's still optimistic that I can pull myself together; we simply need to put together a plan for me to get a new job.

I disagree. How am I going to get a job when I can barely leave Bennet's house? I haven't even visited the room I recently rented for myself in Waltham, paid for with my first paycheck. At this juncture, I'd typically pack up my things and beg my mother to take me in until I could find another job or a hospitable boyfriend. But she's out of the country, in Bali, on a yearlong sabbatical from her teaching job.

Listening to my situation over dinner, Alexis declares, "You need to apply for psychiatric disability."

"Am I really that sick?"

"Look at how much you're suffering! This isn't addiction you're dealing with. This is mental illness. Think of it like being hit by a bus, and now you can't walk."

Suddenly I understand why Bennet leaps to attention every time he hears her voice. Alexis is commanding and self-assured, and even though I'm sure she's my mortal enemy, I follow her suggestion. Despite full-blown anxiety attacks, I make numerous trips to the Social Security office in Waltham and the public assistance office in Somerville, where the waiting rooms swim with foreign languages, the cries of babies, and the smell of stale cigarettes. The disability application process rivals any college application in both duration and complexity. Only here the goal is to gather testimony confirming my inability—inability to manage my life or be an adult like everyone else. I know the records will cause confusion, as my history isn't charted in one continuous, major decline. In some ways, I *am* almost adultlike. Despite the many times I've dropped out of school, I always manage to return, and I finally got my degree.

I used to drink and use drugs; now my addictions are "in remission." And I certainly don't appear disabled—maybe a little frazzled and like I've been crying for two weeks straight, but with some lipstick I clean up fairly well.

To tide me over while my disability application is being processed, I'm issued a welfare benefits card. It gives me a set amount of food stamps, which aren't stamps at all, but a debit system on my card, to be used only in grocery stores. The card also gives me access to a small amount of cash for covering rent and utilities, though the state of Massachusetts must have been using 1950s calculations, for who could pay for housing and the electric bill on three hundred dollars a month?

As the days grow ever shorter and the air sharpens, I continue to stay with Bennet and Alexis despite the pain, and despite the option of going back to my rented room in Waltham. Being with them is a platonic ménage à trois where I'm both trapped and contained, a child desperate for love and also a scorned mistress. I'm unable to break free of a bond that, while upsetting, is also as close to a sense of belonging as I've had in a long time. To confuse matters, Alexis is steadily growing on me. Some evenings the two of us prepare dinner, like co-wives, confiding in each other and discussing delicate information, such as the admirable size of Bennet's penis. We sip tea and revisit the times in our lives when both of us were desperate for drugs. Like Bennet, I've gotten into the habit of hugging her good night. I've missed the friendship of a woman. Also, I realize she's quite hot.

I know that something has to break, and shortly before Christmas, it does. I'm in Bennet's room, and I can hear everything in the kitchen. I can hear Bennet and Alexis playing with Bancha and the stupid cooing voices they use with her, hear them discussing errands that need to be done, and then I hear their usual good night ritual—the hug they give each other while both say, in unison, "Good night. I love you."

But tonight there's a pause and Alexis says, "Not on the lips."

Or maybe she says, "Nothing amiss," or some other small phrase that only a depressed, emotionally strung-out, unemployed, wildly jealous girlfriend would misinterpret. Even though I know they're not sexually involved, they're bound together in so many other ways that I imagine it would be easy for Bennet to fall into treating Alexis like a lover. I imagine that he tried to kiss her good night as he might kiss me, and that image throws the "go crazy" switch inside me.

"What did you just do with Alexis?" I hiss at Bennet as soon as he's in the bedroom pulling off his shirt. "Oh, for Christ's sake, we say good night to each other every night. It's not a big deal."

"But what kind of good night kiss? Full on the lips? Cheek? A peck?"

"She's like my sister! I'm not going to talk about this."

Bennet climbs into bed and I turn toward the wall and sob into the pillow. I fantasize about letting Bancha out into the cold December air, preferably when Bennet is home so he can see the bird pass by the kitchen window and flutter off into the winter sky. I also fantasize about my death. The image of Bennet finding me on his bed, dead from an overdose, flashes through my mind more and more often, especially when I'm in the shower. There, under the hot water, I'm confronted by my body, a pale, hairy thing that feels rubbery and unreal half the time. I can so easily imagine it sprawled out lifeless and rigid, with a note that says, "See what you've done to me?"

I haven't hinted to Bennet about the suicide fantasies, but the next morning it's as if they crept into his dreams. Bennet takes my hand and says, "I think you should see another doctor." I look away, tears welling up. Half of me still believes that if only he'd move out, away from Alexis, the situation wouldn't be so bad. Bennet still has the chance to make it all better! He strokes my back and pushes the hair out of my eyes.

"You're a mentally ill, suicidal drug addict, like the rest of us. There's no shame in that. You just need more help."

I remember how he'd first used that phrase, "mentally ill, suicidal drug addict," at the NA dance. And how he'd said, "Of course we have problems. But I think we should give it a try." We held each other so comfortably, leaning against that tree on the grass island in the middle of the parking lot. In that hour I came to believe that his touch could contain me—that someone might join me and I wouldn't destroy what we had.

2

Girl, Recycled

I take Bennet's advice and call for a consult at a local hospital—the same one my mother took me to after I ran away from home so many years ago. In a small interview room, I sit with Dr. B, an elegant and taciturn Indian man, handsome and compact, with an English accent and gentle eyes. The office is small and bare other than a lamp, two chairs, and a desk.

"What brings you here?" he asks, adjusting his chair.

At first I say it's my boyfriend, but then I tell him the whole thing. I start at the trailhead of my first suicide attempt and try to describe this overwhelming pain I've had for as long as I can remember. I show him the scars on my arms, and I name all the diagnoses I've gotten: depression, anxiety, PTSD, and chemical dependency. I list the medications, therapies, 12-step programs, religions, and nutritional supplements I've tried. I describe my previous stay in this hospital when I was seventeen, put on a ward for the summer before I turned eighteen, and my other hospitalization in college, when I dropped out and went into AA and NA to get sober.

"I've been seeing therapists for almost twenty years," I say, crying. "I've quit every substance besides caffeine and sugar. I've taken every medication psychiatrists have given me. I don't understand why I'm not getting better. Everything I touch seems to turn to shit... I'm back at that place where I don't see the point of going on. I'm just going in circles, like circles of hell, where there's no escape."

The doctor considers his notes for a minute, nods, and hands me the tissue box. "Do you think it's this relationship that caused things to get so bad?"

"Yes...and no... It's like the last straw."

"Do you have any stable or enduring relationships?" he asks.

I shake my head. "I'm lucky if I can hang on to a friendship longer than a year. Two years with a boyfriend is as much as I've done. And when it ends, my life falls apart."

He asks, "Do you have a hard time when you think someone is possibly leaving you or neglecting you?" I nod and feel the stab of pain that always happens when I think of Bennet. I admit that I've sent letters in blood when I've felt rejected, and that there have been times I've thrown fits and kitchenware when a close friend replaces me with a boyfriend. I don't want to make him think I'm a complete nutcase, but I confess that I once believed a boyfriend was having an affair with another woman through telepathy, and that when the three of us got together they were conspiring psychically to meet up when I was gone.

Dr. B scribbles away. "What about anger?"

"I'm terrified of it." He asks if I have problems expressing it. I do. But it's not so much the expression that's difficult as it is the experience of having it inside me so often and having to manage it. It's like being a sword swallower, only I don't have the throat for it. Eventually the anger comes out. And it's usually scary—to others and to me.

"How intense are your emotions, on a scale of one to ten?" he asks. I reply that they're usually somewhere between an eight and a ten.

"Are they fairly steady, or do the change rapidly?"

"Rapidly. Insanely quickly. They exhaust me. They take me over..."

"Do you cut and burn yourself regularly?"

I explain that it depends. When I was a teenager, it was constant. Now it's periodic, mainly after breakups.

"Do you have other impulsive behaviors?"

I don't want to admit how many men I've slept with in the past couple of decades. Or how many credit cards I've maxed out. Or the number of times I've moved (thirty-four at the last count). "Therapists tell me I need to think more before I act. That I don't recognize consequences."

"But you've been able to stay sober."

"Yes. I saw that I was pretty much going to end up dead if I didn't stop. So I guess that consequence made me change."

"How do you stay sober now, when you also want to die?"

I pause here. It's true, I'd rather jump off a bridge than go back to getting drunk and high. Why? And why am I here in the doctor's office when a huge part of me is now convinced I should give up?

Before I can answer, Dr. B says, "Something in you must want to get better."

I'm not sure if it's that, or I'm just here because I'm trying to appease Bennet. Dr. B asks why I haven't killed myself yet, and I suspect it's mainly because of my brother. He died when I was nineteen and he was eighteen. We thought it was a drug overdose, but it turned out to be a brain virus. Every time I get to the edge of wanting to kill myself, I see my mother's face, the way it looked at the hospital when we arrived at the ICU and the doctor opened the door and said "I'm sorry." It's like a software program running in the background. When I have the image of me dead, the memory of her devastation—and my father's—erupts.

"The reason I haven't killed myself yet is because of what it would do to my family," I tell him.

"So you love your family a lot."

"Actually, I hate them a lot."

Dr. B nods. "Would you say you've have some identity issues, not knowing who you are or changing yourself for other people?"

Yes, yes, yes again. A teacher at my high school called me the chameleon. Not because I blended in, as I was the resident freak at school, but because I was always changing—every year a different style. I'm still that way, changing depending on who I date, what music I'm obsessed with, my sexuality...

Dr. B finishes by asking me if I have difficulty with stress. I say the difficulty is so great that I literally go blank and numb when I feel I'm under pressure. "Would you call it dissociation, like leaving your body?" I nod. "How do you see other people when that happens?"

"I don't understand..."

"Does the world seem safe, like you're able to get help?" This question hits a nerve so raw I start to sob.

"No one helps me. My family doesn't understand. Therapy isn't working. I've done everything I can. How can I be thirty and be right back where I was when I was fifteen?"

Dr. B says it sounds like a nightmare. "You have no idea," I cry.

"But I believe I know what your problem is. And it's actually good news, because it's treatable," he says. "It's a type of illness called borderline personality disorder, or BPD. Have you ever heard of it?" I shake my head. "It's a condition of extreme mood instability. A fear of abandonment. An uncertain sense of self." He leans forward in his chair. "Does that make any sense to you?" I nod. "A pervading sense of emptiness," he continues, now ticking off his fingers. "Suicidal behavior. Self-mutilation. Unmanageable anger. Rocky relationships. Impulsivity. In stressful situations, you can get paranoid. Even dissociate and leave your body."

"Yes," I say. "Yes, yes, yes." I'm a bit stunned. It's like acing a test you never studied for. How can this diagnosis from someone I've only just met so perfectly describe what I've been dealing with all this time? The list of symptoms is like a *Reader's Digest* version of my diary. Someone has secretly peered into my soul and given it a name.

"But what does 'borderline' mean exactly?"

Dr. B smoothes out his pants. "Saying you have borderline is just a convenient way of explaining your symptoms. It's a label, a term, to describe a certain type of distress. You don't need to pay too much attention to the name." I nod again. I don't care what it's called: chicken head syndrome, broken personality disorder, whatever. I just want to kiss this man's hand for putting into words this endless cycle of failure and misery. If I have BPD, it means I have something *real.*

"A personality disorder, unfortunately, cannot be cured with a pill," he explains. "Getting better is going to take a lot of time. There's a therapy I recommend you do, specifically designed for BPD. It's called dialectical behavior therapy." He takes a white business card from the pile stacked at his elbow and writes down a number. "There's a program here. Call and set up an intake appointment. I'd also like to try you on lithium, since your emotions are so of control."

This is the first time since we've sat down that I feel worried and mistrustful. Lithium is for manic depression, or bipolar disorder, as it's known these days. Is that another thing I have?

Dr. B says that I might and instructs me on how to wean myself off my regimen of antidepressants over the next couple of weeks. "Don't worry," he says as we stand up. "You are a woman of great passion. You'll learn to channel your energy, to control it, rather than the other way around. You will learn equanimity, and when you do," he smiles, "there will be no need for a diagnosis." He gives me a prescription and we make an appointment for next month.

Out in the winter air, I feel a relief probably similar to what cancer patients feel if they're told the tumor is contained and operable. I've never heard of this strange disorder, and I didn't even know there were personality disorders, but if it means I have a real illness rather than just being a terminal failure, I'm willing to try it on for size. Nothing else has been able to describe the self-destruction, the desperate clinging, the obsession with suicide, and the shifting moods, identities, and perspectives. I have BPD, I tell myself. I'm not a total fuck-up.

Before I reach my car, I call Laura to share the good news. Laura has known me for many years. In fact, she's one of the few people still in my life. We share similar histories: Like me, she became addicted to drugs and alcohol, dropped out of high school, and ran away from home. We both ended up in institutions and eventually landed in 12-step programs, where we met. Now in our early thirties and with a few years of recovery under our belts, it would make sense if our lives continued to parallel each other, but that hasn't been the case.

While Laura got married, bought a house, and is now having a baby, I've been stuck in an endless round of lost jobs and failed relationships. I keep falling apart, while her life grows steadily more settled and secure. I haven't talked to Laura since I called her this summer to gush about my new man, but now I feel like she's the right person to tell.

"The psychiatrist says I have borderline personality disorder!" I exclaim. "And it makes perfect sense!" There's a pause at the other end as she takes in the news. She majored in psychology as an undergraduate, and since Dr. B didn't give me an informational pamphlet on BPD, I'm hoping she might be able to tell me more.

I hear the TV in the background, and then Laura shrieks, "There is *no fucking way* you are borderline!"

I pull the phone away from my ear. "Why not?"

"Listen, borderline is Glenn Close in that movie *Fatal Attraction*. Think stalking, knives, psychobitch from hell. That is *not* you!"

"But I have all the symptoms!" I plead.

"No, seriously. People with BPD are really, really, *really* disturbed. Listen… I know you've had some problems. The twelve steps don't cure everything. But seriously, get a second opinion. You don't want to have BPD on a medical record. You don't want to have it at all."

I don't want to have BPD? Do I have a choice in the matter?

Accepting a psychiatric diagnosis is like a religious conversion. It's an adjustment in cosmology, with all its accompanying high priests, sacred texts, and stories of origin. And I am, for better or worse, an instant convert. In time, I might even be accused of being a fundamentalist. Despite Laura's words of warning, I am convinced, simply from Dr. B's list of symptoms, that this is the problem that's been plaguing me all along. I head over to the hospital's resource center to see if they have any information on this mysterious disorder. A spectacled woman gives me a stack of articles on BPD and a copy of the diagnostic criteria. I ask if there are any books specifically for people with BPD or written by someone in recovery from it, and the librarian shakes her head.

"Oh no, wait," she corrects herself. "There's one you can probably find in a bookstore. It's called *I Hate You, Don't Leave Me*."

Great. *I hate you; don't leave me*. That's exactly what I feel with Bennet most of the time. Though more precisely it's "I hate you, why don't you leave your fucking ex-girlfriend?" I take the materials and head back to Bennet and Alexis's. They're making dinner when I come in, and Bancha is sitting on Bennet's shoulder.

Bennet kisses my cheek and congratulates me on going to see the new doctor. His fingers are covered in garlic juice and bits of red chile peppers.

"The doctor says I have borderline personality disorder."

"Borderline to what?" Alexis asks.

"Good question." I hold up the stack of articles. "Time to find out."

3

The Diagnosis That Dares Not Speak Its Name

There's no question that the diagnosis fits. I have all the symptoms: I have chronic feelings of emptiness and an unstable sense of self. I'm suicidal and self-harming, and I frantically avoid abandonment and rejection no matter what the cost. My relationships are stormy and intense, and my perceptions can shift between black and white at the drop of a hat. My emotions are out of control, I freak out when stressed, and others often find my anger inappropriate. The *Diagnostic and Statistical Manual of Mental Disorders* (*DSM-IV-TR*), the bible of psychiatry put out by the American Psychiatric Association, says this disorder develops in early adulthood, but it seems to me that this isn't true. As I look back, I see that I've had these symptoms, in varying degrees, since I was eleven years old. To say that BPD starts in early adulthood is ridiculous. No one wakes up at age eighteen and is suddenly borderline.

To those looking from the outside, it might seem this illness took possession one day out of the blue, as signaled by some specific behavior: Kiera's cutting herself; Kiera's doing drugs; Kiera's shaving her head. But that's part of the whole problem—no one saw, knew, or understood how long I was suffering and sick. Even my mother thinks it started later, when I went to the private school and began cutting and burning myself. But I disagree. As soon as I read the symptoms, I realize the seed was there all along, watered by pain, secrets, and inattention, and by my own desperate need for relief.

The day after I get the diagnosis from Dr. B, I have my weekly appointment with Anna. I haven't told her about this new consult, so she's understandably surprised when I pull out the list of BPD symptoms and declare that I have borderline personality disorder.

Immediately she declares, "No, that's wrong. You can't have borderline."

"Why not?"

"Because you're not one of *those*."

"Those *what*? Can you explain to me what that is?"

"It's hard to explain," Anna says.

I suspect she's referring to what Laura mentioned. "You mean I'm not someone who stalks people with knives?"

"That's one way of putting it."

Anna is a kind, motherly woman and we've done a lot of work together, though it's never any different from the work I've done with so many other therapists. We dismantle my childhood, my upbringing, and my issues. Every three months we diligently fill out a treatment goals chart. Sometimes we target anxiety reduction; other times, finding a job or improving my self-esteem. All the while, there's a psychiatrist in the background, in a different town, prescribing me medications once a month after I check in with him for fifteen minutes. Anna's been my lifeline through many crises over the past couple of years, and also a font of optimism regarding my potential for growth, but ever since I quit the teaching position and was sucked into the Bennet and Alexis vortex, the tone of our appointments has changed. Now I cry a lot and she gives me Kleenex. Now we discuss things like how I can get out of bed in the morning and how I can avoid dwelling on my desire to kill myself.

I urge her to look at the list of symptoms. "Tell me if this doesn't sound like my life: 'a pervasive pattern of instability of interpersonal relationships, self-image, and affects, and marked impulsivity.'"

Anna peers at the page. As a counselor who mainly coaches people in 12-step recovery, she doesn't trust clinician-speak. "That could mean a lot of things," she finally says.

"I'm the very *definition* of unstable."

"You're an artist," Anna counters. "It comes with the territory."

"So what about all the other symptoms?"

"I'm sure there are other ways of looking at them." She reads off the first of the criteria: "Frantic efforts to avoid real or imagined abandonment..." She pauses for a few seconds, trying to choose her words carefully. "Well, of course you're sensitive to that. Your parents divorced when you were young. You never knew when your dad was going to show up, or when your mom was going to pay attention to you. We've discussed how they weren't there for you in the ways you needed. Anyone with your upbringing would have some abandonment issues."

The topic of neglect is a reoccurring one in our therapy—and in all of my therapies. How much love and attention could a single mother have provided for two young children? How destructive was it to have an absentee, alcoholic father? I know I haven't gotten everything I needed from my parents, but in the Hierarchy of Parental Horrors, my parents were Bob and Carol Brady compared to some of the other stories I've heard.

Plus, I'm more than just a "little sensitive" to abandonment. I used to write letters in blood to boys who rejected me! Anna says that was a long time ago. She says, "You have some codependency issues, but we're working through them."

That doesn't seem to suffice. I've already read *Women Who Love Too Much* and *Codependent No More*, to minimal effect. I've gone to Adult Children of Alcoholics meetings and Al-Anon meetings. None of it has stopped me from throwing myself into the arms of random men and feeling like my life depends on their attention, and then falling to pieces when they look away.

Anna glances at the list again. "I'm not saying your symptoms aren't real, only that they can be explained by things other than BPD."

"So these relationship problems I have..."

"You never had good role models. Didn't your parents stop speaking to each other when you were six? How were you supposed to learn about love? Communication? Emotional security?"

I'm not up for this game of deflection. I know what I see, or at least I think I do. Or maybe I don't know. She passes the list of symptoms back to me. We both look weary.

"Why do you want to pathologize yourself, Kiera? Haven't we worked together long enough for you to realize you can get through these things?" Anna presses her hands to her heart and looks like she might cry. "Can't you see that you're a survivor? You don't need another diagnosis. You just have to start believing in yourself."

Once again, I don't know what to believe about who I am or what I'm dealing with. And that's been part of the problem all along.

❖❖❖

I spend Christmas and New Year's waiting—waiting for a disability determination, waiting for a spot to open up in the dialectal behavior therapy (DBT) group. At my second meeting with Dr. B, he insists DBT will get me out of this hole I'm in. So for the time being, I focus on staying alive and learning everything I can about BPD. Learning about BPD might seem like a straightforward process. After all, the American Psychiatric Association first officially recognized BPD over two decades ago. And while mental illness isn't exactly easy dinner conversation, most disorders are considered treatable. There are ads on TV for depression, complete with bouncing happy and sad faces, talking about all the ways you can get help and treatment. In my research, however, the first thing I discover is that it's almost impossible to get good information on BPD, and even more impossible to find people who claim to have it or recover from it.

I plow through the clinical articles from the hospital resource center, read *I Hate You, Don't Leave Me* from cover to cover, and, like everyone else I've since met who's been diagnosed with BPD, I go online to find help and support, with the hope of being understood and accepted. However, the first sites I come across aren't run by doctors or people with the disorder, but by those in relationships with borderlines. They call themselves "nons" (as in, "non-BPD"), and they are *pissed*. I come across a blog written by a mother who says her adult daughter has BPD. She describes her daughter as a chronic liar who abuses her verbally and lacks even a shred of empathy. The daughter rages, manipulates, destroys furniture, and wrecks dinner parties, and if she doesn't get her way, she threatens to kill herself. The mother is at her wit's end, in a constant battle to control her daughter, who refuses therapy and claims that *she's* not the crazy one—her mother is.

I follow a link on the mother's page to an online community of nons, with seemingly thousands of members. On the website's bulletin boards, they write heartbreaking messages about how they suffer in relationships with people they say have BPD. Words like "cruel," "indifferent," and "incapable of empathy" swarm on the screen. Seen through the eyes of these people, BPD looks nightmarish in ways I can barely fathom.

I am mortified at what I read. How much of what they describe is actually the BPD I have? Am I like what these people describe? Do others see me as a monster—even more than I see myself as one? Now I don't want to have the disorder either. And I understand why Anna and Laura are shouting from the sidelines, "Don't call yourself a psycho!"

I try to find something positive in the family stories. Does anyone see a loved one with BPD get better? Are the relationships ever repaired? At the sites I visit, the answer is almost never. One woman says, "If the person gets better, then obviously she's not really borderline." I'm so disturbed I have to go eat a pint of Ben & Jerry's ice cream. The simplicity and elegance of the DSM symptoms have been scrambled into crime, abuse, and cruelty. The word "sociopath" gets thrown around with alarming frequency. I don't know if I'm looking in a mirror, or if the people looking on are caught in their own distortions.

It seems like it might be better to focus on websites run by people with BPD, and, thank god, there are a couple of them. Not only do they have more factual articles on the disorder, they also have message boards with postings by self-identified borderlines. Finally. My own kind.

I dive in and read, and the first thing I notice is that anonymity is de rigueur. People post under names like "angelofdeath" and "criesforever." I'm shocked by the sheer number of members who are registered to post—thousands of borderlines, from all over the world. And yet the countless messages, the voices of BPD, almost uniformly read like SOS signals: declarations of futility interspersed with cries for help. Unanswered questions cascade down the lines of postings: "I think I have this disorder." "What is it?" "Why do I feel this way?" "How do I get better?" "Does *anybody* get better?"

These forums are lush with suffering and confusion and a quality of camaraderie found only in wars and at bars. People newly diagnosed, like myself, post long descriptions of their ordeals: multiple diagnoses, struggles with addiction, unremitting pain and loneliness, tortured relationships. There is a flurry of connectivity, as one person after another declares, "Yes! It's like that! I'm so out of control! I can't stop hurting myself either. It feels like everyone hates me and I'd rather be dead!"

There's the balm of shared suffering: *Oh thank god you understand.* But then the bigger reality of these postings is how little help is available. I read how there are essentially no doctors willing to treat BPD, an almost total absence of programs for the disorder, and only a handful of programs based on dialectical behavior therapy. And then, further down, I see that "stopthepain" stops posting. And "angelofdeath" announces that she will be killing herself. A handful of moderators plunge in with wads of advice to stop the hemorrhaging, but it isn't enough. These boards feel neither safe nor hopeful for me. At the end of reading these messages, I've gone through ten tissues and feel more lost then ever. Crying for help among the helpless is like trying to get sober in a bar. If 12-step recovery has taught me one thing, it's that to get better, you need to connect with someone who has gotten through it. To believe that you can survive, you need to see that someone else has done it.

In the days after the diagnosis, I spend hours and hours on Alexis's computer, clicking and scrolling, coffee at my side. Among all those websites with descriptions of symptoms, all the scholarly articles, all the bulletin boards of both borderlines and nons, a disturbing and glaring absence surfaces: No one wants to come out publicly as having BPD. This makes me wonder how real a diagnosis it is. Either it's so horrible that none of the estimated two million people in the United States with BPD will come forward, or it's not even real. Maybe it is just a "wastebasket diagnosis," as one researcher complains, set up to collect all the riffraff who either refuse to be helped or cannot be.

This also brings up the question that Anna keeps raising: Does it matter if I believe I have BPD? Look at how much confusion and negativity I've already encountered. I don't need any help hating myself. I'm already filled to the brim with self-disgust. Do I want to put myself in the same league as the incurable? Do I want to throw in my hat with people seen as sociopaths? Can't I just go to the DBT group Dr. B recommended and forget the name borderline even exists?

I've seen other people refuse a diagnosis. And I've seen people who spent time in psychiatric hospitals but never labeled themselves as "mentally ill." But when I look at myself squarely, it's not just that I have a few difficulties or unresolved issues. Unlike those lucky people for whom therapy or medication delivers them back to themselves, I've been suffering from something that was unnamable for most of my life. Yes, I've had periods of relative stability, but the whole concept of "recovery" brings up some painful questions. What do I recover? With drug addiction, you hear that you can recover and reclaim your former self, the person you were before you started using. With other psychiatric illnesses, getting rid of symptoms means you're more or less back to "yourself." But what if you simply don't have a solid self to return to—if the way you *are* is seen as basically broken? And what if you can't conceive of "normal" or "healthy" because pain and loneliness are all you remember? "You were such a happy child," my mother says. But I don't remember that. So what do I recover?

4

Mindfulness and the Big Mac

In late winter a space finally opens for me in the DBT group—and not a minute too soon. Dr. B's lithium diet has resulted in two extreme states: My anxiety level is cresting so high I can no longer go into grocery stores or drive a car without shaking and crying. The other effect is overwhelming horniness. When Bennet comes home from work, I'm waiting like a dog in heat.

"Jesus," he says one night, "whatever problems you're having right now, sex drive isn't one of them." I've never been this orgasmic before, and it's a bizarre contrast to how nonfunctional I am in every other way. When I'm not sleeping twelve hours straight or having an anxiety attack, I'm waiting to be fucked again. Bennet's bed is like a life raft, but it's anchored to my illness. We're both relieved when I get the call from the DBT program saying I can start as soon as I come in for an orientation.

In the orientation and interview, the DBT group leader, Molly, explains the purpose of the therapy: to learn how to reduce my pain and misery through specific skills. She hands me a set of papers listing all the rules of the group, and then she asks me why I want to join the group. I tell her that I can't go on the way I've been living. I show her the broken blood vessels in my nose, from crying so hard and so long while Bennet and Alexis are out at work. Molly's hair is a brown cloud masking the window's light as she studies the side of my nose.

"You want to stop crying."

"I want to stop feeling this way. I just don't know how much longer I can keep dealing with it." She nods and gives me the last of the paperwork to sign. Starting on Tuesday, I'll be attending an hour and a half of DBT skills group once a week.

Dialectical behavior therapy isn't like other types of therapy. You don't sit around sharing your feelings. You don't dredge up memories of the past and analyze your issues. It's an approach that focuses on developing skills to help you regain control over your emotions and behaviors. Dr. Marsha Linehan, a therapist in Washington State, developed the techniques in the early 1990s while working with borderline women who were chronically suicidal and self-harming, and at the time I enter this program, it's the only researched therapy that's shown to actually reduce some of our symptoms (Linehan et al. 1991; Linehan et al. 1999).

When I show up at the group, I expect it to be Borderline Central, and I'm excited and a bit nervous to finally meet other people with the disorder. I carry my copy of *I Hate You, Don't Leave Me* to show I'm serious about this thing. I've been using a highlighter while I read, and by the end, I've painted its pages neon yellow.

"Do you have BPD?" I poll the others before Molly arrives. There are eight of us. We run the gamut from an elegant woman in heels to a sullen teenager with silver hoops glinting from his eyebrows and nostrils, the only guy in the group.

"It's not a real diagnosis," the elegant woman says.

"Sure it is," a girl sitting next to her says, "but only if you piss the doctors off."

Molly sweeps in with a stack of handouts and a small metal bowl. "Diagnosis isn't the important thing here," she says, overhearing our conversation. "Remember the list I gave you? Skills training is for learning how to change the things that cause you misery and distress—to regain control of your mind, your emotions, your behaviors."

The bodies gathered in the room certainly document our lack of control. On several of the women's arms, evidence of cutting rises faintly in pale pink ridged lines. A heavy woman with long, billowy sleeves reveals, in a gesture, circular red burns along her forearm, made from holding cigarettes against her skin. On more than one person, the insides of the wrists are scored with long strokes made by a razor.

Molly sits down with the DBT workbook she's just made copies from. On the cover is a stark black silhouette of a woman's face tipped down as through she were weeping, or possibly hiding in shame. In bold white letters inside her head, the title of the workbook reads *Skills Training Manual for Treating Borderline Personality Disorder*.

I feel like the person pointing at the elephant in the room. If BPD isn't an issue here, why is it in the title of the book? Dr. B said this therapy was created specifically for BPD. Now it's apparently a nonissue. To confuse matters even more, this hospital is home to the most famous BPD doctor in the world. In fact, his office is right across the hall from our group, but some invisible moat seems to divide us from him, or me from getting connected to anything that will directly address borderline. I'm growing upset about this, but there's no time to discuss these things. Molly strikes the metal bowl with a wooden dowel and asks us to focus on our breath in silence, to allow the reverberation of the metal bowl to transition us into another space. While anxiety jackhammers inside me, I try to take some deep breaths and settle in. And I discover that this one minute of silence, of simply being present and breathing, is more difficult than any physical exercise I've ever done.

DBT, as it's done at this hospital, consists of the weekly group where Molly introduces us to specific techniques and skills, and then we focus on exercises and homework assignments meant to help us apply the techniques in our daily lives. The manual has four skills modules, each addressing a specific set of problems. Because we have so much trouble managing our emotions, we'll learn emotion regulation skills. And since we'll do just about anything to get away from intense pain, we'll learn distress tolerance skills. Because we have so much difficulty managing and keeping relationships, we'll learn interpersonal effectiveness skills. And because we experience our own minds, thoughts, and feelings— everything, really—as being out of control, we'll learn core mindfulness skills. Despite what Molly says about the BPD diagnosis being irrelevant to the therapy, I learn quickly from reading the workbook Molly held, Dr. Linehan's *Skills Training Manual for Treating Borderline Personality Disorder* (1993b), that every aspect of DBT was developed with an exquisite sensitivity to the borderline condition.

In fact, Dr. Linehan devised this approach to therapy after discovering that trying to help people with BPD could be like pouring salt in a wound. We can't tolerate criticism and judgment. For us, therapy's constant emphasis on "fixing ourselves" and the pressure to change is like pushing someone whose back is already against the wall—a wall full of spikes. When the focus is solely on change, we tend to flee therapy or stay very angry and defensive. On the other hand, too much unconditional acceptance by the therapist can keep us stuck. In either case, we often get worse. So Dr. Linehan took an approach that no one else seemed to have considered. While her psychiatric training was in cognitive behavioral therapy, which focuses on changing problematic thoughts, feelings, and actions, her personal experience with Zen Buddhism taught her that compassion, nonjudgment, and mindfulness can normalize our experience and help us trust and accept ourselves. The Zen Buddhist and mindfulness techniques in DBT are called acceptance strategies, and the combination of these with the change strategies she initially used forms the core of DBT's "dialectical" approach (1993a).

Although we never discuss the concept of dialectics in group, it's actually critical to every skill and practice in DBT. If you pick up Linehan's *Skills Training Manual for Treating Borderline Personality Disorder* (1993b), you'll see that the concept is presented on the very first page. Even before she delves into the topic of BPD or the skills being taught to help us, Dr. Linehan makes it clear that the theory of dialectics structures DBT on every level. So, what is a dialectic? On the most practical level, it's what happens when opposites combine to create something new. Bringing change and acceptance techniques together is an example of this. On a deeper level, dialectics is a viewpoint that recognizes reality and human behavior as fundamentally relational. According to Dr. Linehan it has three main characteristics: First, that "dialectics stresses the fundamental interrelatedness or wholeness of reality." Second, that "reality is not seen as static, but is comprised of internal opposing forces (thesis and antithesis) out of whose synthesis evolves a new set of opposing forces." And third, that "dialectics is an assumption, following the two above, that the fundamental nature of reality is change and process rather than content or structure" (Linehan 1993b, 1-2).

If you read through this section, it also becomes clear that these aspects of reality are often impossible for a borderline, like me, to grasp. I'm trapped in polarized extremes. The smallest changes in relationships devastate me, I experience myself as cut off and separate from the rest of the world, and I can't see the other side of things because I'm so caught up in my own reality. In essence, I'm not very dialectical. Or as Linehan puts it, BPD characteristics can be viewed as a failure of dialectics (1993b).

As usual, I'm hoping to get brownie points for reading the important text, but it turns out that the actual practice of DBT is infinitely harder than reading a couple of chapters of theory—even something as seemingly basic as mindfulness, which is the first of the four skill sets I'll be learning.

Mindfulness is the technique of simply observing what is happening without any judgment or attempts to change it, and it's the basis of all of DBT's acceptance strategies. For our group exercise, we're instructed to close our eyes and imagine a river flowing past, with leaves floating on the surface. Each leaf is like a thought drifting by. There's no need to grasp onto the leaves—no need to chase them, and no need to deny their presence. Our job is to let everything pass by, even if it turns out there are severed heads and old tires bobbing by. This isn't easy. I last maybe three breaths without getting distracted. Then my brain is off and running. I'm thinking, I'm antsy, and I want the group to end.

After we do that exercise of simply observing, we go on to describing. Now as we watch the stream, we label the leaves: An emotion just passed by. There goes a thought! Stomach is grumbling. The girl next to me smells like cigarettes and roses... I'm better at describing, but I still can't stand how it feels. And how ironic is it that after doing so much LSD as a teenager and trying to be a hippie, I'm getting my first real taste of Zen meditation in a mental hospital—if you can call feeling tortured for two minutes Zen.

As soon as we end group and Molly leaves the room, I turn to the heavy woman with the cigarette burns and take one last stab at the borderline issue. "Were you diagnosed with BPD when you got in here?" I ask her. I grip the book *I Hate You, Don't Leave Me* in my hands, and she holds the *Skills Training Manual for Treating Borderline Personality Disorder* in hers. Borderline seems written all over us in the scars on our arms, all over me in the jagged pathways of my life, ending over and over in a hospital—all fractures and edges, and nothing that can stay the course.

"I don't know what I have," the woman says flatly, tugging her sleeves down. "I don't care what it's called. I just want to stop feeling this way."

When we return the following week and report on how our homework went, I'm humbled listening to how the others practiced the observe and describe homework. The heavyset woman describes her experience with a McDonald's hamburger: how the Big Mac, all warm inside the wrapper, made her mouth water, and how the special sauce dribbled down her chin when she bit into it. She describes the touch of the soft brown bun against the roof of her mouth, the motion of her jaw as she brought her teeth together, and how a lump of Big Mac slid down her throat. By the time she finished, it felt more like food porn than a therapy assignment.

The previous night in Bennet's room with my homework, I too tried to be mindful, to observe and describe how I felt. But it had been another excruciating day. One of the few people in NA I still had contact with, a poet named Brian, convinced me to go to a gallery opening and poetry reading with him, and as soon as arrived, I knew I'd made a big mistake. After so many months of being housebound, my senses went on overload and my heart wouldn't stop racing. I wanted to crawl into a corner and curl up in a ball. By the time Brian found me, I was sitting on the front stoop with my head in my hands. He immediately took me home, apologizing all the way. But I wasn't mad at him; I just hated myself even more.

So later that night, I sat at Bennet's with my mindfulness homework assignment. Bennet and Alexis were visiting his mother. I decided to be mindful of the horrible feelings inside me. I would observe and describe it all: The bird flapping in my chest, raking me with its claws. *Observe*, I told myself. I imagined sitting on the banks of a river and instructed myself to calmly watch the flowing water. But nothing came to mind. And inside that "nothing" lives something awful: a falling through black, blank space with my insides on fire. I knew I needed distance between myself and my feelings so I could observe, but just being with my feelings was like being possessed. I didn't need mindfulness; I needed an exorcism.

Perhaps a minute passed, maybe five. The possession was in full swing. *I don't think I'm doing this right,* whispered a part of me. Another part began a familiar litany: *Nothing is working. I can't stand this. I am so fucked-up. I can't even sit for one minute without falling apart.*

I went into the bathroom and got one of Bennet's disposable razors. I hadn't cut myself in years, even through all of the turmoil with Bennet, but this sudden encounter with myself felt intolerable. Seeing all the scars on the others' arms in group tipped me back into the realm of possibility. And then impulse took over. The blade drew a slim, beaded thread of blood along my arm, and another. And perhaps not surprisingly, I grew more mindful as the slow rhythm of bloodletting rinsed me with clarity. It wasn't dramatic; it was familiar and reassuring. I was all business, making sure not to press too deep. I etched the lines in orderly rows, and after I was done, I swiped with alcohol, blotted the skin, and applied gauze. When Bennet and Alexis returned late that night, I was in much better shape—and wearing a long-sleeved shirt to bed.

"The exercise didn't go too well," I report to the group when it's my turn. "I tried to be mindful of my emotions, but I got overwhelmed."

There are some nods. "Sometimes it's too difficult to be mindful," a beautiful, gaunt girl sighs, "when it gets to be so much."

The others in the group agree. To be mindful of overwhelming pain seems all but impossible.

"That's why you're here," Molly says. "Mindfulness isn't supposed to be torture. It's a tool. When you're aware of something, you have the ability to work with it. That's why learning about states of mind is important. You can say to yourself, when you get into a lather, 'Oh, look, I'm in emotion mind.' You can learn to control your attention and skillfully choose what action to take." She thinks for a minute, then turns to me. "I suspect that while you were trying to practice being mindful, you were actually judging and reacting to your emotions."

DBT describes people as having essentially three states of mind: emotion mind, reason mind, and wise mind. The handout Molly gives us shows a picture of two overlapping circles. One circle represents reason mind. The other circle represents emotion mind. And in the space where reason and emotion mix is wise mind. In discussing the different states of mind, it's easy to understand that reason mind is all about logic, while emotion mind is all about emotions, but wise mind seems beyond my grasp. It's described as the integration of the two other states of mind. Sometimes it's also called wisdom mind or wise knowing, but whatever you call it, Molly says it's that part of yourself that's intuitive and yet also based on direct experience.

"Is it like déjà vu?" the boy asks.

"Think of it more like a well or fountain inside of you. It's always there, but because you're been fixated on emotion or reason, it's hard to access it. When you bring all ways of knowing together, wise mind emerges."

I know there's something more to my mind and reality than whatever I think and feel in the moment, but so far my only proof of it has been out-of-body experiences while I was on drugs. My state of mind at those times definitely wasn't wise.

I think the hardest aspect of understanding wise mind is believing that something exists within me that's actually reliable. Where inside me is this wisdom? How do I access this calm, intuitive, go-with-the-flow awareness?

Back at Bennet and Alexis's, I try to do the breathing exercise where you watch your thoughts and emotions and simply label them: "thought…," "emotion…" I don't find wise mind, but once again I discover how intensely painful it is to just be with myself. As I try to sit, an image from an old *Life* magazine takes hold. It's a Tibetan monk, sitting in his robes, on fire. I remember reading that the monk set himself ablaze to protest China's occupation of Tibet. I know that my feeling of being burned alive is much less noble, and completely invisible, but that's how I feel, sitting with myself: on fire. Dr. Linehan uses a similar image. She says that people with BPD are like emotional burn victims: We've lost all of our protective skin (Linehan 1993a). I wonder if wise mind can give me protection from that. I wish it were like a Magic 8 Ball. Just shake your head and an answer will appear. I wish there were a wise mind drug. DBT says that's inside me, even now. And that is the hardest thing to believe.

5

Saviors

Social Security officially deems me disabled, so now I get a big fat monthly check for five hundred dollars. This means I can at least pay my rent in Waltham and some of the outstanding utility bills my house-mates have been shoving under my door for the past couple of months. I'm still avoiding staying there, but the house is just two miles away from the hospital where I have the DBT group, so I try to stay at least one night a week. My nights at "home" feel like I'm huddling under a tarp in the arctic. My room is warm enough; it's the isolation that freezes and paralyzes me. I've never understood why I freak out like this, but now I know it's a borderline symptom: intolerance of aloneness and a pervasive sense of emptiness. So the first night I stay at home, I try to practice mindfulness as I sit in my room. A leaden and pulsing sensation in my chest gets heavier with each breath until it's too heavy to carry. Once again, I don't know how to manage it.

I tell myself, *Just observe—observe and describe.* I notice that I feel horrible. I feel hopeless. I don't expect that it's really going to help, but watching the feeling and naming it does put a little cushion between me and the pain. I also notice my intolerance of it, how the desire to escape this feeling sweeps over me like a wave. Someone in the group mentioned "urge surfing," a DBT technique for learning how to ride out each feeling and impulse rather than habitually escaping it though various modes of self-destruction. Over the past decade, I've somehow learned how to apply this approach to drugs, but in 12-step recovery this involves believing you're powerless and asking for help. DBT is completely different. It doesn't maintain that we are powerless. On the contrary, it sees the other side of acceptance as the ability to change, and it focuses on developing the skills to do just that.

We spend two weeks on mindfulness and, indeed, the next module we enter is focused on change—the other part of the dialectic. It's called interpersonal effectiveness, and it's about learning how to ask for and get what you want in a relationship. There are numerous complicated worksheets and exercises, and the module is quite long. Molly warns us that we could spend at least two months on it, maybe more. I'm immediately put off and wish that if we were going to spend two months on anything, it would be distress tolerance. That's the DBT module about how to deal with the feeling of being burned alive. And that's where I'm at right now. Besides, nothing is going to change the situation with Bennet. I'd need explosives to separate him from that apartment and Alexis.

In interpersonal effectiveness, we read a handout of bulleted items about the importance of attending to relationships: Don't let hurts and problems build up. Use relationship skills to head off problems. End hopeless relationships. Resolve conflicts before they get overwhelming (Linehan 1993).

Molly moves to the whiteboard to drum up some participation on the topic of balancing priorities versus demands, but my eyes keep returning to one previous bullet point: "End hopeless relationships."

I raise my hand. "How do know if you're in a hopeless relationship?"

"We're actually on a different section now," Molly says, though not unkindly.

"But if you're in a fucked situation with someone, it doesn't make sense to do all this other stuff, like negotiate."

"That's true, but it's wise not to make any quick decisions about relationships." She turns back to the group. "How many people here have left relationships prematurely?" All hands fly up, my own included. Molly certainly has a point. As a creature of blind impulse, I can just as easily flee from a relationship as I can get lost in one. I definitely need to learn how to negotiate rather than cutting and running when trouble develops. However, I'm beginning to understand that I also stay in relationships that are beyond negotiation, that I stay trapped and hopeless, because I'm too afraid to be on my own—because there's nothing else in my life to hold on to.

The BPD diagnosis might be a taboo subject in the group, but my mind goes to it automatically whenever I think about how I've been clinging to Bennet all these months, despite how sick the situation is making me. I will suffer almost anything to avoid the "chronic feelings of emptiness" that BPD involves. It drags me in like a black hole as soon as I'm severed from an important relationship.

I remember that even when I was just five or six years old, I didn't want to close my eyes at night because the dark inside my head would expand like the space of a starless night and I'd be left alone in it. It's like that familiar scene from movies about space travel, where an astronaut is cut loose from the spaceship and spins away, helplessly cast into the empty void of space. That's what being alone feels like. If I break up with Bennet, I'll be floating again. I don't know which is worse, the pain of presence or the pain of absence.

Although Molly cautions us not to act on impulse, reading that line about hopeless relationships sparks a dead circuit in my mind and there's a sudden recognition—a deep, decisive knowing—that I have to free myself from Bennet and Alexis if I want to get better. Is this wise mind? Other's might say it's simply common sense. Maybe, for me, there's no difference.

<hr />

Later that week, Bennet and I sit in front of the TV. He smells like linseed oil and sawdust, and he's probably worried I'm going to drag him to bed for some predinner sex. We sit on the couch and stare at the TV for a while. And then I turn to him. "It's over," I say. "I can't do this anymore."

Bennet stares at the news for another moment and then looks me. His eyes are baggy and tired. It occurs to me that I have no idea what his day was like, because I never asked.

"I guess that makes sense."

There's no anger, and no accusations from either of us. After all of the fights and drama, all the color and noise, with just the slightest tug on the electrical cord the whole screen goes blank and our story is over. And that's it. I pack my bags and carry them to the door.

"Are you going to be okay?" Bennet asks.

Even though this is my decision and I know it's right, I want to say, "No, I'm not alright. I'll probably hit a tree going home, and it'll be *all your fault...*"

"I'll be fine. Really," I say, holding back the tears. Bennet insists on giving me a big hug, and then I drag my bags out into the almost-spring air and to my car. I want to be proud of myself and feel liberation, or at least release. Instead, panic and rage explode inside me as soon as I close the car door. I start screaming when I turn onto the highway toward Waltham. If passing drivers were to look, they'd glimpse a wild-haired woman-child at the wheel, swerving along her lane, mouth open, eyes like slits, her voice—and her life—trapped inside a vehicle careening toward destruction.

The room I'm now living in full-time is in half of a faded duplex built in the 1950s on the edge of a less-than-savory section of the Charles River. I have the back bedroom, along with a narrow additional room that could be used as a large closet or an office, with a window facing the river. After I unpack my clothes, I sit on my futon on the floor. I regret my decision to break up with Bennet as soon as the room's silence envelops me. I've tried to spruce the place up a bit on my occasional overnights, but it feels like I'm visiting the cast-off shell of a former life—and I didn't really even live here for that life. I'm just sitting in a place I used to avoid. It's still not mine, and I don't know how to make it my own.

I know I should reach out to someone at this point, rely on my supports, as they say. But my options are fairly limited. I consider calling my father. After years of fighting and being estranged, we've come to a reasonable truce, partially because we're both recovering addicts. He's been sober eleven years, and I've just passed my ninth. Although his support as a father was minimal, at least we now share some understanding about addiction. The disadvantage is that any problem or feeling I fob his way is met with 12-step speak. Whenever I'm in pain, falling apart, or in crisis, he gives me slogans: Easy does it. First things first. Keep it simple. Ask your higher power for help. Go to a meeting. If I were to call and tell him I've just split up with Bennet (read, *yet another man*), I doubt I'd get sympathy. He'd probably just suggest I do another moral inventory. Fuck moral inventories.

Somewhere in the stack of postcards my mother has been sending throughout the year, I have a phone number for her in Ubud, Bali. Actually, it's the number of a phone booth supervised by a man who takes messages and then forgets about them. Not having my own phone means I need a special card for international calls, which Social Security hasn't factored into my living expenses. But even if I could get through to my mom, I couldn't tell her the truth. If I told her the truth, it would upset her so much that she'd call me a moth later to tell me she hadn't slept since our last conversation. My difficulties completely overwhelm her, and in the end, my pain seems to cause even more pain for her. And though I could call Anna, the eternal cheerleader, who is always encouraging, she has no game plan other than rereading *Codependent No More*.

What solutions would DBT suggest? In group, we're now in the middle of complicated worksheets about goals and priorities in interpersonal situations. I've been in the DBT group for over two months, and my interest and ability to focus on it are dwindling. The worksheets and ideas don't make sense anymore. I know I need more help. In the couple of weeks following the breakup, I barely notice the approach of spring because most days I'm curled up in bed crying. I've been putting it off, but eventually I call Dr. B. We've met three times since he gave me the diagnosis, spending our allotted fifteen minutes going over the change from antidepressants to lithium. Each time, he's asked if the DBT group is helping. I've said that in some ways I'm better, but in other ways I'm worse—that I mainly feel lost in it, and depressed. I'm getting terribly depressed. When I ask him about the BPD diagnosis, he's vague and encourages me not to focus on it, saying that the most important thing to know is that I can get better; it just takes time.

Time. Now I leave a message on Dr. B's answering machine, telling him that I'm so depressed I can barely move. I know it's because of the lithium. I can barely lift my fingers to pick up the phone. In my message, I say, "Maybe it would be a good time to go back on an antidepressant."

Then, out of desperation, I call Bennet, weeping and asking if he might reconsider.

"Do you want to be with me because you love me," he asks, "or because you can't stand being with yourself?"

It's the last time I call him.

When I tell Dr B. that I feel like I'm falling through a giant hole and nothing's ever going to catch me, he agrees that I need to get back onto the other meds.

He asks how my individual therapy is going, and I explain that Anna isn't interested in the BPD diagnosis or DBT. "You should have a DBT therapist," Dr. B says. "Get a referral from Molly."

So at the next group, with a bit of Zoloft finally pumping through my brain, I ask Molly if she can refer me to someone trained in DBT. She shakes her head. "There's not much available right now."

"Are there *any* therapists in the area trained in DBT?"

"Unfortunately, no."

"What about a therapist who specializes in BPD?"

We both glance across the hallway at the famous Dr. M's office. It continues to upset me that I can't get more support or information about BPD even as one of the high priests of the diagnosis does therapy across the hall. Knowing the location of his office also gives me a vague stalkerish feeling. What happens behind those doors? What kind of therapy does the man give to the borderlines? Do they get better? The women (and they are mostly women) waiting for appointments with him look as uniformly unhappy as we do, though they are, on the whole, very attractive; "refined" might be the better word. I suspect he takes only self-pay, as I'm sure insurance isn't exactly generous when it comes to reimbursing famous doctors.

"What about Dr. M?" I venture. She looks at his office and scrunches her face up. "Well, maybe… Maybe I could get you an appointment for a chat." She doesn't sound hopeful.

"A chat?" She makes it sound like sitting by a fireside with tea and scones.

"He's very busy. But he might be able to take you on—if it seems right."

Good enough, though it sounds more like a date than a consultation, this "chat." What kind of borderline would tempt Dr. M into taking her on? The question intrigues me, and soon enough I'm studying the women outside his office with more than casual interest. These women are obviously sophisticated, probably rich, and clearly interesting to him. So I know exactly what I need to do, how to catch him: I need the perfect outfit. From what I've read of his case studies, Dr. M feels special sympathy for the waiflike girls who hurt themselves. I'm not a waif, but I know how to dress like one, how to smudge my eyelids with black liner and tousle my hair, making the curls fall over my eyes. When the day arrives, I dress in tailored clothes, and as I sit in the waiting room, I thumb through *The Economist* rather than the *People* magazine I'd normally snatch up. When Dr. M comes out to invite me in, I make sure I'm not slouching. It's like auditioning for a boyfriend, a teacher, and a father all at once.

The "interview/chat/date" lasts only ten or fifteen minutes. I explain that I have BPD, which I hope will entice him, but of course everyone he sees has BPD. I tell him I was at the hospital before, as an adolescent. Even so, Dr. M doesn't seem to think of this as a clinical discussion. He asks about my career and interests. When I say I'm an artist and writer, this takes him on a tangent into twentieth-century literature, and before I know it, he's giving me suggestions on good novels, shaking my hand, and showing me to the door. In my mind, a little voice is chanting, *Help me, help me, help me.* Should I show him the scars? Burst into tears? I wonder if I made a tactical error in telling him I had BPD. Now the mystery is gone. He can't discover me; I've come to him already named, like a claimed continent. Perhaps the thrill for him is in planting his own flag?

The next week, Molly asks how the meeting went. I shake my head and tell her I don't think he's interested. But I still have that feeling like on the days after a tepid date—I can't help but wait for another call. On a date, I can usually give a blow job to keep a guy interested. What would be the equivalent offering for the most famous clinician of BPD?

The heavy wooden door across the hall remains closed, and I'm not invited back again. Later that spring, as I sit in the waiting area before DBT, unshowered, in my pajamas, and engrossed in a *People* magazine, Dr. M walks through. I look up and smile hopefully. His eyes pass over me and the others, and then return to me for a second, quizzically. He knows me from somewhere, but it seems he can't place it. He smiles and nods, and goes back into his room.

Though I rarely believe in myself, I've always believed in saviors. Perhaps that's why I haven't given up and am always reshaping myself into an ideal image for my chosen savior. When my mother sent me to a born-again Christian Bible camp at age eleven, I changed my name to Kiki, developed a Southern accent and took Jesus Christ as my lord in the span of three days. Even then, I'd do about anything to guarantee eternal love from a man—even if he was bleeding and hanging from a cross. We sat on benches around a wooden table with our Good News Bibles those summer afternoons, and at the end of the study group, we prayed to be saved. I'd sit, head bowed, and try to take this man Jesus into my heart, hoping, begging, that his ministrations would purify me and set the world straight, the same way I'd later get on my knees in front of other men, for other reasons, or sit in therapy rooms and 12-step meetings naming my demons and confessing my latest sins.

The world is full of saviors, both professed and unwitting. But so far, no one has saved me, and I continue to feel like I cannot help myself. Now only one person other than my father regularly checks in on me: Raymond. Raymond has actually been hovering in the background for ten years. He's my mother's ex-boyfriend, and unlike my father and stepfather, Raymond has never been kicked to the curb, had his face cut out of family photographs, or forced my mother into changing the locks. He's the handsome prince my grandparents undoubtedly prayed my mother would find before she lost her virginity. Unluckily for all of us, by the time my mother and Raymond met and fell in love, the obstinacy and ingrained habits of middle age made it all but impossible for them to merge their lives. Plus, Raymond has deep-seated commitment issues, which is too bad, because he's the first man my mother loved who was truly a responsible and successful adult. He has an Ivy League doctorate, his own company, no issues with his mother, and the kind of heart that is able to feel other people's pain without getting overwhelmed or turning away.

For me, this means that he has never disappeared from my life. Over the past decade, Raymond has kept a calm eye on me without interfering, but now with my mother out of the country, he checks in on me periodically. Since I quit the addiction education job, I've been downplaying my struggles and trying my hardest to put on a strong front, because our relationship has never included bailouts. But by the beginning of spring, Raymond is worried. I haven't contacted him in months. He tracks me down and takes me out to dinner.

I love dinners with Raymond. I can order filet mignon, prime rib, or anything on the menu. I point to the most expensive, finest cuts of beef and he just says, "Go to town, kid." Now he wants to know what's *really* going on, so while I stuff my mouth with bloody beef and tear into the basket of fresh rolls, I try to explain the process of my latest disintegration, from quitting the job to going on psychiatric disability to getting a new diagnosis, doing another kind of therapy, and trying different medications.

Raymond looks more than a bit alarmed. "Are you getting the best treatment?" I tell him that I don't know what the best treatment is, that I've never met anyone who's "recovered" from BPD, but that the seeming authorities say the therapy I'm doing now will help. By the time the crème brûlée and cappuccino arrive, Raymond's brow is deeply creased and he shakes his head a lot. As an economist, his job is to analyze and calculate, and from where he stands things aren't looking too good for me. He asks if my mother knows what's going on, and I admit that I haven't told her everything because it will only upset her. When he asks about my dad, I say, "He thinks I need to go to more meetings."

"And your grandparents?" I look away. When I say the words "addiction" or "mental illness," they either leave the room or change the subject.

Raymond continues to shake his head and asks what he can do to help. I admit I don't know. I thought getting the right diagnosis would finally turn things around, and that going into DBT would put me on the right path. We're now in our third month of interpersonal effectiveness, and it's driving everyone crazy. Already two members have dropped out, complaining they were stuck in the fourth circle of Linehanian hell. I have no clue what to do next. Neither, it seems, does anyone else. I've run out of saviors.

6

Full Circle

During the spring, I spend most of my time in my room, sleeping and reading. My bed is the ultimate refuge, though I do try to make forays into the other parts of the house, where the two women I live with putter around. Marcy, a nester and a pack rat, works temp jobs and continues to nurse a broken engagement from four years ago. The minute she gets home, she changes into fuzzy slippers, makes tea, and watches TV in her room. My other roommate, Patty, is a high-energy saleswoman, cranked up on caffeine and with a sex drive that rivals my own in the best of times. One night I wander into the kitchen to make tea and discover her having sex on our kitchen table. It's only 9:30—not exactly the most appropriate time to be having a kitchen tryst, especially with everyone home. Public sex doesn't especially freak me out, but doing it on my kitchen table does. After all, I eat granola there every morning. I know I'll have to confront her on it, despite how much I hate conflict. As it happens, in group we're still in the interpersonal effectiveness skills module, so I try to make it into a homework assignment. I plan the whole thing out, and the next time I see her in the kitchen, I use DBT skills to explain how her behavior is affecting me and request that she keep her sexual life in her bedroom.

Patty throws down the dish towel and turns to me. "You have a problem with me being sexual?! It's not my problem that you're sexually repressed."

"Excuse me?"

"And it's my house too."

"I am *not* sexually repressed," I huff.

"Yeah, what*ever*." Patty sits down at the (recently sterilized) kitchen table, crosses her long legs, folds her arms, and stares me down.

I turn to the fridge and don't say anything. My heart palpitates and races as I hunt through the fridge, looking for something to pull out so I can leave the room. When I turn around and meet Patty's eyes boring into me, I have conflicting urges to punch her and to run from the room crying. And in the back of my mind, perhaps I'm jealous—jealous that she's still such a "bad girl" and that she's getting away with it, being all saucy and bringing lovers home. In comparison, I'm like a stripped storefront mannequin, living a denuded replica of human life.

Patty and I stop speaking to each other, and from that point forward, home doesn't feel safe. I listen for noises before I venture down from my second-floor room. I stockpile crackers and juice boxes in my room, and my ears prick up at the slightest noise, hypervigilant for any sign of her. I share in DBT group that my exercise in making a request didn't work so well.

"Obviously she's a bitch," one of the girls says. Molly nods. There's a caveat to all techniques for being effective: Sometimes the environment refuses to change, no matter how skillfully you ask. In this case, it's the "bitch factor." If that's not in Dr. Linehan's skills training manual, it should be.

In early summer, Raymond sends me a package. It's a fancy new cell phone with a note: "Keep in touch, kid." He says not to worry about the bill. I program his number into it, along with Anna's and my father's, and I carry the phone with me in a little black pouch clipped to my waist like I'm a doctor on call. When I go out to the supermarket and can't breathe from the anxiety, sometimes I open it up and pretend to listen to messages or call the operator just to ask for the time.

But it feels like time is standing still. Why is it that the more pain you feel, the slower the seconds tick by? My father calls one night when I'm literally in a stupor of despair. I can barely talk, and he accuses me of abusing my medication. "I'm not taking any more than usual," I sob. He doesn't understand. He tells me to go to a meeting and to remember that I'm in recovery.

That word again, "recovery." Its meaning is always related to progress: the journey from illness to wellness, from being incapacitated to being effective, reclaiming the parts of yourself buried under problems you're finally overcoming. This word has been in heavy rotation in my vocabulary for so very long, with the basic assumption that when you hit bottom, you'll finally admit to having a problem and ask for help. Sometimes people never bottom out—or at least don't realize they've hit bottom. In AA and NA, I've seen some people lose everything in their lives and still not stop getting high. I've seen people die instead of getting better.

But I know this isn't the case with me; I'm a "help seeker." Whenever I hit bottom, I look for some way out. And from reading the online BPD message boards, I know there are others like me: people with BPD who are desperate for help, who can't find therapists, who join a DBT group and discover it's like trying to hold back a tsunami with a beach umbrella. Yet even with my help-seeking nature, it's all getting to be too much. For all my efforts, I feel worse than ever. If I posted on those online boards, I'd be the person with a screen name like "fuckitall." Anna looks scared when I talk now. I'm scared too, because the part of me that wants to live is shrinking by the minute. I don't want to try anymore.

Keeping old meds is BPD insurance. Even in times when I'm not seriously suicidal, I hold on to big bottles of pills. They have incredible appeal. Candy-sized, the pills can be consumed instantly, and they're also controllable, collectable, and not as messy or uncertain as other suicide techniques. For some people with BPD, the need to escape is so overwhelming and the pain so intolerable that no thinking or planning happens. They attempt suicide the way crack addicts do crack, habitually and impulsively, using death to alleviate the compulsion and pain. These attempts aren't necessarily planned. And a lot of times, they're instantly regretted. I have a less stereotypical relationship with suicide. I don't attempt it often, and usually only after enduring a long string of incremental sufferings. Suicide is like a little cyanide capsule in my pocket, just in case the enemy comes too close—always there, but only to be used when facing seemingly insurmountable odds.

My first suicide attempt was at age twelve, but already I'd been fantasizing about my death for over a year. The immediate reason I wanted to kill myself was that I'd lost my math notes for a test. This was no ordinary math test: A passing grade would grant me admission into one of the most elite and expensive private schools in the country—not because I'm a genius or because we had tons of money, but because my mother worked at the school as a teacher. Passing the entrance exam would mean a free education and the opportunity to become, like earlier graduates, a president or a millionaire.

"Just get in," my mother chanted. It was one of the reasons she took the job—that, and so we could live on a campus stuffed with delights beyond the scope of almost any other high school, from pool to theater to hockey rink to Gothic chapel built of stone. Everyone said that if I could get into this school, my life would be changed. And I did need a change. Already I'd been caught stealing, cheating, and lying by my family, and by a couple of teachers at my middle school. I didn't know why I did those things; I just felt this immense pressure inside of me and a weight of misery that I couldn't push away.

When I discovered that my math notes were gone, I was sure I'd fail the test, which meant no private school, no golden future, and no escape from the relentless bullying of the local kids. So I took a pill bottle out of my mother's bureau drawer, hidden under a stew of lace underwear and smelling of rose sachets, and swallowed the contents—a handful of chalky nibs that reminded me of miniature mints until they passed down my throat and I tasted their bitterness. I didn't know what the pills were, and though I wondered if they were too old, I wasn't particularly concerned with the bottle's expiration date; the pills looked serious enough, and after all, they were hidden away. I felt like a failure—like I couldn't do anything right—and these pills seemed to be the antidote

The next morning, I discovered that I couldn't even die right. In the morning I was still there, just with a buzz in my head. I got up, got dressed, and took the bus to school. The faces of the other kids in my seventh-grade history class were fuzzy and their voices echoed in my head. I had the urge to throw up all through math, the test blurry under my eyes. Claiming dizziness, I went to the nurse's station, where I was allowed to lie down for the afternoon on a padded cot under an empty square of window. I didn't tell anyone. I already knew I would try again.

On a logical level, I know that everyone feels pain. Everyone suffers. Is my pain really that much greater, or am I just weaker? Where is the line

between normal and abnormal emotional suffering? I come across "The Pain of Being Borderline," an article written by another famous BPD clinician, Dr. Zanarini. It says that in comparison to people with other personality disorders, borderlines experience greater levels of worthlessness, anger, abandonment, and hopelessness—that more than others, we feel like bad, damaged children, shunned by the world, and better off dead (Zanarini et al. 1998).

This is my second encounter with the idea that our internal experience can be characterized by a defining emotion, not just "instability." As Marsha Linehan says, we're like emotional burn victims (1993a). Dr. Zanarini views this specific kind of pain as a characteristic of the disorder itself: borderline pain. We're emotional epileptics, thrown from one fit of horrible suffering to another. Poisoned by what's inside us, and vulnerable to anything outside us. I've spent my life chasing relief from this pain, only to find myself more deeply mired in it. How can it be that after all of this work, killing myself once again seems like the only option left?

One afternoon in early summer, I pick up the phone and call Anna. I'm dizzy from spending too many minutes looking over the edge. It's like I'm on a cliff and the smallest breath of wind might topple me over. I *want* to fall, and to release myself from this endless cycle of suffering, but I also resist it. Something in me still refuses to give in. I don't understand this tenacity that duels with the death wish, but it's still here, and it pushes my hand to the phone.

"I'm in trouble. I need to see you," I cry to Anna's voice mail. She calls back and tells me to drive right over. Once I'm in her office, I say, "I can't do this anymore." I curl up in the chair, shaking, a continuous chant of *no more, no more, no more* in my head. For a moment, it looks like Anna's going to give me a pep talk. But she doesn't; she asks if I need to go to the hospital. I nod and sob. An hour later, I'm in an ambulance going to a psych ward. It's been ten years since I've been an inpatient. Ten sober, "I'm in recovery, taking my meds, and seeing a therapist" years. And now I'm back at the hospital where I landed when I was seventeen, brought full circle to this place where my mother deposited me, a drug-addled teenage runaway, to put me into someone else's care.

PART 2

Last Resort

7

Short-Term Solutions

During summer and early fall, I'm hospitalized three times. After the ambulance drops me off at the hospital's evaluation center the first time, I'm placed in a ward called the short-term unit, aka the STU. It's a stereotypically bland place with pale blue walls, anonymous doors, a glassed-in nurse's station, and plastic couches. Three bored staff sit behind the glass with books and snack food. It takes ten hours of waiting for interviews and insurance clearance before I get a bed. By the time I pass through the doors, it's 2 a.m. and the ward is hushed. A middle-aged man with a belt cinched under a thick wad of stomach welcomes me and offers a blue hospital johnny, a toothbrush, and toothpaste.

I know that mental hospitals are supposed to be full of horrors, loss of human dignity, and bad starchy food, and that you shouldn't feel such relief at having your freedom taken away, and yet... And yet when I climb into bed, the white hospital sheets feel as cool and fresh as peppermint. On some level, I am dangerous to myself. And yet... here I am not.

"The goal here is stabilization," says Dr. M, the attending psychiatrist, when we meet toward the end of my first full day. He looks over some papers and asks me how I'm feeling. I've spent one night in a private room and did nothing for most of the day except stare out the windows and eat snack food, yet I'm feeling better. The quiet containment, the fifteen-minute check-ins, my name written in red with little boxes next to the daily groups I should attend—all this keeps me away from the edge of the precipice. I'm still panicky and hopeless, but the realization that tonight I'll be tucked into crisp white sheets and looked after with the sweep of a flashlight, over and over, keeps me feeling calm. I am no longer alone. I want to tell the doctor this, yet I worry I'll be kicked out if I do. And I don't know how I'll feel once I leave. The idea of going back to Waltham and being cloistered in my room immediately fills me with dread. So I tell the doctor I feel horrible, and that I don't know what to do.

I spend five days on the short-term unit; two of them are over the weekend, when nothing happens. You sit and stare at the TV. You look at old *Vogue*, *GQ*, and *InStyle* magazines. I've never understood how ogling the home decor and perfect bodies of the rich and famous helps anyone feel better, especially mental patients sitting around in hospital johnnies. The only distraction on the unit involves "walks" where we're led around the campus in a grouping shaped by the disorders possessing us: the manic ones rushing ahead and racing back, the depressed dragging their feet, the paranoid skirting the edges. By the second day, my privilege level is raised, so I can go on the walks, which I immediately love. They're so measured and routine as we wend around the stately brick buildings and the green lawns like kids at camp following a counselor through the thick summer air.

Come Monday morning, Dr. M sits down with me again. We go over my medication options and he adds a non-lithium mood stabilizer. Then I'm passed on to a social worker, who, looking at my chart, notes that the time in the hospital seems to be helping. I'm starting to understand why people say that hospitalizing borderlines is a bad idea because we get addicted to the care. Of course we do! We're watered, fed, and walked, and it is a balm to every aggravated nerve. Plus, for the first time in years I don't have to put on a public face and pretend that everything is okay. As a result, I'm actually at ease with the other patients and with myself. By the beginning of the week, I've started greeting the new arrivals like I'm the STU welcome wagon. I make flowers out of napkins and coffee stir sticks. I've also developed a full-blown crush on one of the young guys on the staff. The last thing I want to do is go home.

"You're going home," the social worker says when we meet next. I wonder if she's got a message from Dr. M: "Get rid of this one. *Now!*" All the comfort of the past five days drains away and tears well up. It's like being cast of out of the womb prematurely. Wait! I'm not developed! My toes aren't yet fully formed!

"I really don't think I'm ready." I have the same horrible image of my lifeless body on my bed, and then my mother's face.

"We're going to put you in a day program here," Carol says, handing me a folder.

"Is it for borderline personality disorder?"

She shakes her head. "It's for mood and anxiety disorders. Looking at your chart, you certainly qualify." She asks if I can handle showing up every morning for a day of intensive groups. I nod. Although I haven't been able to get out of bed regularly in close to a year, I've had little reason to. Besides, being on the hospital grounds for a day program is almost like being on the unit. Maybe I can tag along with the patients as they're being walked and no one will notice.

The program I'm placed in is called MAP, for mood and anxiety program, and is based on cognitive behavioral therapy (CBT). Every day from 7:30 a.m. to 4:00 p.m., I attend groups inside a questionably air-conditioned three-story wooden building. Now I can't complain that I'm not getting enough therapy. And even though the focus isn't on borderline, I know I'm among kindred spirits. If ever there were a dumping ground for the middle-class dispossessed, this is it. Forlorn housewives, wrecked businessmen, spastic college freshmen, midlife crack-ups, despairing elderly, haunted young women—all are herded from one forty-five minute meeting to the next. At the end of each session, a bell sounds, and depending on level of meds and type of disorder, we dash, stumble, or meander toward the next room, with a few venturing out into the heat for a few drags off a cigarette or a cell phone call.

I've never seen so many groups happening in one building. We meet for cognitive behavioral skills, assertive communication skills, depression and anxiety (I'm level one, the beginner's group), behavioral scheduling, relapse prevention, and impulse control. There's also stress management, self-assessment, mood regulation, positive events scheduling, family issues, life transitions, community meetings, treatment planning, and contract writing. After I've met with Scott, my case manager, and signed a contract committing myself to goals and groups, it dawns on me that I'm no longer just in therapy; I've entered cognitive behavioral therapy boot camp.

The techniques in this program are very similar to the change strategies of DBT. The focus is primarily on how to manage and control your thoughts as a way of modifying behavior and feelings. Susan, the tall blond woman who runs my first CBT group, says, "If you come away from this program with anything, this is what you need to remember: How you think affects how you feel and behave." At first this sounds like a new age platitude: Think good thoughts and all will be well! But when Susan takes us through an exercise showing how a thought like "I'm fat" can lead to a behavior like starving oneself, the importance of thought grows clearer.

It takes some time for me to adjust to the new language of CBT. Here we're taught about the CBT triangle of thoughts, feelings, and behaviors, whereas in DBT we were always referring to the intersecting circles of emotion mind, reason mind, and wise mind. But if you strip away the terminology and some of the details, both come down to the same thing: To regain control, we need to develop awareness—and not just about childhood issues. Whether it's called "mindfulness" or "self-assessment" or "grounding," this is the first and most critical step toward understanding the forces that are tearing us apart. In CBT, some of this awareness involves observing, but the focus is on analysis and assessment. We rate our feelings, look at our thoughts for common types of distortions, strip our experiences down to the facts, and generate new strategies to substitute for habitual reactions.

By the end of the week, I'm more saturated with CBT theory than I was after six months of DBT. It makes my DBT group, with its one and a half hours of rambling group sessions and weekly homework assignments, seem like Sunday school. Now I'm in the seminary and there's another gospel. It's all about change. We're here to fix ourselves, and that takes work, work, work. I love creating the little graphs and diagrams and lists; it makes me feel more in control of what's happening inside me if I can map and record it visually. But for some of the other people, it's too rigorous and brain-twisting, especially when meds and sleep problems make focusing difficult.

Even though I appreciate the approach and can grasp these ideas, I can barely tolerate sitting in the groups. Distractions as small as a woman tapping her foot grate my nerves, and the small, hot rooms are a breeding ground for claustrophobia. There's a lot of discussion around triggers, or what DBT calls "prompting events." A large part of developing new awareness and changing behavior involves seeing how situations, and our interpretations of them, cause habitual reactions. Being in a small room with other people is one of my biggest triggers, it appears. My heart races, I start to think people are staring at me, and the pressure builds until I feel like I'm going to explode. All I want to do is escape the room, and I often do, going to the bathroom to splash water on my face and sitting on the toilet until my heart stops racing. Bathroom escapes are probably one of my first and most enduring emotion regulation strategies, but given that I'm in a program full of people with similar problems, I seem to always be standing in line.

I soon realize that my triggers go beyond simple social encounters: being alone, thinking about the past, dealing with money, feeling ignored… In fact, I'm growing more convinced that almost everything has the potential to trigger me into being upset. It's a lot like Dr. Linehan (1993a) described it: Having no emotional skin leaves me raw and vulnerable to even a feather's touch. And as my life falls apart, my defenses against these triggers seem to diminish, so that, increasingly, I'm almost always upset.

With the prompting of the counselors, I try to be aware of every thought and reaction: My favorite counselor doesn't smile at me and I'm sure she's mad, even though I have no real proof of it. I think about my parents and how they don't care about me, and then I remind myself that their idea of care differs from mine. I try to name and rate every emotion that comes along, and true to my borderline nature, they come fast and furious, and are often contradictory. It's like riding a bull, this kind of mindfulness.

For a couple of weeks I'm holding on quite well, until one of the guys in the program starts to get under my skin. Rather, I want him under my skin. Todd, who must be ten years younger than me, is heavily medicated due to an extreme case of bipolar mania, Jesus-style. He's also unselfconsciously very cute and reminds me of the boys I knew during the Grateful Dead days, singing Bob Marley songs to himself and wearing an occasional tie-dye.

I'd been immune to him at first, but during lunch, as I sit under the large, dying oak outside the cafeteria, I hear Todd's voice on the patio. I put on my sunglasses and stare at him: hair in his eyes, muscular legs, wearing a faded T-shirt and flip-flops. A cigarette burns down toward his fingers as he describes, too loudly, how he's going to replace Kurt Cobain and bring Nirvana back together as soon as he can convince Courtney Love he is worthy.

Something in me melts. Don't ask me why. I do a self-assessment. I can't believe it, but I feel the stirrings of an idiotic, misplaced, and inappropriate lust for Todd. No, wait, there's a judgment in there—which calls for another self-assessment. Sexual desire: Scale? Burgeoning. Unbecoming. Pathetic. Why not at least have a crush on a doctor? On a scale of one to ten, what's the rating? Three, thank goodness. But that could shoot up to ten like one of those carnival games if the hammer finds its mark.

I try to practice awareness of this sudden infatuation with Todd because I know that desire is a huge trigger for me. Even a fantasy can strip me of self-determination. And even though I'm being all insightful and self-assessing with this Todd feeling, I don't want to change it. After six months of nonstop pain and despair, my body has suddenly come back. I'm almost tingling, and, to be honest, I don't want it to stop. I feel alive: I feel the grass under my fingers, I smell the aroma of cigarettes and French fries wafting over from the patio, and I'm starting to remember the comfort of being held by someone else.

But as it turns out, I don't need to worry. Apparently Todd hasn't been taking his meds. "Jesus doesn't need lithium," he declares in self-assessment. "Jesus is full of love. On a scale of one to ten, I am the love-meister. Jesus lives to love." Soon he's back in the hospital and I can buckle down again. And oh, how I do. With five groups a day, even my writer's fingers ache from taking notes. Then, at the end of the third week, the news arrives: My insurance has cut me off.

8

Dancing with Demons

It's like going through withdrawal. After I'm discharged from the program, I languish in bed for a couple of days. When I finally get up, I discover that all of my therapists are gone. It's August, apparently the month every psychiatrist, psychologist, and therapist in Boston takes off for Cape Cod, a craggy hook of beach land on the coast of Massachusetts. As soon as the calendar page hits August 1, they pile into their Saabs and Volvos, loaded with kids, dogs, and spouses, and drive away from us, their patients, inching their way down U.S. 6 in a mass exodus they call vacation.

Anna is off for two weeks. Dr. M, who graciously agreed to replace Dr. B because I fired him after the lithium experiment, is away for the entire month. The DBT group I'm about to return to, the cornerstone of my "life as usual," has been put on hold while Molly suns herself for three weeks. As I am now fully aware, having problems with being left behind is part of being borderline. And despite knowing what a cognitive distortion is and how to observe and describe my feelings, in less than a week into this black hole of "nontherapy" I'm against the wall again. One night I eat half a gallon of pistachio ice cream and then make myself throw up—something I haven't done in years. Then I walk back and forth between the bedroom and the bathroom half a dozen times. I know there's a packet of plastic razors in Marcy's drawer. In my head, the usual images of me finally at rest and dead on my bed conflict with the imagined shriek of anguish I can already hear erupting from my mother's mouth as she finds out.

What has gone wrong? Once again I want to blame the therapy and the people, but if I believe that, then I have nothing more to hold on to. I've tried everything, and I know that isn't a distortion. When I get this worked up, my insides go hollow. I'm numb and feel unreal, and I want to raise blood to the surface. I know I'm in emotion mind. I'm aware of the urge to cut. At first it's because I want pull myself back into my body, and then as the night goes on, I want to go further and cut until I can leave my body entirely. I cast around for some alternative, but my brain cannot do one more fucking worksheet assessing and reframing my thoughts. All the skills from DBT glom together, a mass of acronyms without any meaning. I pull out the DBT books and paw through the pages. Something has to help. Then I find these words: "The lives of suicidal, borderline individuals are unbearable as they are currently being lived" (Linehan 1993a, 107).

I instinctively reach for a highlighter when I read this. Maybe that's the moment I undergo a fundamental shift. I don't grab the razor; I reread that one sentence and feel the same relief I felt when I discovered the borderline diagnosis. It's the balm of truth. Why doesn't anyone else recognize this? The programs I've been in keep insisting I'm going to be fine, even when I'm constantly on the edge, and then they push me out. But Dr. Linehan knows: We borderlines are in a living hell, even when we look okay. I am so relieved at reading this that I start crying. I remember again Linehan's description of borderlines as emotional burn victims (1993a). *I'm on fire again*, I tell myself. *Just get someplace safe.* I call my insurance company and then drive to the hospital with a packed bag. I am immediately escorted upstairs and interviewed by a doctor. When he notes that all of my therapists are on vacation, he signs the papers and I'm let through the door into the STU, and even into the same room.

My second stint on the STU lasts only three days. But something finally happens. And though it seems insignificant, it changes everything. The social worker, Carol, meets with me again and says, "If you keep this up, you're not going to end up at a nice hospital like this."

"What do you mean?"

"I mean, people on disability who keep coming through eventually get sent to the state hospital and," she drops her voice, "you would not be happy there, I can assure you."

Does she think I'm happy here? I try to explain for the millionth time that I'm not a slacker. I really do want to get better. I just feel safest here.

"Who is your therapist?" she asks, flipping through my records. I say she's on vacation.

"No, who is she? Has anyone here talked to her?" I can't say there's been any contact. Maybe secret phone calls take place, but I doubt I'm that important.

Carol keeps flipping through the notes and then looks at me incredulously. "Why don't you have a therapist?"

"I thought Anna was a therapist."

"She's a drug and alcohol counselor. You need someone trained in DBT."

"I was told there were no DBT therapists available."

Carol shakes her head and gets up. "Yes, but there are people outside of this place." She looks angry. "I'm going to make some calls." The next morning Carol finds me in my room and hands me a piece of paper: I have an appointment at another DBT program, located in Cambridge.

"I'm going to tell you a little secret," she says, closing the door halfway. "You've never been in a real DBT program."

"I don't understand. I'm in the skills group."

Carol runs her hands through her hair and shakes her head. "A DBT program isn't just group once a week. In a proper program, you have a trained therapist, you get phone coaching when you need it, and you have a skills group. You're not getting what you need."

I can't believe I'm hearing this; it's insane! I finally get the BPD diagnosis, and then no one will talk about it and Anna still denies it. I'm told DBT will help me, and now it appears I'm not even getting real DBT. And all along, I'm asked why I'm not getting better—what I'm failing to do. Who can I trust in this process? What if Carol is just as deluded? Does *anyone* know how to help?

"Listen," she says, "this isn't going to be easy. At this other place, there's a waiting list for therapists and the DBT group, and the intake isn't even for another month. But you've got to change something. You might not end up here the next time. So whatever you do, don't miss that appointment."

It's probably the fear of being locked up in a back ward in a state hospital that makes me agree to keep this appointment, because at this point, even a non-borderline would throw in the towel. It pushes me in a new direction, so I try to hold on—and hope that my insurance will let me stay in MAP until the next leg of this insanity begins.

I'm discharged from the STU into MAP again, with a new set of contracts and groups. This time Scott, my case manager, is more concerned with my aftercare planning, as it's obvious I'm not going away easily. He agrees that getting into another DBT program is the best direction to take. And he wants to get my family involved, especially given that I have no money and don't feel safe where I live.

The idea of asking my family for help, or even just revealing what I'm experiencing, feels like reopening a giant wound in my chest—a wound I'm always sewing up with barbed wire and hiding from sight. And if my past has shown me anything, it's that my illnesses trigger all kinds of negativity in my family: fear, anger, blame, rejection. I'm not willing to add any more of this to my life, so I tell Scott my parents are too far away, and that isn't a lie. My reality and theirs do not coincide.

But I do need to start preparing my mother, as she's returning from Bali for the start of the school year. In the few phone conversations we've had, I've explained to her, in the least graphic detail possible, the facts of my decline. Now, as soon as I tell her about my latest hospitalizations, a painful and familiar chain reaction occurs: All the way from Bali her voice trembles, and on the edge of crying, she asks me what I've done to fix the situation. It's like she's channeling Scott and the doctors in the STU, only with my mother my failure to thrive isn't just a self-inflicted burden. It oppresses her because she feels my pain so intensely that it's overwhelming for her. So she turns away.

"I don't know how I'm going to sleep at night now," she says, "knowing you're like this!"

"When you come home, I'll give you some of my sleeping pills."

"This is serious!"

I wonder what she thinks is more serious, my current nightmare or how it makes her feel. While my father knows about my situation and keeps his distance, my mother dives into my despair without an oxygen tank, only to surface minutes later, hauling ass for shore. I once had a dream that the two of us were trapped in the wheel of a water mill. We tried desperately to extract ourselves and save each other, but one of us was always dragged under the water, only to emerge and watch helplessly as the other got pulled down.

All year I've been waiting for my mother to return—and dreading it, because as soon as she understands the full extent of my situation, it will practically destroy her. Our fragility shatters each other, over and over again. And yet I need her. I always need her. Her presence is as soothing as it is distressing. I still have the urge to crawl into her lap, to feel the soft skin of her cheek, to have her hold me.

I feel like I'm driving a spike into her when I tell her about my hospitalization. "What about the therapy?" she asks, "and the new medications? And Anna, what does Anna think about all of this?"

By the end of the conversation, my mother is crying, I'm crying, and we both say, "I don't know what to do."

A new set of groups is added to my MAP schedule: life transitions, behavioral scheduling, and aftercare planning, all preparation for my imminent discharge as soon as my insurance company decides to pull the plug. Scott gives me another two weeks, three tops, before the gavel comes down. I'm now considered a "heavy utilizer" of mental health services, and apparently, the more you need services, the less willing insurance is to pay for them. I pretty much keep to myself except for two girls I've met, Cait and Sadie. Both decided to change their names when they entered the MAP program, so I have no idea what their real names are. I consider doing this too, but in true borderline fashion, every day I come up with a different name. Todd is also back, looking foppishly boyish and more clear-eyed than before. I try to keep my distance.

When not meticulously mapping out my future life in groups, I work with Scott on applying the CBT skills in real-life situations. Since anxiety cripples me whenever I venture into public or I'm under pressure, I try intentionally exposing myself to small doses of these triggers. It's apparently a tried and true behavioral therapy method. If you gradually expose yourself to a cue that triggers anxiety while using new coping techniques, eventfully you'll become desensitized and react differently. So I take a bus to Harvard Square. Once there, sweating, dizzy, and with my heart pounding, I hide in the bathroom of the Harvard Coop bookstore. When I can breathe evenly again, I sit in one of the chairs on the third floor, near the psychology section, and do a work-sheet rating my thoughts and feelings. Later, at Whole Foods Market, when I want to kick the person who lingers in front of me over the goat cheese, I take deep breaths, pull out a bracelet with textured beads, and, closing my eyes, focus on my fingers and not the flashes of violence that streak through me. This is called grounding. Afterward, I do another worksheet, called a mood monitor. I have binders full of them by now.

It must be working a little, because I feel calmer when I go out, and Scott is pleased. If it weren't for Todd, I'd also consider myself as having made progress. Unfortunately, Todd seems tempting to me again, and the more time I spend with Sadie and Cait, the more bawdy I'm becoming. We sit on the grassy hillock outside the MAP entrance during breaks and compare notes on sexual adventures. Sadie and I discover we're fairly well matched in terms of sleeping indiscriminately with inappropriate men and, more uniquely, remembering the name and circumstances of every one of them.

Todd ventures over to us on occasion to smoke a cigarette and listen to our girl talk. One afternoon he declares, "My old girlfriend said that having sex with me when I think I'm Jesus is the best she's ever had."

Oh no. I'm all over that one: "What did she mean by that?" "How did you feel when it happened?" "How often do these Jesus episodes occur?"

After Todd stumbles off, Sadie puts a hand on my arm, immediately reading my intentions. "Chicks, not dicks," she says. "At least here."

But I'm under the influence. Something about his youth—and the buzzing manic energy that no amount of mood stabilizers can suppress—feeds me. I'm back under the tree with the sun on my face, intensely alive. I truly hope it's just a passing crush, but I know I'm in trouble because the next morning I wake up happy. Not happy with content-ment or satisfaction; more of an excited, giddy rush to take a shower so I can get out and see a boy. I dig through my bottomless closet of identi-ties and pull out a hippie dress and sandals, and if I hadn't thrown out my patchouli oil in disgust some years back, I'd be applying it liberally.

In CBT group, Sadie sees me and starts singing "Kumbaya." There's a bounce in my step, and all is well until I finally glimpse Todd in the hallway midmorning. Poised to flirt, I'm crushed when he passes by without looking at me. It's hard to tell if his eyes are unfocused or if he's intentionally not looking. Either way, I'm devastated. It's like being on a trapeze and reaching for the next swing only to find you've leapt into emptiness. No, it's worse. You expect the handoff, and instead there's a flamethrower, blasting you with fire. It's sensitivity to rejection on steroids. This upswing straight into the maw of pain makes assertiveness group difficult to follow, especially because my response to rejection involves more than intolerable pain; it calls up an even deeper desire for whoever rejects me. So now I'm obsessed with Todd. It doesn't matter that he lives in a mental hospital, that I've only spoken to him twice, or that he's incapable of basic conversation. Trapped in need, I just hope he'll revert back to psychosis so I can have sex with Jesus.

"You're vulnerable," Scott says when I meet with him later that day.

I'm shaking and crying. "Why does this always happen?" It's more than a silly crush; it's a reflection of some sort of deep trouble—a desire that eclipses reason and takes me over, shapes me, and narrows all of reality to that one pinpoint.

"You merge with Todd when he's around. You've got to practice grounding and get yourself back."

I nod and snuffle and go off to another CBT group. There, we fill out a chain analysis worksheet for a current problem. In each link of the chain, you put down a thought, feeling, or action that leads you to the place of pain. I title mine "The Borderline Chain of Desire." Here's how it goes: Connection. Disconnection. Craving. Despair. Self-hatred. Suicidality. Desperate attempt to reconnect. More rejection.

I always start out flying high with lust in that first link in the chain, but then end up with the chain around my neck, weighing me down with self-hatred and despair. I have to get over Todd. If I'm going to feel suicidal over anyone, let it at least be someone who can speak in compound sentences.

As I'm the only borderline in my new trio with Cait and Sadie, I find it funny I'm the only one who hasn't changed my name. Then again, they're not the ones who instantly resolved, after hearing about Todd's sex life, to wear Birkenstocks and stop shaving their armpits. Since breaking up with Bennet (and Alexis), my identity has grown nebulous again, waiting to take another shape. Sometimes my identity forms in response to longing, and other times in response to revulsion: swings in self-perception decorated with music and clothes. I'm a bad-ass and wear latex; I'm a hippie and wear Indian prints. The various parts of me cannot seem to coexist. And as the summer progresses and my life keeps bottoming out, my connection to the Kiera who tries so hard, who longs for healing, is steadily dwindling.

Todd's somewhat of a last gasp. I'm not interested in listening to Bob Marley telling me to "lively up" myself. The only music that satisfies me is Nine Inch Nails and Trent Reznor's voice crying through industrial rhythms. In the August evenings, I lie on my bed with earphones, letting his laments roll through me like unrepentant thunderstorms. I envy the courage that carries his voice into the world. He doesn't berate himself for pain and anger; he howls. And this delights me, even though I feel ashamed when my own rage comes to the surface. My anger doesn't signify courage; it's just more confirmation that I'm bad.

❦

I try to not let go of the mindfulness practice. I observe the emotions crest and clash, tidal in the coming and going of perspectives. Opposing forces battle within me: I want to get better. I want to die. I want to be loved. I want to spit in the face of everyone I see. Such drastic shifts exhaust me, and I know they baffle others. And it's gaining momentum again. My mercurial self is clamoring for a foothold, and I'm slipping. Borderlines are experts in wrestling with demons; the problem is, we always seem to lose. Fight long enough, and it only makes sense to join the demons. What other choice is there?

Friday night after MAP, as I lie on my bed listening to Nine Inch Nails with the whole empty weekend looming before me, I think, *You've tried to get help. Look where that fucking got you.* Then I sit up in bed and understand something very clearly: If I want to survive, I have to stop turning my energy against myself—stop being the worker bee, the supplicant always feeling helpless and asking for help, the one who desires, unrequited. I have to transform this despair and anger into power.

The last thing Scott told me before the weekend was that I need to reclaim myself and my power. I agree, though perhaps not in the sense he intended. My borderline "unstable sense of self" notwithstanding, there is some power growing in me, shaped in response to my inner

59

conviction that nothing can save me, that I'm basically fucked and not getting better. Many things can happen when you're in a no-win situation: You can completely fall apart, feeling helpless and victimized. You can run away and hope the world changes. Or you can rise like a fury, go dark, and be the pain—which I've done before. In tenth grade, I woke up one day, cut off all my hair, threw out my clothes, and wore only black. People said I was trying to get attention, that I was purposely oppositional and needed more medication. But if the world is closed to you and all you feel is pain, why keep pretending?

I go down to the basement and open up a suitcase. Inside are the outfits I wear only when I'm in this state: latex and leather and PVC; corsets, gloves, chokers, and thigh-high boots. There's a club in Cambridge called ManRay, where all the fetishists come out on Friday nights. It's a carnival of flesh and spectacle, role reversal, and pain turned into pleasure. That's where I need to go. That's where I can be myself as I am right now. In fact, I'm right back in the latex I wore when Bennet and I met, my wrists and neck encircled in leather, eyes carved black with eyeliner. As I pass through the vestibule into the club, I already feel safer. I feel no social anxiety amidst the brooding goths, latex dolls, and men with dog collars, and the pulse of industrial music and smell of clove cigarettes sends me into a trancelike state almost immediately. It's been a long time since my last visit—since before I met Bennet and took out the tongue and nipple rings, before I fell into that particular hole.

In the enveloping darkness, I sit on a stool along the wall overlooking the dance floor. I sip tonic water and watch two girls in lingerie and a bald man in leather grind together. Wandering into the larger room, I sit on a velvet couch and stare at the video screens above me, showing endless loops of women undressing and binding each other up in plastic wrap. In a far corner, a heavy woman in fishnet stockings secures a man's wrists and ankles to a wooden cross, then draws her leather riding crop over his chest. A group of people cluster around, some waiting for their turn.

I didn't come here to be hurt. Physical pain isn't a turn-on for me. My compulsion to cut has an entirely different motivation—in my world, pain simply relieves another form of pain. In my heart, I don't want to hurt myself, or anyone else, but this is like being at a family reunion, and the sadists and masochists are my cousins. I can be fierce without having to lash out. I can feel sexual and be in control. As the night progresses, the crowd thickens. On the floor, a mass of bodies begins to shift like a school of fish. I step inside the swirl and pound of bodies, and a certain magic happens—my core spins and loosens. In this amniotic fluid of rhythm and movement, I rejoin the human realm. More than sex, more than love, this connects me...as long as no one comes too close. As soon as I sense a man keeping his eye on me for too long, I move. Because I also remember this about myself: As soon as I'm touched, all of my power drains away and I'll become a supplicant again. Tonight I've severed the part of myself that needs someone else's touch. But if I am touched, it will awaken. And I'll be helpless again.

My mother has returned. And as soon as she unpacks, she comes to Waltham to take me out to lunch. Her arms are filled with presents she's gathered during her year away: silver bangles, embroidered scarves, a carved box, and earrings with turquoise stones. We go for Thai food and sit in a window booth facing Moody Street. She asks if I've gone out recently, and I say I went dancing at a club on Friday night, which I haven't done in a long time.

"You need to get out more," she says. "If you only go out rarely, each time is a small trauma. Go more often and you'll grow used to it." I thank her for that insight into my agoraphobia. "And not just to gyrate in dark rooms," she adds. "Try to actually socialize. Talk to people."

The waitress appears with fragrant, steaming dishes. After she puts them down, she and my mother discuss the street food in Thailand. The waitress is an exuberant young woman, and her laughter lingers in my mother's eyes.

"She'd make a good friend," my mother smiles. "She's so...positive." When she sees I'm not sharing her enthusiasm, she shrugs. "I just like people, I guess."

Well, it's not like I don't like people; I just find them disturbing and can't manage their effects on me, positive or negative. It's like having too many nerves on the social end of things.

I can't seem to get my mother to understand this. Her eyes delight in the world, and she thrives on discovering and sharing. This is one of the many reasons we can't reach each other. In darkness, she gropes. And when I name those darknesses with the one tool I can always call on, language, she'd rather paint color into the void, hang a still life over the hole with a big sign for me: "Enter Here."

"I'm just not comfortable with you referring to yourself as 'mentally ill,'" she comments after I've given her the full update on my current treatment and status. I emphasize that I really am sick, not just in a funk. "Calling yourself mentally ill… It's so…you know… If you were schizophrenic, I'd understand. But you're not like that. I think you're just depressed again. And it's probably situational depression. Losing the job and that boyfriend depressed you, but I think you can do something to change that."

I find I'm eating quite fast to quell the feeling in my stomach. Thank god for my medication. Otherwise I'm sure I'd be screaming, "Don't you get it?!" and sobbing right now. Instead, I hoover my pad thai.

"If you call yourself mentally ill," she continues, "you'll just be labeling yourself, and probably, when you're around other people, you'll feel different."

"But I am different! Some people might consider me lucky to be alive, given how suicidal and self-destructive I've been." At that, my mother looks so upset that I say no more. We've already lost my brother. Am I rubbing it in her face that her remaining child has a recurring death wish, and for no reason that she can understand? Yet I need my mother to recognize what I'm experiencing, even if it scares the shit out of her.

I don't know how to make that happen without causing more pain for both of us.

9

Flying the Coop

September arrives and another MAP discharge is imminent. I have three more weeks before I'm interviewed for the new DBT program, and Scott proposes that I transition into a low-stress, part-time job in the meantime. Both he and my mother suggest working at a bookstore. That makes sense: a quiet place with books, intellectual types wandering in and out; it just might work. The most logical choice is the Harvard Coop. From the amount of time I spend there, ducking into the women's bathroom, I probably already look familiar to the staff. And it's in Harvard Square, where I've spent half my life wandering the stores and streets. I'm hired as soon as I drop off the application and feel a moment of complete terror as I realize that I'm going to be back in the world—and at the same time, cut loose from MAP. I remind myself that I'm in emotion mind. The facts are simple: I'm going to work at a bookstore. I've done retail before. In fact, after every hospital discharge, I've been scraped off the ground by some store or restaurant and installed behind the counter.

In the transition groups, people talked about "recovery jobs," and that's what this is. I tell myself, *I'm going to take this job because I have to learn how to be a part of life again. I have to train in managing my feelings and reactions, and not let my distorted thinking and emotions control me.*

I receive a quick orientation with a group of new hires, and then we're assigned departments. I'm given a coveted main-floor position with fiction, memoir, and poetry sections. "Don't worry if there are lines," the manager instructs us. "It'll take a couple hours to learn the ropes, but just take your time and don't be afraid to ask for help."

I'm positioned behind a counter facing displays of featured titles. As luck would have it, they're promoting local female memoirists. I get to stare at the covers of *Girl, Interrupted* and *Prozac Nation* while Dan, the young man assigned to train me, looks on exasperated as my fingers can't pick out the proper codes.

"Have you ever used a cash register before?" he asks. Well, yes. But never in the second week of being put on an antipsychotic medication. Every time I mess up, trainer boy has to call a manager, who takes forever to arrive and then grumbles as she reverses my mistake by entering the secret manager code. I look at the clock and realize only a half hour has passed. It's 9:30 a.m. and I don't get a break until 11. I'm boxed in between the other two registers, where seasoned clerks madly bag books, and the line of customers grows by the minute. I have never seen the Harvard Coop this crowded, and I've been visiting Harvard Square going on two decades.

"What's your problem?" Dan asks, as I once again enter the wrong code. There are, of course, many ways to answer that question, but I know exactly what's wrong. I'm starting to have an anxiety attack. And I can't do a thing about it. I note all of the signs emerging: sweating, chest pains, blurred vision, my fingers shaking and refusing to do what they're told. The line of customers snakes into the travel section in the rear of the store. At that moment, my trainer decides it's time for his cigarette break.

"You'll be fine," he says with a smirk—obviously a sadist. I look at the register and my hands seem miles away. The girl standing in front of me with a tall stack of books looks sixteen. Indeed, the whole place swarms with young, well-groomed Harvard students, emptying the stores shelves like waves of locusts. In the background, the words "freshman orientation" float by.

The urge to flee enters my brain like a crack hit. I blink twice, then dart behind the registers, clutching my backpack in my hands and ducking like I'm avoiding gunfire. Coming around the corner, I almost collide with the lady from the information desk. She is old and wears orthopedic shoes and overly bright lipstick.

"I quit," I say.

"Do you work here?" she rasps.

I run through the doors and into the crowds thronging the sidewalk on Massachusetts Avenue. I imagine a security guard chasing after me, demanding I return the name tag, but that's silly. No one from the store will even call me. I take the bus back to my apartment and spend the rest of the day in my room with the shades drawn and a cold wash-cloth on my forehead. My heart won't stop racing.

I know my mother will be upset. "Couldn't you have at least tried to stay for the day?" she'll ask, the disappointment dripping from her voice like acid. When I finally leave the bed, I'm planning on taking a bath, but once I'm in the bathroom my hands go automatically to the cabinet and fish out a couple of new disposable razors. I dislodge the blades and set up my supplies: paper towels for blotting, alcohol for disinfecting, bandages. I'm not cutting to prove anything, but this one session doesn't seem like a private matter. Every time I draw the blade over my skin, I think of how the marks will horrify others. Subtlety no longer matters. I target my upper arm and carve circlets—blood bangles—around and around: ten, fifteen, until my bicep wears a raw band of red incisions half its length. I'm breathless from the effort, dizzy too. And all I can think is *Fuck you. Fuck you for making me jump back in and telling me I could land on my feet. Fuck you for all your fucking help.*

My mother insists we go out for dinner the next night, since she'll go back to teaching full-time in a few days. When I was younger, I often hid my cuts, or if she did see them, nothing was said. I'm sure she assumed it was the psychiatrist's job to talk with me. And I know that, both then and now, my pain triggers something unbearable in her, as does the sight of my wounds. It's a strange and impenetrable situation: My family's response to my recurring crises is to minimize (It's just depression... Just go to a meeting... You don't really have a mental illness...). Yet at the same time, when faced with the blood or the hospitals, they become so troubled that they distance themselves even more. Recently my grandparents sent me a heart-shaped locket with their pictures in it. I haven't talked to them in months, but my mother must have told them something. The locket is their way of expressing that they know I'm in trouble and they love me, but in my mind, it simply reaffirms that, while I have family, I don't have their support. A picture of love is not the same thing as being present and walking through this with me.

I decide not to cover the fresh cuts. Like clockwork, when my mother sees my arm, she cries. But something has changed, because she doesn't turn away.

"I'm not leaving you alone tonight," she insists after dinner. She doesn't realize that almost every night is like this. At the table, she'd given me one last present from Bali, a necklace with a stone Buddha set in silver. I put it on, and the Buddha rests on the middle of my chest, over my heart, sitting peacefully in his cross-legged posture. I don't know much about Buddhism, only that Dr. Linehan's dialectical behavior therapy is partially based on it. For now, I just know that the Buddha looks so calm and collected, so obviously unruffled by anxiety attacks and self-hatred, that it can't hurt to absorb a little of his peace.

"I want you to hold the Buddha whenever you start to feel upset," my mother says as we climb into my bed. "I want you to believe in your own goodness." I wrap one hand around the necklace and drape the other over my mother. Hanging nearby is the gold locket with my grandparents' faces inside. For the first time, I wonder: How much of what I feel as neglect has been fueled by the force of my constant need? How much can any person hold another who is perpetually falling? Yet my mother is here now, and insists on watching over me tonight—and gives me a Buddha that grows warm against my heart.

I wish this could be enough, but it isn't. It's a raindrop that falls on land barren from decades of drought. In a day, the private school job completely absorbs my mother. Her role is to take care of other children, and I am not a child anymore. I remember Dr. Zanarini's article on borderline pain, how we feel misunderstood and think that no one cares about us and that we are bad...damaged children, shunned by the world (Zanarini et al. 1998). How much of this is feeling I have right now is fueled by a belief, and how much is reality? And if, as DBT maintains, there can be a dialectic of opposites, is it possible for both to be true?

All I do now is wait for my appointment with the potential new therapist in Cambridge. When I get to the point where I want to start chopping fingers off, I go to NA meetings, where I meet up with Brian, the poet, and his wife, Maureen. My reliance on them is an uncomplicated version of what I had with Bennet and Alexis: a couple who have room in their lives for a third wheel, only Brian and Maureen are married and in their fifties. When I tell them I'm mired in mental illness, they nod and list all of the medications they're currently on. Maureen insists I call her if I ever need help, but I can't imagine putting the weight of this nightmare on her.

Lately I've been fantasizing about carbon monoxide poisoning. Pills seem too uncertain now, and I'm not very good at swallowing them. My car's exhaust, on the other hand, is rich in poison. In fact, it's in such bad shape that I can practically kill myself just by driving with the windows rolled up. I mull over the benefits of carbon monoxide poisoning until my suicide seems dreamy, almost romantic. I'll have a last meal, park at the edge of a field, watch the sunset, listen to Nine Inch Nails' magnificent double CD *The Fragile*, and slip out of my body as I drink in the fumes. All I need is a hose.

While I continue to wait for my intake appointment for the new DBT program, the night arrives when I cross from fantasy into action. Relief is all I want—that, and a long hose. It turns out that Sunday night isn't the best time to find an open hardware store. The only place open is Petco. There must be rubber hoses in the fish section, so I wander among the blue tanks and supply displays. I find bags of pebbles, miniature castles, fish food and turtle food, glass tanks, and aerators, and, finally, plastic tubes. But they're only about two feet long and no bigger around than my index finger. There's no way I can run the exhaust from my tailpipe into my window for this plan. I'd have to lie on a lawn chair under the bumper to suck the exhaust.

It's amazing how powerful vanity can be, because the image of me found dead under my car with black soot in my mouth is enough to dissuade me. I return to my room, feeling the way I sometimes do when I go shopping for a pair of shoes and come back empty-handed. Now there's some distance between me and the urge again, enough that I have the presence of mind to call the hospital and pack my bags. Like always, they'll ask if I'm a danger to myself or others, if I want to die and if I have a plan. The plan is very important. Then they'll ask for a suicide history, but they don't seem to be interested in all those times when a person has been on that edge for hours, days, or weeks; they only want to know about actual attempts. Apparently getting that close and then backing away doesn't count. But from my side, it's like racing toward a brick wall in a car and then swerving at the last minute.

Afterward there's adrenaline and relief, but no way to get out of the car, and the compulsion to careen toward the wall comes again and again.

This third time, checking in isn't so easy. I come with three bags in tow and the word "borderline" all over my records, and it's obvious that the clinician doing the intake mistrusts my motives for coming back. When I say I've been suicidal for a lot of my life, he raises his eyebrows. "Maybe you should start learning how to live with it."

"But I need to be safe. Right now!"

He keeps his eyes on the paperwork, and when he looks up at me, I sense anger, or maybe dislike, almost like a vapor coming from his eyes. Though it's just a small hint, I feel rage bubbling up. I want him to see my scars. I want him to see me bleeding and smashing my head against the wall. I want him to know what it's like being me.

This time I'm put in the "rapid recovery unit," a place that's about as antithetical to recovery, let alone a rapid one, as you can imagine. The door opens, and the first thing I hear is men bellowing—not shouting or screaming, but bellowing in another language. Several black men in white scrubs, obviously the overnight staff, argue over the TV station in the common room. Their voices send me into a panic, and I turn to the nurse who is gathering my bags for inspection.

"Can you call someone? Get me switched?" I plead. "Isn't there a women's unit or something?" She shakes her head and tells me nothing can be done. I feel like I'm going to throw up as the realization that I'm locked up—really locked up—hits. So far, hospitalizations have felt comforting. I've not wanted to leave. Now I'm trapped. In my room I start crying, then it turns into howling. I don't care who hears me. If there's any place where screaming and sobbing is typical, this is it. The person doing night checks wears stiletto heels, and every time she does rounds it sounds like small firecrackers being thrown down the hallway. I don't sleep.

The "Rapid Recovery Unit," or RRU, is really just a euphemism for a holding tank. I'm the only woman not in a chemical straightjacket from all the meds, and for the first time in my mental heath career, I'm an ethnic minority. The attending doctor is the same one associated with MAP, and he looks saddened to see me here, especially when I say I'm being held here against my will. "But you checked yourself in last night."

"Not here!"

"You can't leave until we figure out why you keep coming back." He sits in a chair, looking dapper in his tailored suit, and I sit on my bed with a blanket wrapped around me, eyes swollen and throat sore. We review my current treatment: medication, 12-step meetings on occasion, the DBT group. He tells me that we can continue adjusting the medications, and that I can return to MAP until I'm in the new DBT program, but he wants to know what will give me hope again. It's the first time anyone has asked me that.

"If I have hope, I'm only going to get crushed again," I say tearfully.

"If you could have anything in the world, what would it be?" he asks.

"Love," I say without a second's hesitation. "But that's the biggest setup of all."

When I call my mom and tell her I'm back in the hospital, she exclaims, "What happened?!"

"Nothing happened. It was just another day." I'm sure she won't be able to visit, but she promises to come the next day. I ask her to bring me chocolate—and a file in a cake. She arrives the next day, bearing expensive dark chocolates, mango body lotion, and a book on van Gogh's drawings. ("He had borderline!" I declare when I see it, and she sighs; not even high culture can escape my preoccupation with mental illness.)

"I want you to try to focus on other things," my mom says, unpacking a sketchbook and some charcoals I mentioned I'd run out of. "This place depresses me," she says, and asks what they're doing for my treatment.

"Why don't you talk to someone and find out?" I say.

"I just don't understand why they're not able to help," she replies. "You're on medication, right?"

I explain that meds don't fix borderline, and that I'm going into a new DBT program with a new therapist soon.

"Good. I never liked Anna," my mom says, "ever since the nipple ring incident." Oh god. After I got my nipples pierced, I asked Anna if she thought it was appropriate to tell my mom about it. "What's the worst that could happen?" Anna asked. That was admittedly a disastrous decision on both our parts. Some things you should never tell your mother.

I share the chocolates with the lunch crowd and give away the body lotion. In two days, I'm discharged back into MAP.

10

Chalice of the Hopeless

People want to know the exact moment or the circumstances of my turning point. Is there a bottom with BPD? Does something happen that changes everything? This will sound bizarre, but yes, I've figured out what did it: rage. Ultimately rage, not hope, hurls me into recovery when I finally understand that it's not simply my illness, but incompetence and avoidance from the mental health system that has created my "incurable and hopeless" condition. And if there's one thing that motivates me, it's justified, self-righteous anger. The tipping point comes when I request my medical records from the hospital, both from my current stays and from back when I was seventeen, so I can discuss them at my upcoming intake interview for the new therapist and DBT program.

It only takes a week for the manila envelope to arrive from the hospital, filled with a small stack of intake and discharge summaries. The current records don't surprise me, I practically could have written them myself. It's the one from fourteen years ago that turns the tide, that makes me decide I am not going to let this illness or the negligence of others destroy me. Call it a variant of "Living well is the best revenge." When I read the discharge summary from so many years ago, it plainly states that my Axis II diagnosis was borderline personality disorder—meaning that for years and years doctors knew and kept it a secret.

The room goes white when I read the words. Why didn't they tell me? How could my psychiatrist allow me to leave a mental hospital without knowing the illness that was destroying me? I call my mother up.

"What did they tell you at the hospital in 1987? What did they say my problem was?"

"They told me you were depressed and using drugs."

"No one said anything about BPD?"

"No one said much of anything, Kiera. It felt like they didn't want me involved. And I was already overwhelmed."

I don't know who to believe. It seems just as likely that the doctors did tell my mother and she promptly forgot. Yet there's no way I can blame her for not knowing. That summer before my eighteenth birthday was a nightmare. In those few months, my brother went into drug rehab, I was in the mental hospital, and my mother's thyroid was diagnosed as malignant and needed immediate surgery. But I can blame the doctors, the hospitals, and the therapists, even if their intentions might have been to "protect" me from the stigma of BPD. This could be considered black-and-white thinking, but given the treatment I've received for my BPD, this much is clear: The whole system is fucked. I've had the diagnosis for almost half my life and no one told me. Even after getting the diagnosis, in this past year not one professional has given me information about it outside of Dr. B's original fifteen-minute discussion of my symptoms. Even my meeting with the famous BPD doctor didn't touch on the subject. I've been on six different medications, and now I discover that the hospital's "DBT program" is a sham, even as I'm still being told it's the critical element to helping me get better.

We hear many stories of desperate parents who must fight with doctors to get proper mental health treatment for their children. Less frequently, but on occasion, we hear of people with mental illness who fight for treatment. But in 2001, no one with borderline is publicly demanding proper help and treatment. Here we are, immersed in a sea of shame and self-hatred beyond reason, and on top of that, our illness is considered too shameful to even admit to, and apparently no one else wants to deal with it. By now, after almost a year of supposed treatment for BPD, my symptoms of inappropriate anger, paranoia under stress, rapidly shifting emotions, and all of the core feelings of being neglected, alone, and helpless aren't symptoms of the disease anymore; they're a response to real conditions. I finally realize that a diagnosis of BPD will create a response in the mental health system (and others) that can actually trigger these so-called symptoms, locking you into the borderline criteria. The clinical term for this situation is "iatrogenic," meaning a treatment that causes more illness.

This is what does it. This is my turning point. I'm so pissed off that I become determined to fight—for my survival, and for my borderline brothers and sisters. We do not deserve to be trapped in hell. It isn't our fault.

By late September I'm a MAP veteran, an old-timer in a place where the typical shelf life is two weeks. Cait and Sadie, and even Todd, have left. The groups proceed with the same topics, people come with the same broken lives and tortured souls. I get my tongue pierced again (though I stop short of the nipples; the last time was just too painful) and I show up for groups in combat boots, fishnet stockings, and dark glasses. I go to ManRay and "gyrate in dark rooms," despite my mother's plea for normal socializing. I wait.

Scott is determined to get my family on board before insurance pulls the plug. "You need their help and support," he insists, "especially given your housing situation." It's true that things are worsening: Patty's lovers are multiplying, with a new man shuffling through the downstairs every few days, and the landlord has announced a rent increase I can't afford. Scott hands me applications to fill out for disability housing and department of mental health client status. He says that it will take months for them to be processed. "In the meanwhile, you need your family. You need them now. You need a 'family meeting.'"

I'm used to this last desperate grab for alternatives. No one invites my parents to the table until insurance runs out, then suddenly they're important again. Meanwhile, my parents have long ago dissociated themselves from my mental health, and each other. If you want to see an example of "splitting," said to be such a borderline trait, look no further than my parents. Divorced by the time I was six, my mother used to tell us that my father was a "bad man." She could barely look at him those weekends she'd hand me and my brother over for visitation. Was this bad man the same person who took us for ice cream and told us he loved us? What monstrous thing caused my mother to never talk to him again? What made my mother's parents turn their backs on him so completely? I thought he might have been a murderer, a bank robber, or a vampire—which confused me, since she always handed us over to him for weekend visits anyway. But as I'd eventually come to learn, he wasn't a monster. He was, in fact, a lot like me: a disappointment, a drunk, inconstant, and irresponsible. My mother hated him because he ruined her dream of the perfect marriage. And he did little to redeem himself over the years, breaking our hearts with his absences and failed promises time and time again.

It was only after my brother died that my father and I became friends. Ben's death was sudden and shocking—a freak brain virus that killed him within hours, and destroyed the last remains of our family, as well. It finalized my mother and stepfather's decision to divorce.

It prompted my mother to flee her grief that next year by traveling alone around the world for her first teaching sabbatical. People have said how brave she was to leave everything and travel. All I knew was that she was leaving me, and though I'd finally gotten my GED and had been accepted into a liberal arts school in upstate New York, I was utterly, nightmarishly alone. Expected to pay my own way through school, I could barely make it to midday classes, while my using escalated to the point I was carrying bottles of whiskey around with me and driving regularly to New York City with theater students to score crystal meth for weekend binges. Yet that black hole also restored my father to me somewhat. When I was nineteen and utterly, nightmarishly alone and devastated, my father called, visited, and brought me cigarettes. He took me to AA and NA meetings and held my hand. He arrived just when everyone who said they loved me disappeared into their own grief. He didn't turn away from my pain.

My brother's funeral was the second to last time in my memory that my parents talked, sharing a few words at the memorial service, next to the grave. The very last time was a decade ago, at the hospital where I got sober. Just as Scott is now suggesting, the therapist called them together as a last resort to help find me a place to live and offer me some financial support. I know Scott's effort now will be futile, just like ten years ago, but there's nowhere else to turn. So one evening at the appointed hour, I wait outside the MAP building for my parents to arrive. My father shows up first, here from New York. He stands with me for a bit, hugs me, and tells me it's going to be alright, but I can see how nervous he is, that he doesn't know what's expected of him, or what my mother will say or do. Ten, fifteen, twenty minutes pass, and still my mother doesn't arrive. This is so unlike her that I wonder if she got into an accident.

Then her car careens past the building and disappears down the road. I wait. The car approaches again and I try flagging it down, but it passes. From the brief glimpse I get of her face, she looks absolutely frantic—so frantic that she can't slow down enough to see that she's passing the building over and over again. Finally I stand in the middle of the road and flag her down, hoping she won't hit me or go off the road. Once out of the car, she's breathless: Classes ran late, then traffic was a nightmare, and she almost got into an accident. She hugs me and tells me not to worry, that everything is going to be okay. I so wish I didn't have to go in there with them.

An hour later, my parents and I walk to the cafeteria, where we sit and try to make sense of what to do. My goal of getting their help somehow collapsed in the meeting. The collision of my parent's perspectives, combined with their limitations and ideas about what I'm supposed to be doing, dismantled the conversation so quickly that even Scott was scratching his head. At the end of the meeting, he says, "I think it's best if you keep talking about this yourselves."

"I have to tell you what I need," I say when we're settled at a Formica table. I look down at the cheat sheet Scott helped me put together the day before. "I can't support myself financially and I need your help. I have a mental illness that you guys don't seem to understand. I need you to learn about it. I need you to work together with me. I feel like all my life I've been on my own. And every time I can't take care of myself, you just get more angry and frustrated—or you ignore me completely." Somehow, my list of "needs" quickly turns into an escalating rant about how neglected I feel. And, since this is the first time in two decades I've had their audience together, without a therapist or a funeral procession, I'm not reining myself in.

"You two have done nothing to help me with this. I'm sick of fighting on my own. It's been a constant struggle, and you're always blaming me. Why can't you support me?" I start crying. "Why can't I get your help?"

"I've been supporting you your whole life!" My mother erupts, in tears now too. "How can you accuse me of that?"

"You mother's right," my dad says. "If there's anyone here who should be blamed, it's me. Don't do this to her."

I look at the two of them. This is unreal! He's backing her up. Maybe they'll have a bonding moment and go out for dinner when all of this is over.

"I think," my father continues, "it's those student loans of yours. You're overwhelmed with the idea of having to pay off so much money."

My mother rebukes him: "Can't you understand that's the last of Kiera's worries? She's been in this hospital half the summer!"

My head is spinning. I was hoping they'd each pledge me a bit of monthly money and agree to some family counseling. My mom is crying hard. My dad holds his head in his hands, sighing deeply. I take my mom to the restroom.

"We're in a mental hospital," I say. "If there's any place it's okay to lose your shit, it's here."

"I hate this! I don't know what I did wrong."

I try to assure her that she didn't do anything wrong, that I'm just really sick and need a lot of help, that I've needed a lot of help that no one has seemed to be able to give me. She shakes her head. "I don't understand why all this treatment isn't helping."

We go back to my dad. "I'm sorry," he says, "but I've got to drive back to New York." My mother wipes her eyes and says she needs to leave too; this whole meeting has exhausted her, and she's got classes to teach in the morning. The three of us walk to our cars and drive away in different directions. Family meeting adjourned.

When my appointment for the new therapist and DBT program finally arrives in late September, I interview for an hour with an older woman doctor and a younger male therapist, Ethan. My responses are fairly wooden. It's like coming to the end of a maze and realizing the exit points you right back into the tunnel. When I say, deadpan, that nothing in my life gives me pleasure except Starbucks coffee, the young therapist stifles a smile. I'm clutching an empty Starbucks cup in my hands, a chalice of the hopeless... And while the doctor in her cashmere shawl nods seriously and makes a note, Ethan and I meet eyes. I'm not quite sure why, but I suspect he gets it: how insane this situation is—almost comical, if I could only keep myself alive.

So this is Ethan, my new therapist. He's about my age, thirties-ish. He's neither tall nor short, and except for that one smile, his face, topped by dark, cropped curls, is as blank and smooth as white marble. He's part of the DBT team at this new hospital but specializes in CBT and anxiety. When we stand up, I notice he's wearing his pressed black slacks just a bit higher than most people would, old-man-style, and that his white oxford shirt balloons a bit too much the way it's tucked in. It gives him a nerdy air that, combined with his glasses, offsets his attractiveness and makes it hard to think of him in bed with me—an image that eventually enters my mind with almost any attractive man, especially one I think of as a savior.

"When can we start?" I ask, trying not to sound desperate. They confer over Ethan's PalmPilot and set a date two weeks away—not a long time for most people, but an eon when every minute is pure survival.

"I don't want to sound like I'm threatening," I tell them, "but I'm not sure I'll make it till then." Ethan doesn't look at all alarmed. He nods as though that makes perfect sense and writes down the numbers for his office phone and after-hours pager. I look at the card with suspicion. Therapists always say you can call them in an emergency, but what they really mean is that you can call between the hours of 9 a.m. and 4 p.m., leave a message, and they'll get back to you the next day. And their answering machines add, without fail, "If this is an emergency, please call 911 or go to your nearest emergency room."

Since I am pretty much a walking emergency, I highly doubt that Ethan is serious about this offer, but he leaves me with these instructions: If I feel like I'm in trouble, page him or leave a message. He will get back to me. He is my therapist now.

11

Safety

I don't know what to make of Ethan as we finally sit down for therapy. He's dressed like before, his face unreadable and his eyes clear as he sits across from me with his hands folded. I expect us to follow the same routine I've gone through for decades: hashing over the details of my fucked-up life. We'll begin with my childhood, climb over the demolished landscape of my adolescence, and survey the desolate wasteland of my adulthood, figuring out what to fix as we go.

Ethan clicks open his pen and looks down for a moment at the blank legal pad on his lap. Then he says, "The first thing we need to do is establish some goals." He scribbles something on the pad. "The first is to get you safe. That means managing self-harm and suicidal behavior—not hurting yourself. And making sure therapy is safe too, for both of us."

Safety. Always a big word in therapy. I have a good idea of what I need to be safe: Give me a place to live where I don't have to fear leaving my room. Give me a way to make money that doesn't kill me with anxiety and exhaustion. Give me a lover who isn't entangled with an ex. Give me a medication doctor who doesn't make me feel like a lab rat. Give me proof that people with BPD get better. Give me someone who understands.

Ethan gives me a worksheet.

Oh dear god. If Ethan insists on three mood monitors a day, I don't know what I'll do. I've already signed a contract committing myself to working with him. And yet I signed a similar one for the previous DBT group, and if I'd known I'd spend the next seven desperate months being dragged through a meandering confusion of worksheets, musical chairs, and philosophical discussions on Hegelian dialectics, without the help of a trained DBT therapist, I would have had second thoughts—if I'd been able to think clearly. I've been hoping that Ethan will take me down a different road, but seeing another worksheet makes me cringe.

"It's a diary card," he says.

"I keep a diary." Well, I call it a journal.

"It's a DBT diary card. In order to be in therapy with me, you'll need to fill one out every week. It's part of the treatment."

I look down at the diary card. It's got all of the DBT skills listed, so that each day of the week you can check the ones you've used. It also has a section where you rate all your urges for self-destructive behavior and your negative emotions, an area to list the drugs you've taken, and a place to rate your level of joy. Ha! There's even a little box to declare how badly you want to quit therapy.

"So this is part of the therapy I never got before." Ethan nods. "What else are we going to do?"

He explains the phone coaching sessions. When I'm feeling like I need help outside of therapy, I can page him. He'll call me back and provide skills coaching. He clarifies that the phone calls are not therapy sessions. "It's like having a coach on the sidelines while you're playing the game."

"Can I call you at 2 a.m.?" I ask. A lot of my game gets on after midnight.

"No."

Actually, Ethan doesn't have to worry about that with me. Getting me to call will be the hard part.

We go over the diary card and determine I'm pretty much overwhelmed with every negative emotion, and while I'm not acting on my urges, I still want to die, still want to hurt myself. I am instinctively afraid of revealing this to him. My symptoms overwhelm people, even those with professional credentials. I need too much. I am impossible to please. I try to pick up on Ethan's body language, the set of his face, anything that might confirm he feels I'm dragging him to the edge of the cliff with me.

He hands me a piece of paper with my goals written on it and a stack of diary cards. I tell him I don't have much faith that this will work. Even if the previous program was incomplete, I've learned the DBT skills and am even more familiar with the CBT skills. I don't understand how I can have so much information in my head and still not be able to change.

"Marsha Linehan says that people don't fail DBT," Ethan tells me. "It's the therapy or the therapist that fails them."

"Really?"

He nods. "She also says that therapists are jerks."

"I'm liking this Marsha."

So for now, the plan is that I'll see Ethan twice a week to go over my diary card, address my self-destructive urges, and work on my living situation. I'm to page him if I feel the need, and he promises he'll call back. I'm to end things with both MAP and Anna. As soon as the new DBT group has a spot, I'll enter it.

When I leave Ethan's office with my diary card and the promise of another session in three days, I'm relieved and terrified. This could be a whole new beginning. Or it could be yet another false start. I can't count the number of blank journals I've bought, or the date books with their numbered pages and little graphs for listing plans, or the self-help books, all with the expectation that this time it will be different. It's the same way with every therapist and medication. Maybe you have to be delusional to keep going back—or masochistic. But now I have that other motivator: the anger. I'm not going to let this thing kill me.

And then there's Anna. Sweet, ineffectual Anna. I have to break up with her once and for all. After three years of working together, I sit in her office and explain that I'm going over to Ethan. She's upset and wants to know what this new therapist can provide that she can't. When I explain that he's trained in DBT and CBT, she shakes her head. "You need someone who really cares about you, who you can talk to. These new therapies, they're formulaic. You might find them interesting, but they're not the solution."

"What is the solution?" I ask, reminding her that despite all our work together, I was only getting worse.

"Sometimes it's darkest just before the light," Anna says.

"Or sometimes you just have to try something new," I respond.

She shakes her head. "I wish you the best of luck, Kiera. I really do, but I'm certain you'll be back. I can almost guarantee it."

I take my backpack and thank her for all of her help. And I really mean it. She tried her best. But I know that even if Ethan doesn't work out, I won't go back.

During my third session with Ethan, I ask him his opinion of the BPD diagnosis.

Like everyone else, he winces, but since it's Ethan, it's just the faintest little cringe. "It's not a very positive association to have," he says.

"And yet, I have all the symptoms…"

"Do you think you're a 'borderline'?"

"I think I have BPD. I don't really know the difference between having BPD and being a borderline."

"Well, I'll tell you why I'm not comfortable with the diagnosis. You might have the symptoms, but with BPD, the rest of the world typically reduces the person to the disorder, which isn't fair or true. And it's still classified as being 'inflexible and enduring.' I'm not sure that's the right attitude to take if you're looking to get better."

I know on some level that Ethan is being sensitive, but encountering yet another deflection incites me. And Ethan is no longer looking like a therapist I want.

"I'll talk about it with you," Ethan adds. "About BPD tendencies, symptoms, the ways it affects your life. But I'm not calling you a borderline."

I'm still suspicious. "Do you know anything about the disorder?"

Ethan nods. "And I also know that in getting better, it's not helpful to form your entire identity around the label. Any label. You remember Linehan's concept of the dialectic? That two things can be true at the same time? I'm willing to say that you can have BPD and yet not have it."

I nod, a little reassured. "Also," Ethan adds, "insurance doesn't cover it."

"How is that possible?"

"Welcome to managed care. So right now you 'officially' have depression and an anxiety disorder."

This is a whole new aspect of the BPD situation I hadn't yet encountered, another facet to this insanity. I have the image of lemmings pouring over a cliff while a group of suited "managed care" providers cluster around with clipboards, marking down a decrease in therapy costs. They obviously don't need to pay for people who are dead! The bad rap with BPD is seemingly endless. Therapists won't talk about the diagnosis or disclose it. Insurance companies won't pay for treatment. And even within a therapy like DBT—which Dr. Linehan developed specifically for BPD—no one mentions it. I still wonder how you get treatment for something unspeakable.

I'm about to learn. I pull out my diary card, and we go over the week's emotional highs and lows. I haven't cut myself since the Harvard Coop incident, and I'm not fantasizing constantly about overdosing, in no small part because I can call Ethan in the evenings when I'm crawling out of my skin and he'll give me a DBT skill to try (self-soothe, distract, opposite action). So this is progress. Every session we look at the diary card and comb through my self-destructive urges and the moods I've rated on a scale of one to five. The problem, of course, is that being the unstable borderline I am (sorry, Ethan!), I can flip from two to five in an hour, then back again, so how can I rate an emotion's level for an entire day?

"Do a daily average," Ethan suggests, "unless you want to keep a notebook and rate your emotions on an hourly basis." Even for me, that is a bit much.

Now it's November again, which is always the worst. The short days are dark and empty; the long nights even more so. Without a day program, job, or lover to engage me, the overwhelming emptiness returns, along with depression. I've stopped going to ManRay because I can barely roust myself out of bed, let alone get it together to be a bad-ass. On the one hand, having Ethan keeps me going from day to day, but on the other, I'm actually feeling an increase in my hopelessness, especially since time is running out with my apartment and travel continues to be a horror now that my car has died.

It takes two buses and a half-mile walk through Cambridge to get to Ethan's office, and as I go past the beautiful houses on my way to therapy, I'm consumed by envy. The diminishing autumn light sharpens the life behind those windows, each of them a diorama of unattainable treasures. I'm not envious of the polished dining room tables, the damask drapery, or the oil paintings hung on warm-colored walls. What I long for is the sense of belonging these people must feel, or that I imagine they feel, as Ethan points out when I describe this to him. He says, "You assume they are all happy in their lives."

"Happier than me," I reply.

"So if you felt like you belonged somewhere, you'd be happy?" Ethan asks. I declare that it would be a good start. And certainly I wouldn't be happy homeless. So far I've visited two halfway houses and made appointments with three social service housing agencies. There's a possibility I'll be able to get into a state-run halfway house, but that isn't an option until I'm officially a client of the Department of Mental Health. Scott helped me fill out those forms at MAP, but it might be a year before the application is processed. The last housing option for someone on disability with no other funds involves getting a voucher for a state-subsidized apartment. Anyone on disability has the right to this assistance. The housing vouchers are distributed according to your position on the waiting list, and also by a periodic lottery. But the waiting lists are long. Even the inner-city subsidized places have at least a year's wait, and the closer you move toward the gentrified parts of the city, the longer the wait. When I call the city of Cambridge to put my name on a list, the receptionist can't stop laughing. When she finally calms herself, she tells me it will be twelve years.

Our focus in therapy these first couple of months is entirely on safety. Not only to keep me from harming myself, but also to make sure our therapy isn't jeopardized by my behavior, or by Ethan's, for that matter. DBT takes the therapist's behavior as seriously as the client's. It's an unusual contract in this sense, as is the fact that this DBT model, true to Dr. Linehan's original vision, involves Ethan's participation in a consultation team. So each week he meets with other DBT therapists to discuss cases and give and receive guidance. This is a bit unsettling, knowing strangers are privy to my personal details, but I'm also reassured that, for once, I'm not like a baby bird in the hands of one person. I'm more than a handful, that much is certain. And I'm terrified of being dropped.

The problem with this focus on safety is that I always feel unsafe. As Ethan and I look at the architecture of my life and try to figure out ways to build in more external support, I feel overwhelming grief. It's not just my behaviors that make me unsafe; it's how I experience the world and how I feel I've been treated, and how I experience my own emotions and myself. I don't realize this is a common BPD trait until

I read about borderline core beliefs. Cognitive therapists analyzed the perceptions of people with BPD through questionnaires and concluded that we tend to share three basic assumptions: The world is dangerous and malevolent; we are powerless and vulnerable; and we are inherently unacceptable (Beck et al. 2004). Dr. Zanarini (the researcher who wrote about borderline pain) made a similar list: We are endangered; we are like small children; and we feel uncared for (Bateman and Fonagy 2004)

As Ethan and I go over my current living situation and joblessness, he points out that my assessments are colored by a lot of these same beliefs. When I get on a bus, I perceive people as dangerous. When we talk about possible solutions, I have no faith that good things might happen. I feel helpless and vulnerable, and like no one cares for me.

"Is all of this true?" he asks. "Because on one level, you're not being helpless. You're looking for housing, doing your diary cards, and taking control of your therapy."

I don't know how to answer that, because although I am trying, as usual, to make things better, I continue to feel like I'm drowning, with no one to grab onto. Somehow, I don't count Ethan as a helping hand, which is odd, given that he's now the central person in my life and is actually helping me. I'm not entirely alone. My parents are also available—not in the way I want, but they haven't disappeared. So how many of these core beliefs are colored lenses as opposed to truths? It's not like I came to these conclusions out of the blue. Most of my life I've been unable to manage myself and looked to others to take care of me. This certainly resulted in my feeling like a child: powerless and vulnerable. And the people around me behaved in ways that, if not intentionally hurtful, still left me feeling neglected, misunderstood, and unprotected. So do I feel unacceptable because I have distorted beliefs in my mind, or because of the way people responded to me as I was growing up? Other kids called me a freak. I was often told that my behaviors didn't make any sense, that I was paranoid and unreasonable. Those are hardly the kinds of messages that make people feel good about themselves.

I've arrived at one of the most important questions I will ask myself, and keep asking: How much of what I perceive is accurate, and how much is a distortion? Ethan points out that I'm coming up on ten years of sobriety. Certainly that shows I'm able to take care of myself on some level. I agree—and yet I don't. I am capable—and yet I'm not. Ethan tells me to remember the dialectic. It's not either-or. My experience right now is "both." I am an adult and a child; protected and vulnerable. Ethan reminds me that DBT isn't about discovering ultimate truths; it's often about tolerating seeming contradictions.

How do you do that? The borderline mind is trapped in polarity. It needs to be trained to tolerate these multiplicities and ambiguities, but right now I can't hold two things at once. In Dr. Linehan's DBT textbook, she says that one of the primary goals of DBT is to "increase dialectical behavior patterns" (1993a, 120), both in our thinking and in our actions. Ethan points out my small successes. Yet all cheerleading and small pieces of evidence aside (Yay! I've showered today!), a backward glance at my life reaffirms that I've been caught in a cycle of failures and breakdowns for decades. This evidence outweighs everything else. In the dialectic of "I'm helpless" versus "I'm capable," I need evidence beyond my own life. I need to see that others have moved beyond being stuck in this downward spiral. I need a faith, of sorts, that can create an actual dialectic, because right now, despite my determination to get better, the situation is "I'm fucked" and "I don't know how to get better." Whether you call it faith, or hope, or proof of recovery, I need some sort of evidence that on the other side of pain and helplessness is what Dr. Linehan calls mastery, and that it can eventually result in having "a life worth living."

As I wait for my spot to open in the DBT program, I read much of Dr. Linehan's textbook, *Cognitive-Behavioral Treatment of Borderline Personality Disorder* (1993a). It's over five hundred pages and isn't required reading for anyone in a DBT group, but as I discover, it offers an unprecedented level of insight into the borderline condition. I'm in Starbucks one afternoon, trying to get a better handle on how DBT is actually practiced in a program (I'm not going to be suckered again), when I come across a list of DBT goals and stages on a handout, adding a fourth stage to the three Dr. Linehan described in her textbook. Stage one is exactly where Ethan and I are now: focused on the DBT skills and decreasing suicidal and self-harming behaviors so that I can stay alive. Stage two, which is supposed to happen after safety is established, involves dealing with emotions and traumatic experiences from the past, exposing yourself to triggers, and learning to survive them. The handout, a FAQ from Linehan's training organization, describes this stage as addressing "inhibited emotional experiencing" and moving "from a state of quiet desperation to one of full emotional experiencing" (Sanderson 2008, 2). Stage three is related to working through problems of everyday living, dealing with ordinary happiness and unhappiness. And stage four (I begin to cry when I read this part) says that a person with BPD will "move from a sense of incompleteness toward a life that involves an ongoing capacity for experiences of joy and freedom" (Sanderson 2008, 2).

Four stages. Linehan doesn't use the word "recovery" to describe this process. But I will, because this is what I've been looking for. Some kind of map or path that shows how someone with BPD can cross over the border—or, better yet, transcend it. Discovering this list is the closest I've come to envisioning a way out.

PART 3

Shifts in Light

12

Keys

After four months out of the hospital and three months with Ethan, I suppose you could say I'm getting stabilized. From the outside, it seems I've made gains: My typically constant crisis mentality is becoming more periodic, and I haven't cut myself since September—not that I haven't felt the urge, but Ethan and I have contracted for safety. I committed to calling him before I do anything self-destructive, and this safety net, the Ethan-net, holds me surprisingly well. Finding the right fit between therapist and client is definitely an elusive science. Ethan admits later that the reason we were assigned to each other was because no other potential clients showed up that day for an intake. He also says that, despite his training, postdoctoral work, and current position on the DBT team, he's probably only three pages ahead of me in reading through Marsha Linehan's textbook, *Cognitive-Behavioral Treatment of Borderline Personality Disorder* (1993a). We're freestyling it in some ways, but in other ways, not at all. He has his DBT consultation team, and I have our therapy sessions, homework, and phone coaching. All I need is a life.

I'm coming to see that the DBT stages aren't necessarily sequential, and that I'm often in multiple stages at the same time. Some days it's all about survival, but the next day, I may be grappling with issues of daily life, which is stage three. DBT's catchphrase of developing a life worth living means you're not just surviving; rather, you have good reasons for living. I'm also getting better at keeping another dialectic in mind: On the one hand, the disorder decimates all relationships and social functions, so you're basically wandering in the wasteland of your own failure, and yet you have to keep walking through it, gathering the small bits of life that can eventually go into creating a life worth living. To be in the desolate badlands while envisioning the lush tropics without being totally triggered again isn't easy, especially when life seems so effortless for everyone else.

The most pressing issues at this point are where to live and what to do with myself day to day. Having no structure outside of therapy isn't helpful. I spend too much time in coffee shops nursing lattes, feverishly writing in journals, and hating people. I hate that they have things I don't: love, purpose, discretionary cash, functional lives. My sense of being dislocated, trapped on the other side of a glass wall, doesn't diminish. In fact, I actually have a better view of how barren my life is now that I'm not fighting quicksand every minute. Every day I come home knowing that as soon as January arrives, I won't be able to afford rent. Yet even the mention of real employment unhinges me. I've worked probably ten jobs in the last ten years, from washing dishes to giving lectures, and there isn't one among them that I could survive.

Just like in relationships, I make great first impressions at jobs. I show up and get gold stars. Yay, Kiera! But it doesn't last. Performing under stress, showing up at regularly appointed hours, enduring criticism, and playing the politics—all of it eventually wears me down to one raw nerve, and I disappear, just as I did with the job at the Harvard Coop; though there I didn't last long enough to make a good impression—or probably much of an impression at all. I don't have any options for good references. And it doesn't help that for most of my life I've heard that I wasn't living up to my potential, wasn't trying hard enough, wasn't giving things a real chance, or was sabotaging my success. But when every excursion into responsibility feels like being dropped into a pot of boiling water, any job seems like a setup for devastation, not an opportunity to practice my skills.

These days there are a couple of programs for people with mental illness that focus on "psychosocial rehabilitation," but none for BPD. Now that I understand this disorder, I know that I have different needs, and that the way people treat me and the environment I enter will have a huge impact on how I react and perform. If I get triggered, I need to be able to self-soothe and calm down. I need a way to moderate the pressure and stress so I don't freak out. I need a workplace filled with Ethans—or at the very least, one where I can keep him permanently on speakerphone.

The house/job/money crisis is not a new one. And each time I hit this place of need, I feel ashamed of myself, and angry—at the world, my family, and whoever stands too close to me in the supermarket. Most painful is how everyone (except Ethan) seems to think I just need to get back on the horse that threw me. Phone conversations with both my mother and my father are barely endurable. Both give advice and suggestions without understanding the illness, and I end up defending myself or mindlessly agreeing with them just to end the call. I'm ready to raise the deflector shield even with Raymond, who takes me out for dinner toward the end of December and suggests I do some reception work for a friend of his. I tell him that having to perform and be "normal" seems beyond my capacity right now. Raymond disagrees and says it's the simplest job in the world: I'll answer phones, run errands, and do some photocopying in an office run by his best friend.

"I don't know." I push the mashed potatoes around my plate. "You know my track record."

"I'm sure you can handle answering phones, Gamine." (Raymond's nickname for me is Gamine Brioche, which can be roughly translated as "Waifish Street Urchin French Pastry.") "What you need is a place where you feel valued. Someplace with low stress and good people." We stop talking for a moment as the waiter refills our glasses with Pellegrino.

"And answering phones is something they'll value?"

"Don't underestimate yourself, child."

"But I'll be alone..." He promises I won't. He's renting a room in the office for his own company, so I'll have insta-Raymond—and no lines of impatient customers. Plus, they'll pay me as much in one week as I get in a month from disability. Raymond coaxes me with crème brûlée and hints of a Christmas bonus if I can stick it out.

I'm to start next week.

With Ethan's pager number written on both of my hands, I arrive at a brick building in the heart of Harvard Square. The office spans parts of the third and fourth floors, with windows looking out over Massachusetts Avenue and Brattle Street, and by an odd trick of entranceways and atriums, the company sits *directly above* the Harvard Coop. It seems I've moved up in the world!

When Raymond said it was a low-stress environment with good people, he wasn't exaggerating. The word "office" automatically brings images of people in suits and cubicles, phones ringing, and heads buried behind computer monitors; instead I discover Renee, my new boss, covered in glitter and bits of ribbon, working on the company holiday cards in a glass conference room. The office itself is all skylights, interior windows, and iron detailing. From the reception desk, I can just glimpse the crosswalk of Harvard Square, the intersection of many of the lives I've led. Now I'm going to be a receptionist, though my first week is total arts and crafts: cutting and pasting pieces of paper, tying bows on the cards, and running across the street to Starbucks for Renee, who insists on paying for my mocha lattes as well. The president of the company, Richard, visits our card production line on his way out to rollerblade the first afternoon and oohs and aahs over our handiwork. He's wearing a hoodie and sweatpants, an interesting contrast to his white beard and hair. If Santa worked out every day, he'd look like Richard, right down to the warm, amused eyes and delighted smile.

"Nice work," he comments, looking at my bows. I worry that he's joking, but he isn't. Mass producing miniature bows, watering his plants, making a dinner reservation for visiting clients—all receive the warmest thanks and appreciation. That isn't normal, and I realize this isn't a normal office. A small crew of international economists and engineers leisurely arrives by midmorning, dressed in jeans and sweaters. The office kitchen brims with fresh fruit, nuts, candy, and handpicked tea. Richard takes everyone out for Indian food on slow Friday afternoons. And at least once a week, Renee makes strawberry smoothies for everyone. She puts them on a silver tray with bendy straws placed in every drink and delivers them to the offices. Now that I'm here, I get to carry the tray.

The situation, and the menial tasks I engage in, make me think of my prep-school classmates, now working on Wall Street or as international diplomats, teaching Greek and poetry at Ivy League schools, living in nice homes, and raising children. Yet I'm lucky to be alive. This is a new feeling, and a precious one, where carrying a tray of smoothies for Renee is a triumph.

Despite showing up at work every day looking nonchalant and self-confident, I'm terrified. Committing the smallest error can detonate an emotional bomb in me, and although Ethan tells me to page him, my hair-trigger reactions and sudden shutdowns can eclipse that option. One day early on I use the paper cutter to crop some fancy paper for the last batch of cards and end up with a mess of rectangles instead of squares. Richard's assistant, Gail, waits for me to hand them over, and I'm dizzy with panic when I do. I've disfigured the last of the specially ordered fancy paper. There's no way I can fix the situation. Trapped between admitting my mistake and wanting to blame the paper cutter, I do a fast drop-off on Gail's desk and head toward the conference room where Renee is wielding the glue gun. I'm hoping she's in immediate need of a white chocolate Frappuccino.

"Kiera?" Gail calls out.

I cringe. I'm not sure what's worse—messing up, pretending I haven't messed up, or being caught doing both. I return to Gail and she holds up my handiwork.

"These aren't exactly the right size," she says. Gail is an elegant older woman, and a true old-school executive assistant in the sense that she takes care of everything, seemingly effortlessly, and has worked for Richard forever. A mother of three children and married to a lawyer, Gail knows how to handle people. But she hasn't yet worked with a borderline—someone who can't tolerate the least bit of criticism because it feels like being punched in the face. I stare at the paper in her hand and tears well up in my eyes. Then I feel anger. Why did they make me use such a crappy paper cutter? Why are these cards such a big deal? Do I critique her bows? Then I look away, ashamed. I'm getting paid more for a week's work here than I'd get for a month of disability. And I'm here to make these cards.

Gail sits in her chair, polished and patient, and watches me struggle with my reactions. This is a moment I've had with so many people: when they first witness my break from reasonable Kiera to emotional Kiera—the moment when the borderline takes over... But before I can react further, Gail sets the paper aside and pats my arm.

"It's okay," she says gently. "I've had trouble with that paper cutter before. I'll just trim them down a bit more. No need to worry."

It's like Gail just defused a bomb. I almost cry with gratitude, but I'm still in complete emotion mind—and terrified. I go to the bathroom and splash my face with cold water. I stare in the mirror and whisper, "It's okay, it's okay." Yet I imagine Gail pulling Renee aside later. They will powwow and then break it to Raymond that I'm not cut out for even the simplest tasks. In a preemptive maneuver, I call Raymond that night and tell him I really messed up.

"What did you do?"

"I cut the paper wrong."

Raymond pauses. "You cut the paper wrong, huh?"

"Yes, and I haven't even made it to the phone-answering stage." As I hear myself talk, I realize how ridiculous I sound. Raymond assures me I won't lose my new job. But I'm not so sure.

In my next session with Ethan, he asks, "What skills did you use with Gail?"

This is now a typical question: What skills did you use? Oftentimes I can only think of what skills I should have used, in retrospect. This week most of the days on my diary card are blank because I'm so exhausted from the bus rides and office work. We're doing a behavioral analysis, a DBT practice that reminds me of the elaborate CBT worksheets from the summer—except that with a behavioral analysis, no detail is considered irrelevant. In analyzing my situation with Gail, it appears I'm more upset with myself than anything else, and I can't recognize what I did well. After some prodding, Ethan gets me to admit that I did observe my feelings: I knew I felt anger, fear, dread... And I didn't react in a way that made things worse. But still, that little inner hurricane wrecked the first seedlings of my confidence at this job. And that's one of the things I really hate—*hate!*—about BPD: that such a small incident can topple my inner composure, causing me to feel so vulnerable and out of control.

Ethan has become my reality check. For every claim I make, he asks another question. Was I really out of control? What I did I do after the incident? Well, I went to the bathroom and splashed cold water on my face, right? I calmed down. Then I sat in the stall and talked myself down from the impulse to run away. I realized that unlike at the bookstore, I'd have someone to answer to, with future steak dinners and crème brûlée hanging in the balance.

"So you self-soothed and thought about the pros and cons of your behavior—both DBT skills."

"I guess... But why can't I just react like everyone else?"

"Why do you want to react like everyone else?"

"I want to have normal reactions because the way I feel things is wrong."

"What's wrong about it?"

I can't come up with a rational answer. All I know is that my feelings are intolerable, and to me, anything intolerable is wrong.

Raymond is often downstairs in his third-floor office, and at odd times he pops up onto the fourth floor and checks in on me. It's like having a secret doting uncle, and just seeing him coming up the stairs calms me down. "So you like it here?" he asks.

I do. I want to sit at this desk behind the high marble counter, tend to the silver candy bowl, answer the phones, and send FedEx packages and sign for them. I want to work with Richard, Renee, and Gail in this quirky consulting office where people show up late and rollerblade at lunchtime and the VP makes everyone smoothies.

"So all is good," Raymond concludes. Umm, no. Actually, soon I'm going to be homeless. Okay, that's an exaggeration. If I can keep this job, I can afford the rent increase, but living so far away and hiding from Patty is wearing me down. Just dragging myself out of bed before noon takes all I've got.

"Why not get a place near Harvard Square?" Raymond asks. Right... That's like suggesting I stay in the Ritz-Carlton. "There's no way," I tell Raymond.

"There has to be a way," he replies. "There is always a way." He digs up the email for a private Listserv for traveling scholars, and I'm stunned to discover that within an hour of signing up, I have my pick of cheap local living options. Do I want to room with an Israeli physicist in a two-bedroom in Porter Square? A bioengineer with two cats in Central Square? Or, could this really be possible, a Harvard Square studio on the top floor of a historic Victorian, three blocks from work? I email the landlords and meet with them the next day. A married couple and longtime Harvard professors, they're used to renting the studio to traveling scholars, not former mental patients, so I know I have to put on my game face and present myself as capable and self-sufficient. I tell them that I'm an artist, looking for a quiet place to work when I'm not at my day job—which is true. Remember the dialectic: Two seemingly opposite things can be true at the same time.

The professors take me up two narrow sets of stairs, and we emerge into a square studio with windows on all sides—a veritable box of light, outfitted with a couch, a table, a kitchen nook, and a surprisingly large bathroom. The ceiling is low, enough so that the husband needs to stoop a little. But I clear it by a good four inches. It's also completely furnished, which is good, since all I have is a futon.

I say that I'll take it, even though I don't how I'll come up with all the deposit money. Ethan coaches me on the phone before I call my parents to request financial help, but when I ask, neither will commit without knowing what the other is going to do. I turn to Raymond, who in exasperation offers to pay whatever my parents won't, and in a week, the three of them have put together the money for my move.

On an unusually warm January afternoon, my mother and I pack up my boxes in Waltham, load them in her station wagon, and drive to Harvard Square, where we carry them up the two narrow flights of stairs. She surprised me by offering to help with the move and has been full of exuberant optimism all day. Her ability to find promise in opportunity is unyielding, which either bolsters me or negates me, depending on the hour and my mood.

"This is perfect for you," she says, after we've unloaded all the boxes. We're sitting on the daybed, which is too lumpy to be a bed but too high up to be a couch. "I wish I could be so lucky. You can go to lectures at Harvard and go out every night to see movies, and you can get a cappuccino without having to drive twenty miles. I'd give my eyeteeth for a place this close to the square."

Yes, I am lucky. And I agree, the place is perfect, though not for the same reasons. That night when I'm alone, I drag the futon over to the corner of the room for the best morning light. Piled along the walls are the usual boxes of journals, drawings, books, and clothes. I have one wooden box filled with my brother's clothes, which I sometimes take out and put on: a Guatemalan shirt, army pants, a tie-dye. Sometimes I go through the box and wish I was the one who died ten years ago. Other times, wrapped in one of his shirts, I feel grateful to still be alive. Yes, I'm lucky to be here, but not because I'm so close to movie theaters and academic lectures. I'm not interested in being cultured; I want to learn about survival. Now I have a ring with two keys in my hand: one for the studio, the other for the office. Each opens a door to the chance of having a life worth living.

13

Leaving the Dysregulation Zone

My first few evenings at the studio, I sit on the carpet surrounded by piles of books and empty cardboard boxes—just sit and stare at my things. My relief at being away from Patty and having my own space is colliding with an even sharper edge of isolation. This is so familiar: I run from the "oppressor" and discover that my own presence is just as oppressive. I stare out the windows at the bare tree branches and avoid filling out my diary card. A different kind of despair enters me. Is this stage two? Despite having more safety and a sense of purpose, the term "quiet desperation" certainly applies here.

More then ever, I'm living a double life. Kiera the Borderline struggles from minute to minute to manage her inner demons. But then there's the outer persona, Kiera the Receptionist: "Good morning! How can I help you?" Actually, there's another part: I'm the official "artist in residence," one in a series of struggling creative types hired for the receptionist position in a tradition Richard established long ago. Right now I'm more just struggling than artistic, but it gives me an identity that the others value outside of my ability to fix paper jams in the copier. And being a receptionist isn't so bad—if I can get away from the conviction I must win the Nobel Prize or publish the great American novel. I try to stay mindful and focus on the concrete: watering plants, unloading the dishwasher, answering phones, getting coffee for Renee (which she keeps insisting on treating me to, as well). And I have one last role: I am the espresso machine whisperer. Despite an office filled with Ph.D. engineers, I appear to be the only one who can decipher the blinking lights, calibrate the grind, and make steam flow from its silver spout, probably because I'm the only one who's bothered to read the manual.

Through January and February, I go to work and I wait for the spot in the DBT group to open up. I continue to work with Ethan on my diary cards and on applying the skills moment to moment. Life develops a rhythm of sorts: work, Ethan, visits to the local gym. Nights and week-ends remain the most excruciating. They form an empty canvas, and all of the submerged tensions, fears, and pain of the day splash onto it as soon as I stop moving and sit down alone. Without a computer or cable TV, I have so few distractions that some nights I find myself crawling over the carpet on my hands and knees, picking up the bits of rock and leaf my shoes have tracked in. Or I take out every piece of clothing, refold, and reorganize. Beneath me the professor couple murmurs and laughs, or the sound of the TV floats up the stairs. Each of them has a private study, and the husband's displays a row of books he's published. (I know this because they asked me to feed their giant orange tabby cat while they were away, so I explored a little.) As I pick the lint off the rug, I can practically hear them editing each other's work in bed.

Some days I don't think I can make it through work. If two calls come in at the same time, I'm hyperventilating. If a visitor walks through the door while a fax is transmitting, I can't focus my eyes. Anything that comes suddenly, intensely, or at the same time as something else undoes me in a second.

"Go talk to Renee if you need help," Raymond tells me. I've figured out at this point that Renee knows that I'm a special case. I never ask Raymond what he told Renee about me, but I suspect it involves my difficulty with stress and tendency to fall apart. One afternoon shortly before I need to leave for a session with Ethan, one of the engineers asks me to print out ten long documents and do fancy bindings—which will keep me from making my appointment with Ethan. It's been a bad day; the small frustration of a jammed stapler has been pushing me into panic and tears. I've kept control, but I know I have to get to Ethan. If I see him, I might be able to exhale without exploding. So, in tears, I go to see Renee. I don't want to fall apart on her, and I feel ashamed that I'm in such a state.

"What's the matter!?" Renee asks when she sees me so upset. I can't stop crying, and I'm sure she thinks there's been a death in the family.

Finally I choke out, "Steve wants me to stay late and I can't!"

I expect Renee to roll her eyes or tell me I'm overreacting. Her brow is furrowed as she hands me a tissue box. "So tell Steve you can't. If you have an appointment, you have to go."

I'm so surprised at her response that my tears stop. "How do I tell him that?" I don't understand. I thought I wasn't allowed to say no. I'm the receptionist.

"You have a life. You have to tell people what you can and can't do. Tell him that he has to give you more heads-up, that you can't drop everything for him because he forgot something." She smiles gently. Renee: smoothie maker, coffee provider, and now adjunct therapist. I can almost feel the simmering chemicals in my brain cooling off. I go back upstairs, hit the bathroom to splash cold water on my face (self-soothe, ground…) and then approach Steve. This is big moment for me. I don't know how to do these things. I'm afraid of what will happen, and I'm trembling as I tell him that I can't do the job.

"Okay." Steve smiles, looking up from his desk. "No problem. Sometime tomorrow then."

When I'm in session with Ethan, he asks what was so intolerable about the situation with Steve. I know I felt trapped and overwhelmed, and certain that Steve would get angry or criticize me if I didn't do what he wanted. From that perspective, my whole life might have changed if I'd done the wrong thing. Maybe I'd get fired from the job, then I'd lose my studio and be right back where I started. That short interlude at work reminded me of standing behind the counter at the Harvard Coop: my emotions cresting, people demanding things of me, and feeling that I couldn't escape. I don't know what other options there are except to submit or flee. But this was different, Ethan reminds me. I saw other options and took another direction.

Am I doing things differently, or is it this office and Renee, nurturing me in a way no job ever has? I suppose I could have freaked out on Steve and simply left. I did try something new by going to see Renee and asking for help, despite how ashamed I was. Perhaps the difference is that my skills and the environment are finally working together.

At the end of February, the promised spot in the DBT skills group opens up. From the moment I join the group, I see that it's dramatically different from my previous DBT group. No more freewheeling discussions or spending an entire session on one person's homework. No more musical chairs or sidetracking into Hegelian dialectics. Simon, our group leader, is the antithesis of Molly. Whereas over the course of an hour Molly might pace the room, perch on a desk, and swivel to and fro in her office chair, Simon's body laconically drapes over his chair and moves only with the tide of necessity: a turn of page, a gesture to one of our raised hands. The rhythm of our progress is similarly unhurried, but systematic. Each week we begin with a quick check-in: I'm fine, I'm not fine, I'm totally freaking out. It doesn't matter where each of us is. Simon doesn't put out our raging fires, which are many. As with my environment at work, the space he creates in group holds us in the room, despite our urges to flee. And sometimes people do get up and leave. I haven't so far.

Based on the textbooks and materials, DBT can seem so formulaic. But as I see the contrast between this DBT program and the previous one, I'm growing increasingly aware of how, at heart, this therapy involves the seamless weaving of multiple strands, and that even one broken thread can unravel a supposedly solid treatment. If you can't tolerate sitting in a group of people, for instance, how can you learn the skills? If you have trouble with being around men and it's a mixed group, how do you endure it? Some people get triggered by the smallest glance and have angry outbursts, while others dissociate the minute a voice is raised.

In my all-women DBT group, almost everyone is either married or involved. Maria, with her fur coat and Gucci bag, is married to a dictatorial businessman who sounds suspiciously overinvolved with his Italian heritage. Darcy dates a boy who can't keep a job and spends most of his time smoking pot in the living room. Jenny, who is three-quarters blind, has both a service dog and a boyfriend, though the boyfriend is confined to a wheelchair. Robyn is a quirky, petite artist married to a musician, both recently transplanted from Alaska. And then there's Natalie, a stunning goth chick with an on-again, off-again boyfriend who occasionally beats her, and vice versa. She's constantly in the midst of court proceedings and legal details involving her daughter and restraining orders. None are happy in their relationship except for a quiet older woman, Monica, who talks about a mysterious and loving man: "her David." Plump and serene, Monica doesn't seem to share our ongoing crisis and misery until she discloses, during a homework review, that her urge to kill herself is unremitting. Our one lesbian, Misha, is single, but she's obsessed with her ex-girlfriend to the point of stalking. Ah, borderline love.

Except for our goth beauty, everyone in the group appears fully committed to learning the skills, which also seems critical to the success of the group. We aren't rowing our own little lifeboats. The skills, like a language or a sport, develop through sharing, in addition to practice. I feel lucky that I've learned to share in groups. AA and NA taught me to tolerate the distress of exposure, once I understood the benefits. Here, the benefits include hearing how others with demons similar to my own try to tame and master them. At last I'm not entirely alone.

I am, however, the only self-identified borderline. And while this program is much more comprehensive than the last, it too doesn't involve education or discussion specific to BPD, nor does it go into the philosophy or theory that Marsha Linehan based her therapy on—theories that grow more important as I examine my symptoms and how the DBT skills help reduce them. For example, Dr. Linehan (1993a) uses the word "dysregulation" to characterize BPD, not "instability" as the *DSM-IV-TR* does. All of the DBT skills, therefore, offer some means of regaining control of (or coming to terms with) our dysregulated selves. It might seem like a small shift in wording, but as our DBT group enters the emotion regulation skills module, this concept of dysregulation takes on immense importance. In her skills training manual, Dr. Linehan says that "from a DBT perspective, difficulties in regulating painful emotions are central to the behavioral difficulties of the borderline individual" (1993b, 84). This means that many of our "symptoms" can be seen as "behavioral solutions to intolerably painful emotions" (1993a, 149), including cutting, suicide attempts, desperately clinging to others, dissociating, getting high, jumping into bed with strangers. "Anything to stop the pain" might be a good subtitle for BPD.

So we need to learn how to work with our emotions. Mindfulness starts to teach us how to be aware of them, but we need to go further. When Simon asks us to define what an emotion is, no one in group can explain it, which is ironic since we are all people who have been consumed by emotions our entire lives.

Simon explains that emotions are complex physiological processes. When we look at an emotion, we tend to view it as a single event or experience, but in reality, many things are going on. He gives us a handout with a flow chart, and we take a trip down emotion lane, from the "prompting event" (like seeing a hot guy), to chemicals in the brain that cause changes in the body (arousal), to the urges that develop (Fuck me!). Then there are the actions we take (seduction, or avoidance, or shaving our legs), and then the aftereffects.

In the life cycle of an intense emotion, if it isn't acted on, it eventually peaks and then decreases. But as Dr. Linehan explains, people with BPD have a different physiological experience with this process because of three key biological vulnerabilities (1993a): First, we're highly sensitive to emotional stimuli (meaning we experience social dynamics, the environment, and our own inner states with an acuteness similar to having exposed nerve endings). Second, we respond more intensely, and much more quickly, than other people. And third, we don't "come down" from our emotions for a long time. Once the nerves have been touched, the sensations keep peaking. Shock waves of emotion that might pass through others in minutes might keep cresting in us for hours, sometimes days.

I can see it happening in group every week. We're like a pack of skittish animals sensing a brewing storm even as we try to sit calmly in our seats. Any sudden social noise can send first one of us, then the pack, into a tizzy. As anyone with BPD knows, the charges so often leveled against us include being overly sensitive, overly reactive, and emotionally intense and unpredictable. Luckily, DBT doesn't present these tendencies as pathologies; it views them as basic biological vulnerabilities. They aren't symptoms to be cured, but inherent qualities that we haven't learned to manage. If you look at people's personality traits in general, it's obvious that tendencies don't always become disorders. Not everyone who has a temper ends up throwing furniture, and not everyone who's depressed ends up in a mental hospital.

So why do some people who are sensitive and reactive develop BPD while others never do? Marsha Linehan (1993a) speculates that BPD behaviors and experiences develop through a combination of biological vulnerability and an environment that is unable to respond adequately to our special needs. She calls this the biosocial model. In one sense, it's like growing a plant. You have the seed, but you need to give it certain elements: sun, water, soil. We have the seed. But how do you grow a borderline? Her word for the environment that cultivates our disorder is "invalidating." She doesn't use the term "abuse" or even "neglect," but "invalidation" to describe how a vulnerable child's inner experiences—thoughts, emotions, sensations, and beliefs—are either disregarded, denied, erratically responded to, punished, or oversimplified by caretakers and nurturers. There is a "nonattunement" of response in the family (or school, or even culture) that ends up aggravating a basic biological vulnerability. According to Dr. Linehan (1993a), invalidating environments put a premium on controlling or hiding negative emotions. Painful experiences are trivialized, and blame is put on the vulnerable person for not meeting the expectations of others and living by their standards.

The biosocial model describes a horrific feedback effect: Every experience of invalidation compounds the intensity and dysregulation of our emotion, and feelings of abandonment, isolation, and shame increase. Because we don't know how to manage the feelings, our behaviors grow ever more destructive and desperate, which results in more invalidation and blame. The end result is a person with all of the BPD symptoms who has learned to expertly invalidate herself.

What makes DBT therapy so critical to BPD isn't just the skills. It's the approach to the borderline tension between needing to be accepted and validated versus needing to be pushed into making changes. I see this with Ethan: He always recognizes my perspective and how I feel, while also showing me that there are other ways of seeing and responding. The difference between being told "There's no reason to feel that way" and "I can understand how you feel that way" is the difference between taunting a rabid squirrel and giving it a tranquilizer. Ultimately, we need to learn how to validate ourselves, but right now that's beyond me. I need others to do this for me, and as anyone with BPD knows, getting this kind of support is all but impossible.

But I am making progress toward self-validation. Understanding my emotional life and the biological basis of my experience is a start. And embedded somewhere in DBT's skill sets, especially the emotion regulation techniques, are the skills necessary for moving into stage two: learning to deal with emotional experiences. But to do that, we have to understand what emotions are and investigate the myths we've believed about them. We have to understand that some of our core beliefs increase the intensity of our inner pain: beliefs that our inner experiences are evil or meaningless or not worthy of being understood, that emotions are bad, that there are right and wrong ways to feel. In my sessions with Ethan, I've discovered that I view all negative emotions as enemies, and changing that perception isn't easy.

In DBT group Simon explains that emotions serve a purpose. "Despite how horrible they feel or how much trouble they seem to cause, they do important things for us: They communicate. They motivate. They self-validate. They give our lives richness and meaning." As the season turns, I try to find meaning in my intense loneliness without concluding that I'm a pathetic loser. My work at the office remains steady, challenging, exhausting, and occasionally satisfying. My walks to work become my mindfulness practice. I try to notice my body state, the thoughts that run through my head, and all the smells and sounds of a Cambridge morning. This year spring appears and then retreats like a jack-in-the-box. The daffodils poke their heads out of the soil only to get bombed with snow. As soon as the snow melts, they rise up again, yellow prongs of hope, only to be battered by freezing rain. I never realized how foolishly enduring nature is. Or maybe it's blindly determined? Where does that power of endurance come from?

On my mini fridge, I put a magnet with a Zen quote: "Barn's burnt down... Now I can see the moon." I'm trying to value the simplicity of this new beginning and hold onto the notion that from destruction comes creation. But what I wonder more and more often is *who* is creating? For decades I've been a tangle of crossed wires, misdirected impulses, distorted views, exaggerated emotions, facades, and aching, exposed nerves. Even right now, there's the me who wants to kill myself, the me who is ripe for cults and controlling men, the me who sleeps for twelve hours just to recover from a grocery shopping excursion, and a host of other identities I can trace all the way back to Kiki at Camp Good News, desperate for a savior. And now, there's me the reception-ist—the lonely and increasingly horny receptionist.

Despite the reoccurring snow squalls, students returning from spring break mimic the flowers in their hope for warmth, baring their skin and wearing bright floral shorts and flip-flops in the slushy streets. The couples emerge too, strolling, holding hands, cuddling. When I see them, I have chest pains and feel possessed with envy and the conviction that I will never be loved that way.

It's been over a year since I've been touched. I've been so well behaved. No more lusting after young mental patients. No more ManRay. Therefore, sessions with Ethan involve a higher-pitched lament of loneliness. How intense is it? On a scale from one to ten, it sucks beyond that. And this longing is no longer confined to the night; in daylight I feel chilled inside, hollow, and achy, and then I catch a glimpse of a messenger boy on a bike, tattooed, wearing shorts, and sweating, and I'm flushed and disoriented with desire. Harvard Square blooms with bared skin as the weather grows warmer—a festival of privileged flesh parading through the crosswalk between Out of Town News and the Harvard Coop. The bodies pull my eyes so hard that walking is difficult. Men, women, young, old—it doesn't matter. I want, I want, I want... I want a connection with someone, anyone.

Good relationships are said to be the greatest factor in happiness after basic material needs have been met. And yet BPD symptoms sabotage relationships. So it's a vicious cycle. Being alone is torture, but so is being close to others, needing them, having them. You're like a starved baby unable to draw milk from the breast, or a diabetic hooked on candy. Worse, you can't explain this in rational terms to anyone. And now, wanting a relationship brings on an onslaught of fears and uncertainties: Am I healthy and stable enough? Can I control my behavior better, not get so triggered that I start screeching when my boyfriend looks at another woman?

I've now been in therapy with Ethan for over seven months. Between the two DBT groups, I've been attending skills groups for over a year. And I am making progress: I'm not hacking myself up, not thinking every ten minutes that I might as well kill myself. There's a saying that pain is the craft entering the apprentice, and while I've felt pain all my life, the emotional hell I've been going through these past six months is actually yielding positive results. This is clearly due to the DBT skills—and to finally having a cohesive group of people supporting me in effective ways: Ethan in sessions and by phone; Renee, Gail, and Richard at work, and Raymond nearby; the DBT group in our weekly meetings. The doctor who's now prescribing my medications is doing a good job. Everyone, even my parents to some extent, understands that, despite being thirty-two, I'm only now learning how to live, and I need their help. If I didn't have this unusual patchwork of support, I'd be clinging to the first person who looked at me kindly, and sucking them under in no time. I've come to realize that if I put all my eggs in one basket, I'm setting myself and the other person up. The question now is, can one of those eggs be a lover, and can I stop making such a mess that eggshells end up all over the floor?

I'm no longer in stage one. I'm not trapped in the dysregulation zone, bombs constantly exploding. For long moments, I can see the eternal optimism of the flowers and taste the air without thinking of emptiness and bitterness. I've found a small perch, and I'm able to look around without falling or jumping off. From here, I'm able to see how my fears compete against each other: fear that if anything changes, I'll fall again, and fear that this sprawling, empty loneliness will destroy me just as easily. Another dilemma of the borderline: Connection gives us our life, yet it also threatens to take it from us. But like the flowers, I have to move toward the warmth if I'm to grow at all.

14

No Blow Jobs on
the First Date

At my next session with Ethan, I declare my intention to do online dating. He nods. Someone else might ask if I'm really ready for such a step. Instead, Ethan wants to know what my goal is. What has my motive always been? To be loved, cared for, protected, affirmed, and kept away from the great black hole in the center of my soul. And I want sex. It's been a while.

You can view this need as pathological, or see it as the most natural thing in the world. For me, it's often both. Inside all this hunger for someone else is a simple yearning for companionship, human touch, and connection. I just never know how to separate these out and proceed accordingly. When Ethan asks what my greatest challenges are about dating, I hesitate to tell him. I remember that when I was in my twenties, one of my therapists made the polite suggestion that I not give blow jobs on a first date. I promised to try, but inevitably, I'd relapse. To clarify, I didn't just go around giving blow jobs to anybody. It's that once I'm approached by someone attractive, my longing for touch blurs my reason, and the next thing I know, I'm on my knees. Contrary to folklore, it's the easiest way to a man's heart.

Ethan fiddles with his pen a little more than usual as I explain this habit in detail. "So I guess," I conclude, "I don't know how to develop a relationship. I sleep with people, and most of the time they choose me. My boundaries are obviously not that strong."

I reason that online dating can at least provide some artificial boundaries. I'll have more control over the process. For example, face-to-face, a cute guy might steer me into the shrubbery with a couple of kisses. That would be more difficult through a computer screen; at least, I should hope so. Making informed decisions is not an easy task when you're under the sway of BPD-induced loneliness and a sex drive that, despite Zoloft's deadening effects on my clitoris, can overrule all reason. As Bennet once said, "You love indiscriminately." I can fall into a delusion of eternal compatibility before I even know a man's last name—and then fall out of it a week later with a conviction bordering on religious faith. If there were a way to slow this process down with some external speed bumps, perhaps I'd be less impulsive and operate more from my wise mind. Dr. Linehan might call this approach "structuring the environment." Match.com calls it "guaranteed compatibility." It's like man shopping, and I get to drink coffee while I do it.

But in order to enter this new mating dance, I must create a profile for others to see. Attraction, seduction, and all the small nuances of romance now boil down to this public offering, a canvas of self-promotion where you try to paint every last interesting, compelling, appealing detail of your existence without giving any hint of desperation. I'm somewhat at a loss as to how to do this. Putting yourself out there isn't easy in the best of circumstances, let alone when you have a personal history that reads like *Go Ask Alice* and a diagnosis that makes grown men run for their lives. Ethan asks me what kind of partner I'm looking for, and one thing is clear: I need to be with someone who can understand and accept BPD. My family might not want to discuss it. The DBT groups may avoid it. Even Ethan may only speak of "BPD tendencies," but whoever I become attached to better know what my issues are and how we can deal with them. Otherwise, it won't be pretty.

I honestly don't know what's going to happen when I finally say to a potential partner, "By the way, I have BPD." Obviously I'm not going to mention this in my profile. I toy around with hinting at a "history": "I've been through a lot," I could say, "and come out stronger for it." Or I could allude to being in recovery through all the various codes, like saying, "I'm a friend of Bill W" (the founder of AA). How about "friend of Marsha"? I spend an entire day wrestling with three paragraphs for the "Who I Am" introduction and filling out the numerous questionnaires and preferences, and in the end I have an ambiguous description of an artsy chick with only oblique references to pathos. I've been working on my profile all day at the office, and after I press the "submit" button, I realize I haven't eaten or peed in almost seven hours.

The next morning I rush to work, hoping to have dozens of messages from intrigued and handsome men. My inbox is empty, but I've been "winked" at twice by overweight divorced men my father's age. Winking, a noncommittal gesture of interest, alarms me a bit. Is it okay to just ignore winks? What's the protocol? I write a carefully worded message to each winker, explaining that he's out of my age range but I wish him the best of luck. After all, I'd feel devastated if I winked and got ignored. Three minutes later, one of the men messages me that he's very youthful for his age and he thinks we'd be quite compatible. He also asks for my phone number.

As I try to figure out what to do next, Steve asks me to copy a stack of papers. I feed the copy machine in the production room while running back and forth to my desk to see if anyone else has emailed or winked. My profile was posted at least ten hours ago, and I wonder if it's a bad sign that no one appealing has contacted me yet. I've already scanned over all of the men in the Cambridge area and added the hottest ones to my favorites list (a crush list of sorts). None of them have emailed me or winked, though a few have looked at my profile and passed by, giving me the pinched feeling of dismissal. This wide-open vantage—knowing who looks at you and having others know who you look at—throws an extra layer of fear and hope into the mix. You don't just look at other people's profiles. Your looking is itself on display. And at any moment, a message might come through—or not. The tension renders me useless for anything other than hitting the refresh button.

Finally, around 4 p.m., I have messages. This must be the time everyone gets bored at work and starts cruising the site. There's a message from a Pakistani man who writes in broken English and, though I am sure he is sincere, my standard of English fluency and literacy disqualifies him. A forty-year-old father of two with a refrigeration business and love of motor homes sends me a message that reads like standard job application. I am hugely disappointed, and when I look at my "viewed profile" list, I see that all of my favorites have looked at me and moved on. I know it's only been a day, and that it's unreasonable for me to expect that my "perfect match" will appear so soon, or that I won't have to sift the wheat from the chaff. I need to be patient and not take every slightest thing to heart.

Yeah, right.

Over the course of a week, online dating possesses my body and soul. I come to work early, stay late, check my email every three minutes, and troll through the little squares of men's pictures and the pages of profiles, wondering at and weighing the possibilities. Even when I want to stop, I can't. Every minute holds the possibility of a connection or a rejection. I send out three emails with carefully constructed greetings and witty comments. No responses. I switch the wording around on my profile, add more hobbies, increase my income level, take my income level off entirely. I say I want children, then decide I don't. I'm losing ground within myself; with each passing day, I have less sense that I'm desirable. I wink at a redheaded yoga instructor with the body of an Adonis; no response. A sculptor who lives in a converted mill for artists sends me a reply: "Thanks for your message, but I'm looking for something different." It seems that all the men I want ignore me, while those I'd cross the street to avoid find me irresistible. By the end of the second week, I've racked up an impressive seventeen winks from men over fifty. I'm ready to pull the plug when I finally hear from some good prospects: a biblical scholar doing work at Harvard and a physics student at MIT. Both look cute and well groomed in their pictures, and both are in their early thirties, like me.

I meet the Bible guy for coffee first. He's nice enough, but we can't move past the religion theme in our discussion. His specialty is the Dead Sea scrolls and mine is Camp Good News. We meet somewhere close to the New Testament but can't make it much further. I see the physicist for coffee next. We have more things to talk about, and I think he's pretty cute. All goes well until we wander over to the Cambridge Common and sit on the potato famine statue and the conversation turns too personal. I'm the queen of self-disclosure. You can't spend a third of your life in therapy and AA meetings and not accidentally lapse into gory details. I don't mention any specific diagnosis, but I say enough that I probably raise numerous red flags along the mating speedway. I don't hear from him again.

"Did you like the physicist?" Ethan asks in our session. I'm not sure what I felt. In my mind, a sense of compatibility doesn't need corroboration with facts. The physicist might have had potential. Then again, if my past scared him, he didn't meet my criteria. But what if I'd withheld most of that information until he got to know me better? I find myself in a dilemma. To appeal to others, I need to not scare them with my past. I have to seem like a happy, well-adjusted person. I've peeked into the women's online profiles while in stealth mode and see that everyone has put their best foot forward. Even the angry punk chicks make it sound like they have their shit together—making good money by day and moshing in the pit by night. What kind of positive face can I put on? I refuse to create a fictional self only to demolish the image when the truth starts to come out. I'm complicated. I try hard. I give good head. What else can I say?

My third date is with a computer programmer who rides a motorcycle and says in his profile that he thinks Rush Limbaugh is a twit. This time we talk on the phone first, a wise tactic I should have used with the first two but didn't. Then we meet for a dinner date. Motorcycle boy is tall and lean, with pale blue eyes and long brown hair. He breaks easily into laughter and is strangely unaffected. He's a curious combination of geek and bad boy, and while his appearance is less polished, having just come from installing a new water heater in his parents' home, he reminds me of boys in high school who didn't know how cute they were. His name is Taylor, and within a week he will become the center of my world.

On our third date, Taylor and I have yet to kiss—a record for me—and I also have yet to broach the B word. As I'm giving him a tour of my studio after a movie ("and here is my kitchenette"), the opportunity arrives. We end up sitting at the little table where my papers, books, and sketching supplies are spread out, sipping herbal tea.

"Is this your handwriting?" he asks, pointing to the pages of notes on BPD I've been taking down. He lines up the papers and I'm afraid he's reading them, but what he's really doing is comparing the script across the pages. I open up a journal and show him how different my lettering is when I'm in different moods.

"That's nothing," he says. "You should see the different types of writing someone with multiple personality disorder has."

I stop flipping through my journal. "You know someone with MPD?"

Taylor opens his month, then stops. "It's kind of personal." I nod sympathetically but have no intention of letting this go, because if he knows someone with that disorder, there's a chance he might understand what I go through.

"Personality disorders are rough," I say.

"Yeah, we were friends for years and sometimes she acted really weird, but I just figured that was something she did—not, you know, a huge problem. But then she got kind of out of control and she told me. So I did a lot of reading…"

I put my tea down and look at him. "Taylor, I have a personality disorder too: borderline personality disorder."

"What is that?"

Oh, how long I've been anticipating and dreading this exchange. Numerous words pass through my mind: "instability," "impulsivity," "disorder," "syndrome," "psychopathology"…

"Dysregulation," I finally say, channeling Marsha Linehan. "It's a disorder of dysregulation." Taylor doesn't understand what that means. "Well, take how I feel. It changes—a lot, and quickly. And I react strongly to things. And my views flip-flop… Sometimes from one extreme to another. Pretty quickly."

"Huh… What's with the word 'borderline'?"

"That's because a long time ago doctors saw the symptoms as somewhere between neurotic and psychotic." I try to maintain a casual tone; I want him to think it's no big deal. I've got this thing under control. But it *is* a big deal. It's like two people having the presex disclosure talk, and one needs to confess to having AIDS. I'm inviting him into my world of shaky attachments, my howling insecurity, my overwhelming passions; it's a world I've mastered on a basic level but have yet to share with anyone successfully.

"Huh," Taylor says again, and looks around my studio. Every book, pencil, and teacup is in its place, my futon sheets are tucked in, and my pillows fluffed. Here, in this sanctuary, I've created the picture of a well-ordered life, and it isn't false. And yet it also isn't true. I don't pick up my tea because my hand could be shaking. "You seem pretty stable to me," Taylor comments. "Working. Paying your bills. I haven't noticed you changing much this past week. Things can't be that bad."

"I've done a *lot* of therapy," I say. Should I also mention that I'm always fairly good at the beginning, and that it's when I get attached that all hell breaks loose?

"Do I need to worry?" Taylor asks. His candor is unnerving.

"I think…I think you'd need to learn about BPD, just the way you did with your friend who had MPD. You're going to need to be aware of how it affects me, and us—if there is an 'us.'"

"It's official," I tell Ethan. "We're dating *and* I haven't slept with him yet." Outside, the flowers burst with fragrance, and I'm giddy, verging on delirious.

Ethan says he's happy for me. His expression, a mixture of attention and distance, ratchets my delirium down a few notches, which is a good, I think. If he were as happy as I am, I'd probably go off the edge. "I think it's important that you don't sleep with him for some time," Ethan adds.

"What?! How long?"

Ethan is scribbling in his notebook and tears off a page. It's a contract: no sex for a month. I whine that it's not fair—everyone else is doing it—but I sign the contract knowing that it's a good plan. Both Ethan and I are aware of how quickly my reality changes as soon as I'm touched. In fact, it's already begun to change. When Taylor looks at me, I feel myself coalescing around him, like I'm a wraith, a thunderstorm, and a scattered puzzle, all gathering into his eyes. I don't feel this with therapists, or with my mother and father. It's only a lover who holds me this way.

I show Taylor the contract. "A month?!" He's taken me to his house for dinner and a video. And as much as he's alarmed by my therapist's sudden imposition on our future sex life, I'm also overwhelmed by the state of his house. When he told me he owned his own home, I was duly impressed. Visiting it, I'm less so. A century-old one-floor bungalow, the house is covered in cat hair and a chaos of papers, gadgets, motorcycle parts, toys, and cardboard boxes. It feels like a hard sneeze could blow the whole place to bits, and I start sneezing as soon as I walk in, even though I'm not allergic to cats.

"I'm a little bit less organized than you," Taylor says when we enter. He grabs a large lint roller and vigorously swabs the futon until its green canvas cover appears. His kitchen is in dismal shape: the garbage and recycling piled halfway to the ceiling in one corner, the linoleum cracked, tools on the table, and boxes cluttered underneath. I'm appalled to see (and smell) the kitty litter box positioned next to the stove. We eat hot dogs cut up into macaroni and cheese, a culinary compromise I'm willing to make in light of the fact that Taylor has been a bachelor for a long time. I try to view everything about his house as the result of not enough female influence, from the dusty curtains he says were the originals, left by the ninety-year-old previous owner, to the lack of food in the fridge. At least he owns a house, which is better than I'm doing.

After dinner, we sit on the fairly clean futon and stare at the no-sex contract. I try to explain that this is necessary for me if I'm to learn how to have a healthy relationship.

"What's wrong with us dealing with the issue ourselves?"

"It's important that I have some concrete structure. I could get really thrown off balance if I jump in too quick."

"I get that," Taylor says. "If you knew me better, you'd see that I move very slowly. And I'm not impulsive, like you say you are. It's the idea of someone else being in control that bothers me."

I put my head on his shoulder. "If it's for the best, can we just do it?"

Taylor fiddles with my fingers and traps my thumb under his index finger. It's the tiniest gesture, but it makes me feel securely held.

He turns to me and asks, "So, can I kiss you?" I tell him I've been waiting for him to kiss me. "Can I touch you?" he asks. I say yes.

That night, we sleep in his bed, chaste spoons covered with cat hair amidst piles of laundry and cardboard boxes. And I am, quite possibly, happy.

15

Empty Room

It would be so lovely to end the book right here and say Kiera and Taylor lived happily ever after. After all, this would be the perfect ending to my nightmare journey, wouldn't it? But it's obvious by now that with BPD, falling in love, intimacy, attachment—all open the trapdoor to yet another dark place. With Taylor, it's like watching a truck barreling toward me in a dream, with my legs stuck in cement. As always, the first couple of weeks are so very good. Taylor is an intoxicant. His sweat smells like spice. The thought of him sends me into a fugue state. When we talk, I feel listened to, deeply. Even when he's discussing brake calipers, I loll in an opium den of feelings, skin tingling.

Taylor and Bennet are similar in many ways. Both are tall, lean, muscular, and at ease with tools, machines, and things with sharp parts. Their minds are similar too. Both are storehouses of information— reason mind to the core. I've exchanged Bennet's long explanations of guitars and amplifiers for Taylor's in-depth analysis of motorcycles and computers. Most importantly, they are both fixers, men who thrive on solving problems and repairing broken things. Bennet restored furniture, rebuilt guitars, and sponsored a gaggle of newcomers in NA; Taylor rebuilds motorcycles and computers and will show up at any hour of the day or night if you need to jump-start your car. Both men have the patience and determination to work with broken things, and that's to my benefit. I need a certain kind of person to grow intimate with: someone who doesn't view my vulnerabilities as weaknesses; someone who can remain calm in the face of my upsets; someone whose own world and sense of self is strong enough to withstand the storms that will pass through it as I learn to trust. Taylor is all this, and more. Perhaps most importantly, he doesn't judge.

There is, however, one last similarity with Bennet, and when I find out, it's like I've been punched in the stomach and can't regain my breath. We're cruising into our third week as a couple and still haven't broken the no-sex contract. I'm leaving Ethan's office after an hour of gushing about how good life is when Taylor calls my cell. He wants to know if it's okay if a friend of his crashes in his living room Friday night. I'm not sure why he's asking, and then he explains that his friend is a *she*.

"And who is she?" I try to keep my voice steady.

"Her name is Tanya." He pauses. "I don't want to freak you out. That's why I called and asked."

"Is she a close friend?"

"Umm…kind of. She's my ex."

I've been walking down Cambridge Street and suddenly the ground lurches. I step under a pharmacy awning, and before I can take a deep breath or do anything I've learned in DBT and CBT, I start crying.

"Crap, I was afraid of this," Taylor says quietly.

"You've never mentioned her before!"

"That's because I didn't think it was important. Or seemed appropriate."

I'm trying not to sob. "Not appropriate until she wants to spend the night with you?"

"Wait. Look, she wants to crash on my couch in the living room, not in my bed. I probably won't even see her. She's coming back from a concert late."

Be good, I tell myself. *Be reasonable.* A part of me knows that I'm overreacting. Another part is howling and wants to bang her head on the sidewalk. Yet another part recognizes and appreciates that Taylor is thoughtful enough to ask my opinion. But I'm *not* going to set myself up like I did with Bennet by being all nice and accommodating. "It's not okay," I say, my heart pounding. He wants to know why. "Because it's inappropriate."

"If you had an ex who wanted to crash at your place, I wouldn't object."

"That's not fair!" Taylor told me at the beginning that he doesn't get jealous—ever. So there's no way I can ask him to empathize with my own storms.

He counters that it's not fair for me to tell him how to handle his relationship with Tanya.

"But you asked for my opinion, and if you know it upsets me, why would you do it?"

I look up and notice that passersby are staring at me. I'm bent over like I've been kicked in the stomach, and I'm holding the phone to my ear with both hands. The tears won't stop.

"I've got to go," I say. I know this is a good time to page Ethan and put those all important skills into practice before I do something idiotic like throw the phone into a wall or jump into traffic. I also want to punish Taylor for having an ex-girlfriend. This wasn't in the plan. I page Ethan and he calls back in a matter of minutes. Sometimes when I page, he asks me pithy questions and can direct my thoughts in a new direction. At other times, like now, thinking doesn't work. I just sob.

"I don't know what to do," I sob.

"Can you try to do a distress tolerance skill?"

"I can't remember any!"

Ethan goes over the list with me—self-soothe, improve the moment, accept reality...

"I don't want to accept reality!" I wail. Ethan waits while I blow my nose.

"How about distracting from the pain?"

I look around me. There's an ice cream parlor down the street... But what do I do after ice cream? I can see what's coming: The thought of this woman will start to blow up like a balloon inside my head, forcing out reason, curiosity, and patience. I'll end up kicking furniture in the bedroom while Taylor and Tanya have a civilized dinner in his dining room.

Ethan suggests that I draw up a plan for the rest of the day—a distraction and self-soothe plan so that when thoughts of Tanya come up, I can turn my attention somewhere else. "And what do I do about this sleepover?" I ask Ethan. "Tell me what to do!"

He won't. He says that when I get back into wise mind, I'll be better equipped to figure that out.

"Look at all of this as *information*," he concludes. "You're gathering data points about Taylor, the same way you would if you were making a decision about anything else. You don't know yet what his relationship with Tanya is. You barely know him. Everything that's happening is good information. Just take note."

I agree to try, but it's hard to look at any of this as data. In my mind, we are already a couple, and Tanya is already a threat. There was a turning point sometime these past few weeks. Was it the kiss, or when he caught my thumb between his two fingers? Whichever small capture, now it binds me.

I feel like I've detoured from the kiddie ski slopes onto treacherous black diamond trails. I'm careening downhill with skis strapped to my feet, and every small bump with Taylor throws me off course. I'd thought that being in a relationship would force me to call on more interpersonal effectiveness skills. Wrong. I'm working with distress tolerance all the time. Apparently the emotional experiences I'm learning to deal with in stage two are all about abandonment, and Taylor's relationship with Tanya lays the groundwork for all of my previous fears to be rekindled. Shortly after the sleepover issue (which we both deftly sidestepped with a version of "don't ask, don't tell"), I arrive at his house for dinner and discover a pair of women's pants on his dining room table. Actually, many odd things reside on Taylor's dining room table: a windup plastic ladybug with tiny wheels and flapping wings, a computer hard drive partially dismantled, finger puppets, mail from the 1980s—and now a pair of women's pants.

I stand in the dining room on the edge of hysteria and point at the jeans lying on the table. My only consolation is that they're a size 18.

"Whose are these?"

Taylor is washing his hands in the kitchen and doesn't know what I'm talking about.

I hold the jeans up as he walks in. "Oh, those are Tanya's."

"What are her pants doing on your dining room table?"

"She stopped by after work yesterday to pick up her bicycle."

"And she just happened to leave her *pants* behind?"

Taylor thinks for a second and I scan his face for guilt. "I think she changed out of her work clothes when she came over." He shrugs. I can almost hear bombs exploding in my brain and the shrapnel trying to force its way out of my mouth.

"What the fuck?"

"What the fuck what?"

"First of all, I've explained to you I have problems with you being close to her. Second of all, I have BPD, and I've told you that this situation triggers me. Don't you get it?"

Taylor shakes his head. "But there's nothing to be threatened by. I'm not even close to her."

"Just enough for her to accidentally leave her pants behind."

"That doesn't prove closeness, just that she's a space cadet."

Talking to Taylor only increases my upset. What do I feel? Observe and describe! I feel rage, hurt, betrayal, and then I want to slam my head into a wall. "I can't talk about this anymore," I say, as the fury inside me builds. *Disengage*, I tell myself, turning toward Taylor's bedroom. *Think of this as an opportunity to practice the skills.* Fucking skills. Just knowing that he doesn't understand amplifies my rage. Usually I'd escalate at this point. As I go into his bedroom, the pressure in my chest becomes unbearable and I notice that my left hand aches. It's as though a dull knifepoint is pushing into the skin on my palm, but when I turn my hand over to see if I've accidentally done something, there's nothing there. I'm craving Taylor's assurance like crack, even though I still want to berate him. Climbing into his bed, I assume he's going to come in and check on me. But he doesn't. Underneath the floor, coming from the basement, I hear the clatter of tools and the cadence of a voice on an NPR talk radio show.

Wait! He's not supposed to do that. He's supposed to apologize and pull me into his arms. Now what do I do with this pain?! I want comfort and understanding, and as the pain increases, I start to cry. The ache in my palm turns sharp, like a stigmata. I hold my hand and sob, and consider my options: Do I go into the basement and say, "I'm sorry; I overreacted," and ask for a hug? I seriously consider whether I'm overreacting. I know the emotions are huge, cataclysmic, but there's no smoking gun—just a very large pair of pants. Still, emotion mind is in full force. I've been triggered, as we learn to say in CBT. The idea of another person taking Taylor away from me is as powerful as Alexis sitting next to me at the dinner table with Bennet. I feel too vulnerable now to go to the basement, so I burrow under the covers, where it smells like Taylor—like when we wake up in the morning, his body fit perfectly behind mine, one hand cupping my breast. I pull the pillows all around me and weep. And when he finally comes to bed, I wrap myself around him like a vine, hair and legs and arms, as close as I can be without breaking the contract. I want to possess him completely.

"What evidence do you have that he's being unfaithful?" Ethan asks. We've spent the past half hour doing an extensive behavioral analysis of the pants incident, teasing out the thoughts and feelings that led to my meltdown. We look at my vulnerabilities, such as spending all my free time with Taylor, not grounding into my own life, not going to the gym and working out, and sitting at a desk seven hours a day with these thoughts and fears constantly barraging my mind. All of this has disconnected me from myself and turned Taylor into the hub of my life. And if he *is* the center of my world, of course Tanya becomes a threat. But how much of a threat is she, really?

At the end of the behavioral analysis, I still don't know. I see I made the assumption that they'd had sex. Then I made the assumption that if they didn't have sex, Tanya left the pants on purpose: to torture me and to sabotage my relationship with Taylor, because she must know he's clueless about these things. That's what is most upsetting in all of this, that Taylor doesn't get how painful this is for me. Taylor and I are so different that sometimes it's like we're living in parallel universes. And yet it's what draws me to him: this counterbalance, our wildly different natures equalizing each other. Taylor sees this as well and jokes that we're like the nursery rhyme: "Jack sprat could eat no fat, his wife could eat no lean." We're polar opposites: I live in emotion mind; Taylor in reason mind. I'm impulsive; he's calculating. I read social sub-subtexts; Taylor recognizes only the concrete and literal. He is spatial to my relational, cool blue to my burning red, earth and rock to my hailstorms and hurricanes. He tells me from the very first, "Don't expect me to know what you need. Be explicit." He'd rather I poke him in the stomach when I need his attention than storm off because I feel ignored, rather that I ask for clarification and information before I jump to any conclusions. This is highly unnatural for me, so it's exactly what I need to practice.

But I need his help. I say, "When I start to get agitated, it helps me the most if you can stay calm, and for you to pay attention to me when I feel unmoored and alone. And instead of trying to convince me I'm being paranoid, just help me ride out the storm, then I'll be able to think straight again." Taylor has no problem with the calm part; he's unflappable in the face of intense emotions. And his sense of curiosity, scientific and probing, means I can tell him anything and his first impulse is to figure it out, not pass judgment on it. He can't, however, see things from my perspective, and, ultimately, this is more devastating than any imagined betrayal, because it feels like I am still alone.

I don't understand until many months into the relationship that Taylor's temperament and way of relating to the world is as deeply entrenched as my own. On one level, this forces us to move closer to a middle ground, reeling both of us in from our extremes. On another level, our opposing natures cause pain—at least in me. There's the ongoing ex-girlfriend issue, and then there's his house, which all the magical brooms of *Fantasia* couldn't sweep clear of a decade's worth of dirt, detritus, and low-grade hoarding. But mostly, it's that despite my freedom to tell him how I'm feeling, he doesn't understand it from his own experience. And so I must constantly remind him: "Please look at me when we're in social situations." "Please ask me how I'm feeling." "Please remember that it's hard for me to ask for things more than once." And "Please, please, *please* move the litter box out of the kitchen!"

Dr. Linehan says that one of the primary experiences of BPD is having a failure in dialectics (1993a). But in reality, this inability to reconcile opposing views and extremes is a fundamental human tendency. Borderlines just have it in a more exaggerated way. So when I finally conclude that Taylor isn't going to grasp things in terms of my feeling states, I have to resist the urge to accuse him of willfully neglecting me or not caring. Rather than digging in my heels and deepening my opposition, I try a more "interpersonally effective" tactic. Instead of asking him to understand my experience, I try to translate it into his. I explain that I have an operating manual, and that BPD symptoms are like dashboard lights: an indication that there may be trouble. I say that there are DBT tools for when I get broken or need a tune-up. I give him some of the lingo, like the word "dysregulated." I ask him to use that term when he sees that I'm getting upset, because often I don't see the emotion coming and I need him to notice and mention it to me. If

I still escalate to the point of being unreasonable, he should step back and not try to fix me. It would be better to say something like "I know you're upset. I'm really sorry you're feeling this way." If I'm crying hysterically, he can offer to hold me. If I'm slamming doors, he can promise he doesn't hate me and suggest I take a break.

I don't rage often, like I hear some borderlines do, but my intensity is the same. I'm a crier extraordinaire. With Taylor, the pattern is that I accuse, we argue, and I cry and accuse some more. If I'm feeling horribly victimized, I might crawl into bed and not come out. If my anger reaches the point where I'm afraid of what I might do, I pick up my bags and head out the door. Although I'm becoming well-versed in the DBT skills and Ethan's pager number is in my phone, my ability to slow down my reactions during an "episode" and consciously choose a strategy seems to disappear when things get rough with Taylor.

In DBT, distress tolerance skills are the first line of defense against making things worse. And for these skills, especially, I need coaching from Ethan or well-phrased suggestions from Taylor. There's something about the other person simply knowing and acknowledging how I feel that shifts the intensity. The first time Taylor does it, I see the change. "You're getting a bit dysregulated," he comments as I storm around the living room, upset that he's made plans with Tanya again. She's planning on moving to Europe, and while this is the best news I've had all year, Taylor, being ever helpful and handy, is helping her with some of the logistics.

"Doesn't she have her own boyfriend?" I ask. Apparently she does, but Taylor has a bigger car. When he tells me I'm dysregulated, my first impulse is to tell him to fuck off. But I don't.

The floor stops spinning and I focus my eyes on him. "It really sucks that you're doing this."

"I know," Taylor says. I'm still pissed, but the anger is loosening. I'm not accusing him of forsaking me. Instead, I take a shower and focus on the hot water hitting my body. I admit, I turn the water temperature a bit too high so it's close to scalding, but it does the trick. I'm soft, pink, and calmer when I emerge. Taylor hands me a cup of Sleepytime tea with milk and honey when I return to him wearing my pajamas.

"Can you understand that I can be with you and still care about someone else?" No. I don't understand how that is possible. But I'm willing to try, if he's willing to give me more concrete reassurance.

We sit across from each other at the dining room table. I take his hands. "I need you to look at me," I say, "and tell me that *I'm the one* you want to be with. I'm the *only* one. And you need to say it often. I'm the only one."

Taylor, for all his own stubbornness when it comes to changing himself, understands that this relationship is my in vivo training and that I need a lot of help from him. He also gets that I'm building up a new life from scratch. I warn him that my tendency is to make the other person my world and then lose myself. Taylor says that he's willing to share as much of his world as I want, and that he supports me in having my own life, as well. The funny thing about awareness, though, is that you can know and acknowledge a problem and yet still make the same mistakes over and over. And so it is with Taylor. I mouth the words "I want a life of my own" and "I need to discover who I am," but I'm constantly attached to him by this emotional umbilical cord, so I can't create the distance necessary for having a separate sense of self. If I think about buying a pair of shoes, I wonder if he'd like them. My musical taste now dips toward folk, as that's what he has in his CD collection. I find that I'm willing to take up motorcycle riding, and even to learn HTML coding—anything that will keep me close to his center. Almost every evening after work I go to his house and spend the night, pitching my Kiera-tent in the midst of his chaos, and actually feeling soothed by the smell of cat pee greeting me as soon as I walk through the door. I find that as long as Taylor is accessible, emailing me when I send a message, answering his phone when I call, and hugging me when I ask him to, I remain on stable ground. But who can do that all the time? As soon as he gets a call from Tanya, doesn't reply to a message, or doesn't say the right thing to make me feel special, the sirens go off and I'm… dysregulated, as we now say.

One the reasons I'm always at Taylor's place is that he doesn't like coming over to my studio. A couple of times we tried to spend the night there. His head grazes the studio's ceiling, and after all, it's only one room, with no TV or Internet. So after a few hours, during which he plays solitaire or fiddles with the kitchenette plumbing, we always end up back at his place, watching a movie. In just a couple of months, my studio has turned into a mausoleum, a giant abandoned suitcase holding the few small scraps of my past lives.

I sit with Ethan and say, "I'm losing myself. I can feel it." We draw up a plan for me to spend a weekend at home while Taylor visits friends. When the time comes, I regret the decision. I think I've mastered a lot of the skills; I mean, I can almost tolerate Taylor hanging out with his ex. But as soon as I'm alone in that studio, I'm defenseless against the pain. Sleep is accompanied by a sense of doom, and in the morning, the bottom falls out so quickly I can only lie on the floor and sob.

My box of light is now a casket. My source of life is gone, off playing stupid board games with his friends. The pain in my left palm flares more than ever, so I hold ice cubes to create a distraction and countersensation—a trick one of the women in DBT group shared. Distress tolerance skills are good for not causing more damage or pain, but they're stopgap measures, holding your place until you can return and move forward. Only I don't see any way out. Taylor's absence strips me of any accurate sense of time.

I page Ethan, who validates my terror and suggests more skills to use. Then I cry, eat pints of ice cream, leave messages on Taylor's phone ranging from hostile to apologetic, and finally resort to praying: *Please make this go away. Please stop this from happening.* I know that my response is because of BPD, not Taylor. It's a symptom and also a wound, a pus-filled, festering wound in my core that opens like a night-blooming flower and unleashes a toxic scent. This is the emotional experiencing I try to avoid at all costs. It's why Jimmy, the boy at arts camp so long ago, got letters written in blood, and it's why I'm now curled in a ball, wailing, while Taylor plays Cosmic Encounter with three other IT guys and eats too many cheese doodles. This is part of stage two. I'm exposing myself to emotions that I cannot, will not, tolerate—that I've never been able to tolerate. And yet I have to experience them. After a lifetime of being an escape artist, I finally understand that the only way out is through.

16

Learning to Ride

All summer I bounce back and forth between being triggered and being in love, between the desire to merge and the urge to flee. I feel threatened one minute and divinely held the next. The most stable parts of my life are Ethan and my work, where four days each week I continue to attend to the trivial details of other people's lives while receiving words of thanks and encouragement that feel like strings of gold stars after my name.

Taylor is currently out of work—the months right after the burst of the dot.com bubble aren't a good time for IT guys—so much of his time is spent tending to his five sport bikes in the basement. When he asks me if I want to learn how to ride a motorcycle, I say yes without any hesitation. I definitely want to learn to ride. Not only will it be a way for us to spend time together, but a part of me has always wanted to be a biker chick: in control of a powerful machine between my legs, decked in leather, hair streaming behind me. Men will gawk and women will be envious as I pull up at a stoplight and casually rev the engine. I have visions of a cat-woman outfit, but Taylor is a safety nut and insists that, before he teaches me anything, I purchase a full-face helmet and a waterproof, full-body, armored moon suit. When they arrive and I put them on, I look like a futuristic gladiator in an unearthly color called high-vis yellow—decidedly *not* sexy.

So here's an odd thing about me: I may have no emotional skin and come undone at the smallest interpersonal upset, but I'd make a great bullfighter or firefighter—anything that gets my adrenaline going and focuses me on a physical target. The motorcycle is all of that and more. When I'm on the bike, it feels like a door opens in my chest and the world rushes in, pure, fresh, and sparkling with clarity. It forces me to approach fear with total awareness and to pull reason mind into the moment of intense reactions. The motorcycle is another place to practice the skills, and before long, the other DBT group members are rolling their eyes as I yet again use the homework to describe a riding experience: how countersteering is a form of opposite action and how stop signs can be a place to practice interpersonal effectiveness.

Taylor is a born teacher. He starts me in a parking lot on a Honda Hawk 650, a sport bike he describes as naked because it's not covered in plastic. It's big and heavy, but that doesn't stop Taylor from pushing me around the parking lot like I'm a second-grader on a tricycle. As soon as I've mastered the shifting, he gets on his own bike (another Hawk) and leads me down the street, a real street, at the bottom of which I forget everything I've just learned, stall the bike, and go down with four hundred pounds of metal while cars back up behind me. I lie on the ground crying, not from pain, but humiliation. Taylor stands over me with his helmet off, smiling.

"Okay," he says, "no biggie. Let's try again."

What?! I may be a trooper, but I have limits, and dumping the bike wearing a heavy, bright yellow moon suit in the middle of the summer heat is a good enough reason to go take a cold shower and watch some TV. I tell him I don't want to.

"But this is the only way to learn," he says, lifting the bike up. "Everyone drops the bike the first time out. There'd be something wrong if you didn't."

This hadn't occurred to me. In my world, you do things right or not at all. Or you practice for long hours alone in front of the mirror and only emerge once you've achieved perfection.

"The two most important things to remember," Taylor adds, brushing the tears off my cheek, "are relax, and look ahead." *Relax... And look ahead...*

I climb back on the bike. How do you relax knowing that the slightest fuck-up could cost you your life? And if you look ahead, what about the stuff immediately around you?

Each day after work Taylor takes me out for practice, and I slowly begin to understand what his advice means. "Relax and look ahead" is his version of wise mind. Relax is the state of mindfulness—awareness of the cars, the bike, the position of your body, the currents of fear and excitement—where you rest, present and with all senses alert. But in order to ride, you must combine this present-moment awareness with reason mind—the moment-to-moment judgments involved in seeing where you want to go and how to get there, making calculations, weighing options, and letting emotions inform your behavior but not control it entirely. The dialectic of emotion mind and reason mind, combined with mindfulness, transforms the Honda Hawk into a wise mind machine. When I get triggered with Taylor, I can't navigate this internal calculus, but on the motorcycle I discover the place inside myself where I can manage the intensity of my feelings and be fully functional at the same time.

I continue building my life one piece at a time: Ethan, DBT, work, Taylor, motorcycles, and now sex, another level of exposure. It's another place to experience emotions, and also a place to avoid them. As soon as the month's contract ends, Taylor and I are fucking on a daily basis. And I have to admit, I'm better on the bike than I am in bed. My system is flooded with antidepressants again, so my ability to experience pleasure is severely at odds with my sexual appetite. It's like my clitoris is on novocaine. I discover that riding a bike for two hours gets my lower regions more sensitized, but even so, Taylor and I must work at my pleasure—work, work, work at it. Unlike Taylor, I'm not a good teacher. He asks me to tell him what to do, but I'm tongue-tied. Part of the problem is that, because of the medication, I don't know what will work for me from day to day. Maybe this should be BPD criteria number ten: instability in sexual response, followed by inappropriate expressions of sexual response, like when we're sitting on a public bench. Sometimes when I see his body or smell his scent, I want to consume him with all of my senses. Then, when we meet skin on skin, it's like hitting a thick glass wall. "It's the medication," I tell him.

"Can you change it?"

"Um, not the best idea right now."

"But doesn't your therapy help you so you don't need the pills?"

I say it might, but I'm not willing to risk it. I've also got depression and an anxiety disorder churning under the surface, along with BPD, and I'm not sure I'm stable enough to make that kind of change just yet.

By the end of summer I'm riding the Hawk to work every day. When I pull up to the corner of Church Street and Massachusetts Avenue in the morning, I pause after I take off my helmet. Perched on the bike, I survey the square. Students are returning. The first breath of fall rustles the leaves. Last year I was running out of the bookstore like I was under sniper fire, convinced even the simplest tasks were beyond me. Now I'm sitting on a motorcycle twenty feet away from that same spot, about to go to work. A lot can happen in a year.

I believe I'm progressing, but it's distressing to realize that as my relationship with Taylor deepens, it unearths even more pain. It reminds me of when I quit using drugs and alcohol. Without the instant numbing power of a substance to manage my inner turmoil, my life actually got worse. And now, as I try to practice mindfulness with each emotion, without reacting or defending or deflecting, I'm immersing myself in new territory, or, I should say, old territory from a new perspective.

Now, at stage two, which involves dealing with emotions and traumatic experiences from the past, the old-school BPD theories about disordered attachments and disorganized personality begin to make sense to me. I go back into the literature to see in what other ways BPD behavior and perceptions can be explained. I know I'm dysregulated, unstable, and impulsive. And I'm using the skills with all my might to manage these characteristics. But why do I still go blind with rage when I think Taylor is talking on the phone with Tanya, when actually it's his mother? Why is it that even when Taylor and I have sweet, intimate moments, I can't surrender and sometimes even go numb and float away? Why can't I put the pieces of a self back together? Why has yet another person become the center of my world? And why do I turn into a fearful child now that touch, love, need, and belonging have fused with Taylor?

Trauma, unresolved issues, core wounds—maybe it makes sense that these demons only resurface when I achieve a semblance of safety. Now that the ground is firm, my inner rifts are more accessible.

I try to put all of my energy into not letting this relationship dismantle my progress. I have gone though all four DBT skills modules in group, from mindfulness to interpersonal effectiveness to distress tolerance to emotion regulation, and am now starting my second, and final, round of them. I'm at the head of the class, and the other women in the group increasingly look to me as a leader. But with Taylor I often feel like I'm regressing. He doesn't turn the radio down like I ask him to, so I decide that means he doesn't care about me and I spend the rest of the day strangled and stupefied by the emotions from just this one slight. I'll feel cozy in Taylor's house until he makes a comment about renovating the kitchen. He mentions wanting to redo the floors as he's carrying a bowl of pasta into the dining room, and by the time he's crossed the threshold, I'm completely offended and huffy.

"What happened between the kitchen and the dining room?" he asks, completely baffled. I'm convinced that he's planning on a future without me if he's thinking of renovating and hasn't yet invited me to move in. When I read a while back that borderlines "test" people, I had no idea what that meant. Now I understand: It's like I'm constantly searching for confirmation of his love for me, and each of his gestures and words, no matter how trivial, can either prove or disprove it. I wish I could just ease up and feel secure. On the other hand, I wish he'd stop doing things that trigger my insecurities. It's a vicious cycle of sorts, but that does make it extremely fertile ground for learning.

And despite all the turmoil and periods of freaking out, I am content like never before. For weeks and months at a time, I live in a cocoon of comfort. I work in office fun-land. Renee and I go on outings to Ikea for furniture and to Costco to fill an entire pallet with office snacks. I started out not being able to make small talk, and now I'm the "Office Goddess" (I have a mug that officially declares this), dipping strawberries in dark chocolate to feed the masses, arranging luncheons and parties with Gail and Renee, presiding over my desk with the silver candy bowl and a "Free Advice" sign, like I'm Lucy from *Peanuts*. At home (by which I mean Taylor's), I sleep, cook and watch TV. He teaches me how to design web pages and how to season a steak. All the while, I continue with therapy and DBT group, ride motorcycles, and grow close to Taylor's mother, who has the same insatiable curiosity as her son and no baggage from the past to throw into the mix of our mutual affection.

It's a cliché, but time really *does* fly by when you're having fun. The flip side being, of course, that when you're in misery, each second feels like a year, boulder-heavy and crushing you. The rhythm of my life follows accordingly: When things are good, weeks flash by, and when they're bad, each second seems like an eternity. I'm still set off by the same things. I feel threatened when even a hint of an ex-girlfriend pops up, including Tanya's underwear, which I discover while cleaning out Taylor's dresser to make room for my clothes. (Apparently, he throws nothing away—*nothing!*) I still feel like I'm being stabbed when Taylor forgets to make eye contact with me in social groups or when he doesn't respond to an email or voice mail promptly, and it doesn't help that my definition of prompt and his are drastically different. I continue to flip in my perceptions and emotions about him depending on my perception of how he treats me, and I resent him whenever I discover that I have very little life outside of the relationship, even as I keep perpetuating that dependence.

Taylor comments that although I'm still often triggered, my times of upset are shorter: I lose my bearings for a day or two, not a month. And I no longer declare that our relationship is over every time I feel neglected.

I agree. My relationship to pain is changing. While the feelings are as intense as ever, they don't take me over completely, and I don't react as quickly. Sometimes in the crisis of the moment I can actually say what I'm feeling, and even do it without accusing Taylor of trying to hurt me. I try to take the long view—to ride these states out, rather than giving in to the story lines that justify their presence. I haven't hurt myself physically in a year and a half now, though the impulse is still there, like a shadow, and it still steps into my conscious mind when the pain peaks. I still have to ride out the urge, have to tell it, "You're an outdated survival tool," and figure out some other way to reregulate myself, from holding an ice cube to going shopping for shoes.

Certain areas of my life, however, aren't evolving so well—my sex life, for instance, where I start to wonder if I'm actually regressing. It's hard to examine this, because I feel baffled and ashamed, but I'm beginning to wonder if I'm a semifrigid sex addict. Like my cravings for love and security, my carnal desires overwhelm me but only lead to more disconnection. I'm passionate and intensely physical and crave being touched and petted like a cat all the time. Yet when Taylor and I are intimate, I don't respond easily and cannot climax unless an hour or more is dedicated to my body, and even then there's no guarantee. And for all of Taylor's tenacity over fixing broken things, he's at a loss as to how to repair this.

There is one guaranteed way I can get excited, and that's if I am allowed to be in complete control. I initially tried to avoid this scenario because I wanted to learn how to be vulnerable and trusting in bed, but soon enough the ManRay girl's boxes of clothes come out, and it's not like I have to twist Taylor's arm to get him to participate. If I take the dominant role and render him completely helpless, I get ridiculously turned on. My pleasure flows most naturally when I'm in complete control.

And having Taylor supine and unmovable allows me to use all of my senses, all of my body, to consume him. It's a ravenous delight that works well for both of us—until I start to grow weary of the dominatrix role. While it's definitely more pleasurable, I don't want to always be in charge and doing things just to him. I don't articulate it, but I feel a growing resentment that this sex is still ultimately about Taylor's pleasure. Even with all the power, I feel like a handmaiden who needs to please a man in order to have any value.

So I tire of this and want to go back to straight nookie. The thing is, when we go back to being simple bodies under the covers, I don't know what will happen. Some moments I'm in the midst of the action, a full participant, feeling great. Then a numbness cuts me off and I'm dissociated, clinging to Taylor and wishing with all my heart I could reenter the waters of passion he's still so happily frolicking in. I want to ride that wave, damn it. I touch myself, call to mind various fantasy images, do a bit of self-coaching (*Relax! You can do it!*), ask him to do this or that. But in the end, I'm just along for the ride, feeling like I did in almost every drunken high school hookup. A boy has turned into a rutting, frenzied stranger. My Taylor, with the lights off, can become a stranger. The worst part is that after what should be a pinnacle of intimacy, I feel horribly alone. I am empty and need more. It's like I want to siphon every last bit of affection he can offer so that I don't drift to sleep with this ache inside me. I want to climb inside him and be comforted like a child. But Taylor, of course, has fallen asleep.

I'm a hypocrite, because if I were being really honest, I'd tell Taylor that the sex isn't really working. But that would threaten our relationship, and without the relationship, I don't know what I'd have. All of Taylor's friends have become my friends by default. I've taken up residence in his extra room while still maintaining my own place, though I never go there. My day is perfectly structured by him—between our routine of emails, phone calls, dinners, and nightly TV shows, I can't fall through any cracks. If Taylor were gone, it would be like pulling the plug in a basin that holds all the shapeless, turbulent liquid of my life. I would drain away.

And so I need to understand: How can I be healthy and functional in so many ways, and yet still be on the edge, without a self? I'm essentially trapped in a paradox of need and love. I keep telling Taylor that I need to create my own life. Meanwhile, Ethan and I work on the skills and examine how I'm avoiding being with myself and how I'm blaming Taylor.

If I can stop projecting everything onto Taylor and see the deeper workings of my mind, I can possibly become more than a "functional borderline," more than a woman now living on the edge. Outwardly, I seem to be doing so well. But it's like I'm wearing a loosely secured mask. Everyone is so proud of me for having come so far, yet as soon as Taylor turns his eyes away, my world is threatened with destruction.

PART 4

Emergence

17

First Touch

I find myself going back to the original rift. Not infancy, where I may or may not have had unlimited access to my mother's breast. Not to early childhood, when my brother was born and undeniably usurped my parent's attention. Back to when I was six years old, playing at the edge of the yard, spinning with wide arms. House then street, house then street, whirling by until they blurred. Only the sky remained still and unchanging, a blue portal with smeared walls. It's an apt metaphor for the shifting focal points in my young life: a divorce and my father's absence, a blur of languages and countries in six short years. When things finally stopped spinning, I'd landed back in the States, along with my mother and brother, with Dutch, Italian, and English twisting on my tongue.

I was lonely. Every afternoon the street clattered with children playing, but I remained an outsider. Then, a babysitter. How old could he have been? Like most six-year-olds, I saw all tall people as adults, but perhaps he was just a teenager, perhaps even just a boy. While our mother went out at night, he watched over us. He let us stay up and watch TV, even though we should have been in bed. He made us popcorn in the brand new machine that melted butter at the same time it popped the kernels. On one particular night, we camped in the living room with our pillows and bedding because the heat was low and the windows were drafty. Only the top of my brother's head was visible as he lay swaddled on the couch across from the TV. On the other couch, I was stretched out with my fuzzy yellow blanket, the babysitter sitting next to my feet.

The metallic light of the TV flickered against us, casting a blue tint. Inside the balloon of warmth within my blanket, a cool pocket of air grazed my ankle. The babysitter tickled my foot and I giggled. Shh, he motioned, his finger to his lips. His hand moved lengthwise under the covers, bringing a cold line of air with it, until he found the edge of my nightgown—a flannel nightie with posies dropped all over the surface and lace around the sleeves and neckline, a gift from my grandmother when we stayed with her after the flight home from Europe.

I watched my babysitter's profile. He didn't look at me. He laughed with the canned laugh track from the television, but from my knee to my thigh, his hand traced my skin so that it quivered. His hand played itsy-bitsy spider, ascending finger over finger. I noticed that the ceiling had lumps in it, as though the floor above had let some of its weight crumble down. My babysitter turned his head and winked as the itsy-bitsy spider climbed higher, giving me shivers. Then it arrived. There.

As the grain of his fingerprints rubbed against my hairlessness, I kept my eyes on him. Both of us were breathing shallowly. A warm panic prickled my insides, and I looked to my brother. He was oblivious, staring slack-jawed at the TV, only his eyes and the sheen of his hair gathering light. What did I feel, with the babysitter's fingers caressing my vagina? Could it have been arousal? Do children even feel such things? Why didn't I cry or push his hand away? As we sat in a bubble of suspended motion, inside I felt an incomprehensible mix of sensations: warmth, prickling, panicky, hopeful—for what? I remained silent, waiting for the next caress. Keeping his eyes on the TV screen, the babysitter slowly moved one of my legs out toward the edge of the couch.

A moment later, the front door opened and my mother strode in with her cheeks stained red from the winter air. The hand under the covers froze, pulling back just as my mother bent over me to plant a kiss on my forehead. I pretended to be asleep.

That year our town was awash in patriotism. American flags draped houses, snapped from poles, and festooned every light post along Main Street. Fife music and the rat-a-tat-tat of drums formed a backdrop to the firing of cannons as my brother and I joined the crowd to watch the bicentennial parade. Somehow, two hundred years of freedom were commemorated by clowns tumbling past and throwing fistfuls of candy. We scrambled into the parade to snatch candy from under the feet of the marching band. Across the street, a house on a sloping hill gave out free cola in cloudy glass bottles.

We lived a quarter mile away from the Old North Bridge, in Concord, Massachusetts, where the shot heard round the world was fired. My brother and I shared a room on the apartment's second floor. Ben needed a nightlight and I didn't, yet he always fell asleep first. Floating above his nasal breath, I didn't want to close my eyes. Not because I feared a boogeyman; I was afraid to close my eyes because if I did, I'd start to float. Unmoored inside myself, the black against my eyelids would expand like the space of a starless night, and I'd be utterly alone in it—like those astronauts in the movies, cast adrift into the empty void of space. That's what closing my eyes felt like when I was six. I wasn't afraid of the dark; I was terrified of being inside myself.

When I ask my mother about it now, she insists I was a happy child. Certainly I was brash when it came to climbing trees, and I enjoyed jumping on the mattress despite repeated orders not to do it. But I remember it differently. Even when I was that young, I was always guarding against nakedness and feeling the eyes of others penetrating me and branding me as somehow different.

I remember grasping Ben's hand as we entered circles of children playing in this new neighborhood, and wondering what they saw in me. My breath shortened and my heart stuttered. Even in a simple game of tag, the complexities overwhelmed me. Not so much how to play; I knew that one person was "it" and that this person must try to pass the "it-ness" on. Chase and tag. Run and shout. But why was I chosen? Why did the small boy with the flared collar single me out and go after me with such force? And when I was "it," why did the older kids wander off to kick a ball across the wide lawn by the mailbox? That troubled me, but not nearly much as when I accidentally grabbed the ribbon on a girl's shirt and it came off in my hand. It seemed I always played too rough, even as I was sensitive to the slightest gestures from others. The little girl angrily snatched her ribbon back and said she was going to tell her father. I was left on the grass, howling inside.

It was nothing—and yet everything.

Some alchemy happened then: touch and absence, words and silence, the reconfiguration of reference points at a time I lacked both inner and outer ground. Not everyone who's been sexually abused as a child develops BPD, but for me this was a critical juncture because before that I was simply a sensitive child. Maybe I lacked a certain solidity of self. I probably was more socially anxious than many other children. If I really wanted to start at the beginning, maybe I'd list the numerous times we moved for my father's Air Force job: the rented houses in Italy and Holland, the interim stays in hotels and friends' apartments; surely that must upset a child's world. And when I left home myself, at seventeen, I continued in this unsettled way, never able to abide too long in one place, a perfect example of Freud's notion of repetition compulsion.

I wish now I remembered birthday parties and the sweetness of frosting, good-night kisses and the crayon art of second grade. But those memories are eclipsed by something larger: the flickering blue light of the television, the shivering and pounding heart at the touch of a pale hand. I've always known that touch marked me. Not so much because it hurt or harmed—though it may have, gentle as it was. His hand on me was almost like the redemptive touch of some dark god. From a swirling nothingness I became the imprint of his gesture. I felt myself take shape in the touch of another.

I wish now I could say it was an isolated incident, but that night in front of the TV was just the first time. Sometimes my mother would leave me at his house, just down the street, for safekeeping. And there, in his room, he would lift me onto his bed and take my clothes off until I was lying naked on the sheets with his large hands passing over my skin. Touching me, he'd murmur, "This seems to be fine. Arms in perfect shape. Neck okay…" And then move on, with a doctor's detachment, to my legs, and then inside me, no part of me left unexplored. I didn't think we were playing doctor; it was too real, and too important, for make-believe. His examinations were a test, and if I passed, he would keep me. Under his touch I became a perfect specimen, made to be loved, held, and stroked.

In time, I discovered the immensity of his erection. And when I did, I couldn't stop looking and touching. Before we'd moved here from Holland, I'd spent long afternoon hours dressing up as a princess waiting to be rescued by a knight. My mother set up the record player with Tchaikovsky's *Swan Lake*, the only music I'd listen to. At the end of the record, the needle would find the clear, silent space and then lift and swing back, starting the dance again, filling the air with ruffled taffeta and graceful swans.

In the babysitter's bed, I could hear the music. I was the princess in the high tower, finally united with my prince, and I wanted to stay locked up together forever, feeling the warm tingle from his hands and his eyes on me. He'd ask how I felt: "And this?... And this?" I existed at the center, and my body kept him tied to me. He never looked away. Why return to the ground, without my prince? What awaited me but a lonely walk home, past oblivious fathers mowing their lawns and mean children playing tag? In that curtained room, I chose captivity over freedom, thinking it meant I'd never be alone. There's no way I could have foreseen that becoming this child lover would trap me in an endless cycle of unmet need and desperate attempts to secure more love, each time offering myself to others in ways that only brought more secrets and shame.

Until I entered therapy at age fourteen, I didn't tell anyone about that babysitter. I simply didn't think it was important. And yet look at me now: a woman in her thirties who still longs to be touched so that I can become yet another imprint. I want to cry for that little girl now, but I can't. I turn to Taylor at night hoping he can be lover, father, doctor, and friend all at once, but of course that's an impossible dream. I try to explain my dilemma to him, how I am both child and adult, supplicant and dominatrix—sometimes all in the span of an hour. He wants to know what he can do to help, but I cannot answer. Deep down in the rabbit hole of recovery, I don't know how to fix this.

I think I was born with this primal nature. If I'd been left in the wild without any sense of shame, I probably would have opened myself to all creatures, rolling in the mud and rain, rutting and howling. Maybe the trauma wasn't simply being sexualized too early, but not being given a choice in the opening of this force I couldn't control, which brought not the love I craved, but a deeper alienation. From that time onward I was pulled into a double life, with the secret knowledge of adults vibrating inside me even as I was still playing with dolls. It was only a quick jump from there to giving blow jobs on concrete steps before I hit age twelve. Choiceless not just in those first interactions, but choiceless from then on because my need meant that anyone could reach out and I would respond, despite the rumors that surrounded me and the word "slut" pinned to my overly developed middle school breasts. More than the sex, it was disgrace that wounded me and trapped me in another repetitive compulsion: seeking redemption the only way I knew how, by offering my body even as I lost more of myself each time. And now I don't even know how to say no to Taylor. When he wants me, I open to him. Sometimes it's a needy child he enters in the darkness, and sometimes it's a woman. And sometimes I roll him over and pin him down, taking whatever I can from him before my body rebels and I'm left alone within the embrace.

18

Exposure

Ethan and I begin to explore this new terrain of my sexuality just as my final cycle of DBT skills group comes to a close. I'm about to graduate from the group and enter life after DBT, a place thousands of us transition into without much understanding of what comes next. So what does comes next? In my case, I'm lucky. My program has a graduate group run by a trauma specialist. As I've mentioned, in Linehan's model (1993a), resolution of trauma is key to moving though stage two, and while I still resist seeing myself as a victim of trauma, it's becoming clear that I have some lingering unresolved issues, despite my decades of therapy.

In DBT, stage two is mainly concerned with exposure-based procedures for working with trauma and difficult emotional experiences. Linehan recommends that this kind of therapy not be done in a DBT skills group. In fact, she suggests that therapists stay away from discussions of past events until stage one, learning the DBT skills and decreasing self-harm, has been achieved. This ensures that the person has a toolbox ready for dealing with the difficult issues that come up in stage two. Stage two isn't formal in the way the skills group has been. I don't get a worksheet to fill out that says now you're going to have sex with Taylor and work on exposing yourself to difficult emotions and traumatic experiences. Acclimating to seemingly overwhelming feelings and developing tolerance is an incremental experience. There are many techniques presented in Linehan's textbook related to this next stage, all of them based on behavioral theory: exposure to triggers, blocking the tendency to react in typical ways, choosing which behaviors to reinforce (and which to not reinforce), and role-playing.

And just as the dance between acceptance and change plays out in life and therapy, both exposure to and protection from these emotions need to be managed dialectically. I am not yet so good at this.

A few weeks before I'm to leave the skills group, I meet with Olivia, the graduate group leader, and Simon to review my progress and get oriented to the new group. I'm completely committed to entering this new group, but I have to ask whether there's any chance the previous group can continue as a peer support group for DBT skills. The skills group is as close to a recovery community as I've gotten, even though it doesn't have a BPD emphasis. I want to keep sharing my recovery with them, and I want to keep seeing their progress. Darcy is blossoming. She broke up with her boyfriend and has a place of her own—and a new haircut that shows off her beautiful eyes. Misha is getting over her ex and finally starting to date other women. Jenny (and her guide dog) has started attending graduate classes in psychology. Like a pied piper, Simon has led us from one skill to another, and we've been traipsing after him as best we can—sometimes stumbling, but also skipping, racing, and even dancing. Sharing in the group amplifies every concept by the power of our individual experiences and feeds us with new options. Robyn practices the distraction technique by building sculptures from found objects. Maria visits her in-laws knowing that she'll be sucked into their drama, and yet able to practice radical acceptance. Goth Chick has switched from punching walls to kickboxing. We share our lists of pleasant events and witness each other identifying emotions. We even survive a cat fight between Maria and Goth Chick. As the fight-or-flight response passes through us like electricity, we all begin to hyperventilate; Simon makes us sit and breathe until the intensity begins to ease. This group meets only ninety minutes each week, so it certainly isn't the center of my life, but it has become part of my foundation. And I need to keep a foundation. I don't want to lose everything just because I'm doing better.

Simon and Olivia shake their heads sadly when I ask whether the group can continue meeting as a peer group after we graduate. They say it's impossible: no resources, no time, and possibly boundary violations and conflicts of interest. I feel upset that they don't understand the significance of this loss, and I even secretly petition the other women in the group to come find me after they've graduated so that we can meet in secret. I imagine us gathering in someone's living room. "Did you do the distress tolerance exercise?" "Shh, I think there's someone at the door..."

In order to prepare for the upcoming transition, I need to look for other supports. I've joined an online DBT Listserv. That helps, since it allows me to communicate electronically with others about the skills, but it doesn't substitute for real people. There's a depression and bipolar support alliance at another local hospital, but I don't feel safe disclosing my BPD diagnosis there, or anywhere at this point, unless I have some assurance I won't be dismissed and judged. In New York City, a personality disorder association gives workshops about BPD for family members, and the National Education Alliance for BPD has recently developed a similar program, but again it's only for family and friends of those with BPD. The one place I keep circling back to is a local personality disorder organization that meets at my old hospital. While it too is set up to help non-borderlines, they say they welcome everyone to their workshops, regardless of status. After reading so many online tirades, I'm more than a little worried about the reaction I might get if I show up at one of their events, but on the other hand, this organization offers family workshops featuring famous doctors and training in DBT skills. It's as close as I'm going to get to a BPD community that doesn't include a computer screen and people threatening to jump off bridges.

So one Saturday afternoon I suck it up and finally go. The meeting, held in a room off the cafeteria where my parents and I met during that summer of last resort, is attended mainly by haggard-looking parents and fretful spouses. I spot maybe one or two other borderlines in the room. How do I know they're borderlines? They position themselves as I do, hunkered down, not making eye contact, already appearing defensive as the conversation will, inevitably, be about "us." It's a bizarre scenario, actually. What if there were no support groups for people with cancer, but only for their families? And what happens when cancer patients actually sneak into in the room, like spies, to hear themselves being discussed? Imagine if none of those cancer patients talked to each other, and they didn't even know how people might recover from cancer; instead, they just sit silently in the corners, feeling their disease eating them alive. That's exactly how I start feeling.

The room is small and there's no airflow. A mother is talking about how her borderline daughter just yells at her all the time. A husband can't get his wife into treatment. A father explains that his son needs treatment, but no one will give it to him because of the common misconception that only females have BPD. My anxiety reaches a critical level, so I flee to the bathroom. First I splash cold water on my face, then I sit on a toilet and self-soothe by pressing my palms against my face and on my neck, patting my arms, and massaging my chest. These physical interventions help a lot.

I go back into the room and discover that the other two borderlines have left. I know Ethan would ask, "Why do you need to be in this group if it's so upsetting?" Why? Because this is the only place I know of where people even dare to utter the word "borderline," and I'm desperate for a community where I don't have to feel like I'm always hiding, and where I might even be understood. I'm quite desperate for it. That could be viewed as a problem—a pathological need for attention, which is often considered another BPD trait—or it could be seen as simply human nature. Perhaps it lies on the borderline of both—yet another dialectic, along with the issue of exposure versus protection. For those of us with BPD, entering into a shared experience means passing through the ring of fire that leaves us feeling even more burned—and in this case branded with a label no one would ever choose to wear.

I'm royally triggered by the meeting, but I go back the next month to another packed room, and listen. This time an occupational therapist discusses job difficulties for people with BPD. I linger for a bit afterward and nervously allow myself to be greeted by the organizers. When asked by Allison, a stately, blond woman with kind eyes, why I'm attending the support group, I say, "I have BPD." Such a simple statement, really, but it feels like I'm disgorging a giant rock from my mouth. Allison smiles when I tell her. Smiles!? I've never gotten this reaction before. Anything she might say after that smile will pale in comparison, because this is truly the first time that admitting to having BPD hasn't caused bafflement, denouncement, worry, or fear. Even with Taylor, who has been so understanding and supportive, it always feels like I'm describing the creature from the black lagoon. He's fascinated, and also unperturbed—unless I start throwing too much muck at him. But this is the first time I've gotten a smile and a hug.

"My daughter has it too," Allison says, embracing me. "Bless your heart for coming. I'm sure it can't be easy." I look down and realize I've got five giant cookies from the refreshment table on my paper plate. Distress tolerance skill 3.4: carb overdose. I thank her and she brings me over to Don, a tall man in a suit whose grown daughter has BPD. And then to Janine and Reggie, a married couple and parents of a son with BPD.

"You don't know how much it means that you're here," they tell me. I feel like a movie star, and I'm flushed from the attention; in fact, it's almost as disturbing as being ignored. They want to know everything, so I give them a rundown of my past few years. Their admiration is unflagging, and I feel like I'm in the twilight zone. It turns out that most of them have received BPD education and learned some DBT skills through the program created by NEABPD. Hearing all of this, I comment that I wish that my family would get involved like they have. The parents nod, and one of them replies, "And many of us wish that our children would come here, like you have."

Across the cafeteria and down a few stairs is the table where my parents and I sat that summer, where I begged them to help me and denounced them for not trying hard enough. Then I think of one of DBT's many dialectics: Everyone is doing the best they can, yet everyone needs to try harder. I put four of the cookies back as discreetly as possible, and Allison hugs me before I can sneak out the door. I'm overwhelmed by their seemingly unwarranted appreciation, and also warmed, like I used to feel after downing shots of whiskey. An inner ease spreads inside me. Such is the power of acceptance and understanding from other people, the power of validation.

This is such an important word: "validation." It means recognizing someone else's feelings, behaviors, and thoughts as legitimate, no matter how problematic or dysfunctional they may appear to be. It's the opposite of "invalidation," which Dr. Linehan points to as a key factor in activating BPD symptoms in those of us with the biological vulnerabilities (1993a). Allison gave me a powerful dose of validation just by recognizing that I have the disorder and understanding how difficult it was to show up at that meeting and how painful my life has been. That validation fills up a small hole inside me. I've tried doggedly to practice radical acceptance and all the other skills, but when these are self-directed, it's only a partial comfort, and I still feel like I'm living a double life, keeping the disorder in secrecy and isolation. Receiving validation from someone else about being a borderline has a profound effect.

The trainings now being offered by family organizations teach validation as one of the most critical techniques in helping someone with BPD. We need this help from outside because we don't know how to do this for ourselves. We start with a deep deficit—a chasm, really—when it comes to understanding and being tolerant of ourselves, and that's even before we go forth to do battle with the rest of world. As soon as someone judges, criticizes, dismisses, or ignores, the cycle of pain and reactivity ramps up, compounded by shame, remorse, and rejection. The act of validation, simply saying, "I see things from your perspective," can help short-circuit that emotional detour. In DBT, therapists are encouraged to always see the grain of truth in their clients' thoughts, feelings, and actions, no matter how challenging, dysfunctional, or dysregulated.

And this is exactly what I've been trying to teach Taylor and my family: not only to recognize the causes of my pain as being legitimate, but to find a way to be loving and nonjudgmental when I react in ways they can't understand. I need them to be aware and present with me in the midst of the storm, not just tell me what to do. The fact that the BPD diagnosis and so much of what we suffer from also isn't validated, either by our loved ones or by the culture, adds another layer to this fundamental problem. Now it appears to me that invalidation has been an ongoing theme in my life—from my adolescence, when my behaviors and feelings were always pinned on being "difficult" and "attention seeking," to my family's continued insistence that there's nothing seriously wrong with me, especially not a personality disorder. It's possible that only Ethan has walked the fine line between recognition and dismissal, with his admission that I have the symptoms of BPD coupled with his insistence that I am more than that. Yet I also recognize this: Even if everyone in the world were to accept me and my illness and validate my pain, unless I can abide myself and be compassionate toward my own distress, I will probably always feel alone and neglected by others.

19

Being More Than One Thing

DBT graduation is simple. At the end of my last group, we go around in a circle and say good-bye. If it were my choice, I'd have cake, speeches, and party favors (little key chains with "Use Your Wise Mind!" printed on them). I'm accustomed to AA and NA anniversaries, where we pass cards around the room and sign them, and a sponsor stands up to describe the person's progress: "When our little Kiera first came around, she constantly wore combat boots and sunglasses! Just look at how she's grown!"

I suppose the purposes of this kind of therapy don't include community building, so you shouldn't expect to leave with a group of friends. It teaches you the skills to create your own life, each skill a building block inside you. You're not supposed to cling to the structure, but instead go forth and create your own. There's just one pestering question: What happens to people after they leave the DBT skills group? As with BPD recovery in general, the future is hazy and incomplete. I keep going back to Marsha Linehan's texts and the research, but I don't find any data on stage two, nor do I find an instruction manual for life after skills group.

In an article in *Psychiatric Times*, I find a quote from Dr. Linehan: "In sum, the orientation of DBT is to first get action under control, then to help the patient feel better, to resolve problems in living and residual disorder, and to find joy and, for some, a sense of transcendence." Yet she also admits, "All my research is at level one, but you can't stop treatment there. If you don't go to the next levels, [patients] will often move back to level one again" (Knowlton 1999, 2).

So the question for those of us with BPD on this path is how to keep moving forward. The stage two work of emotional experiencing that I'm doing with Ethan seems to be helping me stay in my relationship with Taylor despite the numerous triggers, and it also helps me manage the stresses of having a job. But I still confront these inner minefields. I try to step around them as best I can, yet it's obvious that the deeper into life I go, the more explosives I'll need to identify and disarm.

Miraculously, the advanced DBT group appears to be the answer to this next level. In my orientation meeting with the group leader, Olivia, she explains that while we'll still be talking about the DBT skills, this group is specifically designed to help people apply their skills in situations that are connected to past traumas.

"Like what happens with me and Taylor whenever I feel threatened," I say.

She nods. Part of the exposure practice in this group will involve gaining access to the different parts of ourselves that are shut down or in conflict with each other. The technique is culled from a therapy called Internal Family Systems (IFS), developed by Richard Schwartz (1995) while working with severely bulimic women. His patients referred to the different parts of themselves so often that Schwartz began to understand that inner experiences can be organized into separate components of an internal world. This system operates much like a family, each part having its own identity, goals, and values. IFS can seem freaky at first. It's based on the premise that all of us—with or without psychiatric disorders—have a multiplicity of selves, and that these selves, or personalities, are always interacting in much the same way as family members behave within a family, having individual histories, roles, alliances, goals, and conflicts. Schwartz also uses the analogy of a tribe to describe this collection of parts, breaking down their roles into three basic types that contribute to the overall functioning of a person: managers, firefighters, and exiles. Ideally, each part should be supportive, not in charge. That role falls to the self. Acting in the capacity of tribal leader, the self ideally works with all parts effectively, checking in with them, listening to them, and acting wisely, taking all of the parts' needs into consideration.

This concept of parts actually doesn't surprise me. It's likely that one of the reasons I've resisted healing my "inner child" is because I actually have too many inner entities, too many shifting aspects of myself. Schwartz makes the distinction between multiple personalities that are in dissociative states (such as with multiple personality disorder) and the more relational and conscious way our inner parts typically operate. For instance, when Taylor seems to be ignoring me, I can go from happy girlfriend to scorned woman to whimpering child in fifteen minutes. I'm aware of these different parts, so while they're compartmentalized, they aren't entirely split off from me. I can observe that ManRay Girl comes out when being a good girl no longer works or that Hippie Chick can emerge if I think she can get me laid. This awareness of the differing aspects of myself is one of the reasons why the borderline symptom "unstable sense of self" made so much sense when I first heard the criteria. And I can still witness new aspects of myself emerging, as though my identity is not only constantly changing, but adapting—a psychic evolutionary strategy based on my need to belong and feel loved by others. The multitude of parts within me may be a little more extreme, but Schwartz says that parts are inherent in everyone. The IFS model doesn't try to get rid of parts; it sees them as natural and useful. It's only when they're in conflict, frozen in time, or overly controlling that trouble occurs.

Olivia gives me a good amount of reading material to prepare for joining the advanced group, and I also buy Schwartz's manual, *Internal Family Systems Therapy* (1995). The first thing I need to get clear about IFS theory is where "I" really am, given there are so many various parts. Is one part simply in charge of the other parts? Schwartz says no. He makes a distinction between the parts and the self. The self is considered a transcendent aspect: the awareness and discerning intelligence that dialectical behavior therapy calls wise mind—the integration of emotion mind and reason mind. In IFS, the self has characteristics such as leadership, compassion, perspective, curiosity, confidence, and acceptance, and it works with all of the parts. Schwartz likens the self to the conductor of a symphony, able to hear each instrument and yet leading all of the players in concert (1995). In this sense, the relationship between the self and the parts is dialectical. You have to view yourself as being many things, and yet also one thing, in the same way that physics describes light as both a particle and a wave.

There are other similarities between IFS and DBT. For instance, in the IFS model, nothing is static. Each part's existence and movements have an impact on every other part. It's similar to a mobile; when one piece shifts, all of the other parts will reverberate from the impact and move as well. This is considered a systems model, but it's also based on the same kind of common sense that dialectics uses to remind us that interdependence and change are constant and unavoidable aspects of reality.

DBT and IFS are also alike in being nonjudgmental. IFS doesn't judge the various aspects of a person in terms of good or bad, even those that are destructive or harmful. IFS says there are no bad parts, that all inner aspects have a role that serves to protect the self, even if that role is not ultimately effective or helpful. Similarly, in DBT the behaviors and experiences that define the borderline condition are seen as ineffectual ways of trying to accomplish goals. Self-harm, for example, serves the purpose of self-soothing, despite its negative effects. In this way, both therapies use validation, but at the same time recognize that the strategies the person is using may not be helpful.

Joining Olivia's advanced DBT group is like signing on for inner space exploration. The first thing we do is an exercise called the Conference Table. We have to imagine a conference room with a long table and invite all the different parts of ourselves to sit at it. Olivia says a part can be as clear as a voice from the past reminding you to brush your teeth, or as nebulous as a rush of feelings that overtake you in the middle of the night for no apparent reason. Any of the different voices and perspectives that happen inside you can be parts. Olivia asks us to close our eyes, imagine the table, and invite all the parts to sit down.

So I do. And in no time people start appearing: Kiki, the Goth, the Hippie, the ManRay Chick, the Biker Babe, the Writer, the Freak, the Academic, the Mental Patient, the Supplicant, the Obsessive Organizer, the Failure. Olivia asks us to also invite our younger selves to the table, along with the internalized voices and perspectives of other people. The table grows increasingly crowded. My mother takes a place, and sitting on her shoulder is my grandmother. Sometimes they seem to blend together. My father is there, along with an anonymous man, a sort of "watcher." But where are my younger selves? Olivia tells us not to force it, that our parts come out when they feel safe, and some of them don't like to be exposed. But when I look under the table, I immediately find my six-year-old. She's hiding, half in play and half in fear. And then there's my twelve-year-old. She's not playing at all. She's formulating a way to escape.

I'm not the best visualizer. I tried to heal myself through creative visualization at one point during my hippie years, and I never got past the white light exercise. So it surprises me that all of these images have appeared so clearly—even details of the conference room, with wood panels covering the walls and a series of tall windows shedding faint light along one side of the table. I notice a small door at the back of the room. Of course there's a secret door. Assuredly it leads to a room where parts of myself are hidden. As we sit with our eyes closed, imagining all of these parts of ourselves, I don't go near that door.

I tell Ethan about all the parts in our next session. He's been receiving IFS training as well, so he can move through this journey with me, thank god. I want to know what's behind door number three, but he explains that there's a process to working with parts. You don't just pull them out of hiding or force them in any way. First you simply become aware of them. In time you come to understand exactly what their roles and needs are. You have to allow them to have a voice and speak for themselves.

The parts that are most inaccessible and fearful are known as exiles. These frozen and traumatized parts of ourselves hide and feel the need to be protected at all costs. And at least one of mine is behind that small door. Managers try to protect the exiles by managing emotions and developing survival strategies. When the exiles get loose and run through screaming and on fire with past pain, the firefighters emerge and attempt to douse the flames. Despite their good intentions, firefighters aren't helpful; they're the out-of-control behaviors that DBT helps us rein in. And like DBT, IFS understands that those behaviors may be self-destructive, but that they're also survival tactics for dealing with unacceptable pain. My addict part is a firefighter. My cutter part is a firefighter.

"What is my six-year-old?" I ask Ethan. "Is she the girl who was molested? And why is there a twelve-year-old seemingly connected to her?"

Oh my god is this complicated! Of course, I read the entire IFS book before my next group, and have even started making diagrams of all my parts. I'm ready to wow everyone with my in-depth knowledge, but there's no opportunity. The way the group is, each week just one person provides an example of a problem behavior, and for the next hour and a half we do a behavioral analysis, identifying the parts involved and the skills that could be used. There are currently five women in our group, and it's going to be more than month before it's my turn. So I take a backseat and let my perfect student part, who is always trying to manage information and people's perceptions of me, take a break.

A couple of months after I connect with the family organization, they ask me to be part of a discussion panel about living with BPD. Until now, I've told only the people closest to me about my BPD diagnosis. The idea of such public exposure scares me, and at the same time it seems the next logical step in my process. I don't want to spend my entire life hiding because of an unspeakable illness. I also don't want to be so vulnerable that I leave myself open to the judgment and hatred I've seen unleashed on people with the diagnosis. The dialectic of exposure and protection is surfacing again, both required when outing yourself. It takes trust to go forward, and in this case I decide to trust them. A roomful of parents and spouses who, thus far, have applauded my confessions of being fucked up can be extremely reinforcing—especially if you like applause.

So one spring evening I and two other people with BPD take turns addressing a hushed room packed with parents, spouses, clinicians, and even some fellow borderlines who lurk in the back rows. I explain that I've had the symptoms of BPD since I was quite young, and that only now am I getting the right treatment and learning how to live with it. I don't emphasize the gory details; it's the inner pain that I want people to understand—the hopelessness and shame of being who I've been and not having anyone who understands. I've grown up with an ethic, call it a part, that insists I hide my pain at all costs. As I talk, I feel this pain leaking out—not just the core symptom of BPD, but all the years of being blamed or ignored for my condition, and all the years I've blamed others for how I am. It's the pain of being told I was too needy even as I could never get the help I needed. When my eyes start to tear up, I see that the eyes of the crowd reflect mine. That's a mirror I've never looked into because I've been so isolated and ashamed. And in that moment an image comes to me: a million bodies, curled and sobbing in the corners of rooms, hiding under covers, dragging razors along their skin, raging, screaming, and unseen. How many of us are there?

It reminds me of the part in *The Wizard of Oz* when Dorothy stands trembling before the projection of the great wizard. She has traveled so far to petition this powerful figure for a way home, but when Toto pulls back the curtain, she discovers that he's only an old man with a microphone. All of the power and control she thought he had evaporates as she realizes that he's only human. I feel like Dorothy. I've pulled back the curtain to find all of these people, full of fear and not knowing what to do. I think of my mother, a frightened witness to her daughter's transformation from gregarious child into self-hating, angry, and unreachable stranger. I see a long line of doctors who kept giving me more pills because nothing seemed to work. And most of all, I see my own kind, the borderlines, each hiding alone in an echo chamber of judgment and helplessness.

A couple of months later, I'm invited to speak at another local conference, along with a group of parents with borderline children. The experience is the same—fear, release, connection. Afterward, we are surrounded by well-wishers. Parents tell me they now feel more hope for their child. Spouses say they never realized what their partners deal with. Some clinicians say they've never encountered a person with BPD who has come so far. It's tempting to interpret these responses as a sign that I'm special. Who knew borderlines could be so articulate and self-aware, so capable and reflective? But I have to wonder: Am I the exception to the rule? Or has the BPD diagnosis put a muzzle on an entire population, so that there's no yardstick for comparison?

"Your parents must be so proud of you!" a woman gushes, giving me a big hug.

"They are," I agree, cringing just a little. (They're especially proud that I'm not trying to move back home with them or asking for money.) Alas, people have started asking the obvious questions: They want to know how my parents have gotten through this with me. How have we kept our relationships intact? What kind of treatment and education have we gotten together? Have my parents gone through the Family Connections program started by the National Education Alliance for BPD? Have they come to hear me speak? I actually did ask my mother to come but she said she's too busy and that the whole thing makes her feel uncomfortable, anyway. I avoid the questions by pointing to

Allison and her daughter Caroline. Now standing shoulder to shoulder, the two lovely blond women have passed through the bowels of BPD hell together. The hospital put Allison and other parents together for multifamily groups, and as Caroline went through DBT, her mother went through a similar training focused on how to understand and communicate with her daughter through the lens of BPD and all of the difficulties it entails. Now they even give talks together, which impresses me and makes me jealous. Very jealous.

Periodically I approach my mother, my father, and even my mother's parents with pamphlets and the occasional article. Now I have updates on my evolving role as a BPD advocate. Their discomfort with mental illness is visceral. After I share "Family Guidelines," a pamphlet on BPD, with my grandparents, my mother calls me up to request that I never mention BPD again to them. She says it's too disturbing, too complicated, that they're old and don't need to be thinking about such things. So at family gatherings with my mother, I try to stick to the acceptable script. Indeed, I discover that the less I say, the happier everyone seems to be with me. I sometimes wonder if I wouldn't have been better off as a paraplegic or afflicted by some tragic form of cancer. The invisibility and periodicity of my disorder, along with how I often border on normalcy, allows them to evade my need for their understanding. And because our most enduring family heirloom is avoidance and denial of pain and suffering, I don't need much prompting to shut myself down in their presence. It's only with Ethan and Taylor that I cry about it.

At these times, Ethan asks, "Why do you need them to accept you?"

"Because they're my family, that's why! Isn't that what family is supposed to do?"

"But if they can't, why do you keep expecting them to?"

Ahh, the rigidity of expectations.

With my father, I'm more forgiving. Perhaps because of our common recovery from addiction, I have a taste of validation in that relationship. That troubled part of myself is also in him, and we've both had to admit and confront it. And it may be that because I've never found comfort and security with my father, I'm not so devastated by his lack of support as I am by that treatment from my mother and her parents.

As part of my new advocacy work, I begin to attend larger mental health conferences. The years 2003 and 2004 are a good vintage for

BPD research. Technologies such as functional magnetic resonance imaging are starting to show the biology that causes disturbances in emotional processing in people with BPD. Our experience with physical pain, with trust, with aggression, show up as colored patterns in the brain. Parents and doctors take the stage to discuss their knowledge and experiences. These conferences are yet another level of exposure. I have to visit the bathroom to cry when the mother of a sixteen-year-old says she's gotten her child an early diagnosis and that her daughter is now in a teenage DBT group. I'm like a spy in the house of psychiatry, and I feel hot shame and frustration at hearing doctors refer to me and my ilk as "them" and "they" and "those." Going to learn about yourself at these events is like overhearing a conversation not intended for your ears, yet every syllable has meaning for your life.

However, my talks at the local organization have opened the door to the conferences held by the National Education Alliance for BPD, and soon I am standing on a much larger stage proclaiming my illness—and then huddling in the bathroom afterward until the shaking stops. I try to treat it like AA: "Hi, my name is Kiera, and I have BPD." There is total attention in that room, and I want to be honest, but not too honest, because if I told everything—how I still fall apart regularly, how I freak out on Taylor, how I'm still working as a receptionist when everyone in my high school class has moved on to bigger things—the audience might wonder if I'm really all that much better. And I wonder the same thing. At this point, I feel like I have to sleep for a week after I give a talk, almost zombified from the intensity of just standing there, claiming the name, describing the pain. What will happen if I show anger? If I start to cry or get into a conflict with someone? Does that mean I'm a fraud or not truly better? The pressure to appear perfect, something that's caused me to experience so much neglect, creeps into even this work. I feel I can't be symptomatic or I'll be discrediting myself and burning all of these hard-won bridges that might eventually lead me to others who are on the same path.

So there it is: yet another layer of dualism, another dialectic. I *am* better, and yet I can become symptomatic again suddenly and drastically. One day a professor at a local college asks me to talk to his medical students about BPD, and because the hospital is on the other side of town, I have to take two buses to an unknown city campus. My talk goes flawlessly, but as soon as I leave I have an anxiety attack. I can't find the bus stop—can't even find my location on my map. I sit on a bench and sob, and I don't know what to do. I'm a total mess, when just half an hour ago I was bowing to their applause.

Ethan always wants to know what my goal is, and what the pros and cons of each action are. With this new advocacy role, the con is I get totally dysregulated. But on the other side of this brutal exposure, I experience a disarming sense of freedom. The thing that makes it so disarming is that by saying to others, "I educate people about BPD," I am no longer defining myself as the illness. At work, I've started to explain my mission without any apology, and when my colleagues ask, "What is BPD?" I'm able to tell them without appearing confessional or inappropriate. I'm still the "artist in residence" at work, but my role continues to shift toward "psychologist in residence." And not surprisingly, everyone has someone in his or her life who—officially or unofficially—struggles with a mental disorder, including BPD.

20

Control and Blame

I ask Taylor if he'd be embarrassed if I became the BPD poster child. He hugs me, smiles, and says, "I'd be proud of you." Raymond, Renee, Gail, and Richard all pitch in, from giving me unlimited access to the supply room and copy machine, to coordinating days off for my other "career," and even flying me to Florence, Italy, to attend a conference on personality disorders (thank you, Raymond!). Yet I'm not making progress with my family. Seeing other parents at the advocacy events has the same triggering effect that watching happy couples once did. My father is more approachable, even if he does translate everything in terms of addiction, but my mother still flinches at the idea of me talking publicly about anything personal. And while I can tell she's proud of me for making such progress, as soon as I share details she says, for the hundredth time, that she wishes I'd explore something other than my own problems—that I should get more outside myself. It seems that even my triumph over my illness needs to be swept under the rug.

I never planned to ambush her, but it was bound to happen. All my life I've been hearing that I need to get more outside myself and stop being so self-centered. I wish that just once she'd be capable of seeing things from inside my eyes rather than dictating what I should be doing. She calls on Christmas Eve just before I leave work and asks if I'll have dinner with her because her boyfriend changed plans and she doesn't want to be alone. I half dread seeing her, but the idea of her spending Christmas Eve alone is even less tolerable, so I cancel plans and meet her for Thai food. My plan is to stay at the restaurant only an hour, but as it turns out, I don't need to worry about time. A half hour into dinner, my mom is telling me to get out of the restaurant. "Just leave!"

she hisses, throwing down her silverware and burrowing her face into her hands. "Just leave, for God's sake!"

It happens so quickly. We meet and all is well until I realize the conversation between us is completely one-sided. It's only about her life. I start shutting down and thorns of resentment push at my skin. We both know there's really just one thing in my life to discuss: I'm trying to recover from BPD. Therapy, work, even Taylor—they're all avenues toward learning to get better. But she doesn't want to talk about that. I think, *screw that*. It's time for her to recognize what I'm dealing with.

So as soon as there's a break in the conversation, I tell her how much progress I'm making. She beams and nods. "It's so wonderful," she says. "I'm so proud of you!" And I know she is. Then I go on to say that one of the reasons I'm doing so well is because of how much I've learned about BPD and DBT, especially the part about Linehan's biosocial model and how BPD develops through a combination of biological vulnerabilities and an invalidating environment. When I explain what an "invalidating environment" is like, she stops chewing her spring roll.

If I weren't feeling so aggressive and put off by her constant deflection, I wouldn't have gone any further, but now I can't stop, even as I watch her face change from beaming to confused to upset. "I grew up in a very invalidating environment," I declare. "People didn't take my problems seriously. I was blamed for everything I did. When I got upset, no one taught me how to take care of myself. And you were gone half the time on your trips around the world, and when you were around, you were constantly preoccupied. Even with you there, you weren't there. I felt entirely alone."

One look at my mom's face tells me I've a crossed a line. So I backtrack. "I know you did the best you could. And I don't blame you. I really, really don't. But part of getting better involves acknowledging these things and learning how to not repeat them. There are DBT skills you could learn, and ways that we could deal with this together—not keep creating an invalidating environment."

My mother forces her face into the echo of a smile, a half-grimace that tries to mask rage. Through barred teeth she says, "You always blame me for everything." I deny this. I blame my father a lot too, only he wasn't around, so she's the one who actually raised me. "Why do you willfully keep bringing up the past in order to hurt me?!" she cries out.

Her barely contained rage glows around us, a fierce aura, but neither of us is backing down.

"I'm not going to pretend things didn't happen just because you don't like to remember." I counter. "And I'm not trying to hurt you. This is the same stuff your parents did to you: ignoring your feelings, not recognizing what you needed, invalidating you. You grew up never being taught how to be honest about what was going on inside you. You also had to pretend."

"So now you have blame them too? It this what therapy does— teaches you to blame and hurt others to make yourself feel better?"

"I don't see why we can't look at the facts without judging them. No one *ever* talked about what was really going on in our family. We were always hiding, or ignoring, or punishing when things came to the surface."

"That was years ago! If you can't let go of the past, then I don't think you're making all that much progress. And you can tell your therapist that." She's waving frantically at the waiter to give her the check, even though our dinner is only half eaten. "Just go..." she hisses, not looking at me any more, fumbling for her purse. "Just leave."

So I do.

My mother and I don't talk for six months. At first it seems like we both need some time, then it becomes one of those chosen avoidances that grows more difficult to repair with each passing day. She sends me a letter sometime around Easter—half plea, half demand that I let the past rest so we can continue to have a relationship. I tear up the letter. There have been a hundred times my mother has removed herself from my life, so now I have a switch inside me that flips on and off and blocks the thought of her without my even noticing. It's much the same with my father. So while I'm upset about this situation, it's not unfamiliar. Usually my mother is traveling in Asia or Europe, or subsumed under the seven-day work schedule of a teacher at a private school. This time, she's just in another town. But there's one big difference: This time, I'm in control of her absence.

There are many things I want to control; for example, Taylor's house—and the cat situation. He agreed to take Tanya's two cats— temporarily—when she moved, just until their shots and tests for overseas have cleared. Now there are four extremely hairy cats in his small house, and they are *everywhere*. Tanya's cats have some circus-freak gene compelling them to walk atop narrow doorway ledges, jump from appliances, and sail through the air like flying squirrels. Between those in the air and those underfoot, it's hard to avoid inhaling, stepping on, or being knocked over by something feline. And the house reeks. My immune system thinks it's being attacked by an alien horde, and I finally discover what the word "allergy" means—and why people on commercials look so miserable before they take antihistamines.

"It won't be forever," Taylor says. Maybe in six months or a year they'll be put in boxes and sent to Europe on a plane. Thankfully, summer is approaching and we can open the windows. Motorcycle riding season begins and we resume a familiar pattern: work, motorcycle riding, and cookouts with Taylor's best friends, Doug and Barbara. They stage rib-fests that involve three grills, forty pounds of meat, and eight hours of slow basting with pineapple juice. I'm gaining serious weight. I have been all along. Closing in on two years with Taylor, I've gained thirty pounds. I'm still not a size 18, like Tanya, but I soon could be. As far as I can tell, Taylor doesn't notice, and this is both good and bad. He doesn't give me compliments, which is upsetting as I obviously need constant flattery and reassurance, but on the flip side, he never seems to think I look bad, *ever*. He's always happy with me being me—whoever that is at the moment.

It's both alarming and a relief to love someone who has so little concern for appearances. I'm not sure how he got this way. His parents have made long, fruitful careers out of their sensitivity to space and form, color and shape. That he was spawned by an architect and an interior designer and yet doesn't have any concern about his own house's appearance, or his own appearance, doesn't make sense. We're both children of artists, but only one of us seems to care about visuals. I'm at the other extreme: fixated on space and image as though it has a texture that rubs against my nerves. If even one drawer in the bureau is out of place, I have to align it with the others. I can't stand the chaos of his house. It makes my insides feel mashed up, and since his house is the center of my world, I'm in constant conflict with it. Taylor and I embody so many polarities it's baffling: He's immune to his surroundings, and I'm incredibly sensitive to them. His nature is unchanging and steady; mine is mercurial. I love vegetables and he'd be content to rely on iceberg lettuce. The list seems endless.

Negotiating these differences exhausts me. There have always been conflicts between our lifestyles, but as time goes on, different life goals are also emerging; or, better put, I'm creating my own life despite how much I've been piggybacking on his, and it isn't clear how well my new life meshes with his. When we began dating, I was like a newborn. I needed constant support, advice, teaching, and direction. Now I'm starting to find my own way, and it turns out that it doesn't involve sitting at home playing board games with Taylor. I'm traveling to mental health conferences and giving talks. I'm starting to approach mindfulness practice more as a lifestyle than as an occasional technique. I'm considering becoming a vegetarian and going back to school to study psychology. If I had more experience with relationships, I'd say this might be the point when two people begin to drift apart. As I have never been with someone this long, I don't know the signs. Also, I'm still orbiting Taylor despite these new directions. He's not worried about me disappearing, but I'm worried, in that underground gurgling way that will eventually rise to the surface to surprise everyone—except me.

Meanwhile Ethan and I sit down every week and work with my parts. It's a parts party. The more there are, the more I seem to discover, but they can be roughly grouped, like the IFS model says, into the emotionally devastated and frozen exiles, the helpful but controlling and protective managers, and the frenzied, impulsive firefighters. As in the initial exercise with Olivia's group, I continue to home in on the six-year-old. This exile spends a lot of time feeling ashamed and needing to hide, yet her feelings and needs are incredibly powerful, because she craves love at all costs. She confuses sexuality with nurturance. She will fuck Taylor and at the same time recoil because he has become a substitute for a father. She doesn't experience any solid ground, and her language is still caught in other countries. Then there's the suicidal twelve-year-old, another exile, who changed her name to Kiki, drank from every bottle in the liquor cabinet, and felt like she mainlined God's love. But the deepest exile is the part I call "the little dark one." She's primal in her rage, her love, and her need. I can barely get her to raise her head from her knees. She's the one hiding in that small, secret room.

The managers are more accessible but very dictatorial, always making absolute declarations and demanding I do things a certain way. I lump them all into a part I call the manage-atrix. She's the mother of all management: She organizes, plans, controls, and criticizes every action. Her role, supposedly, is to protect me from anything bad, but as I grow more mindful of her, I see that she seems to rule by threats and judgments. I feel bludgeoned by the manage-atrix's unrelenting harshness, her rigidity and insistence that the smallest mistake will cause my entire life to cave in. My mother and grandmother are embedded in her like faces in a totem pole. And for all of the manage-atrix's yearning to keep me "perfect" and "presentable," she's the voice of self-hatred, inner shame, and invalidation. The manage-atrix can be the dominatrix, too, or the image of a vast audience watching me, whispering and judging. Yet this multifaceted thing within me is also the part that struggles to make sure I survive, even at the cost of my hating myself and others.

So, no more diary cards. I'm obviously becoming well versed in the DBT skills, but the most critical now are mindfulness and acceptance. This "parts work" requires a deeper attention to what happens within. Just as in stage one, I have to learn how to not react and not try to escape from what is. Thank god for Ethan and for Olivia's group. Because if anyone else heard me talking about the parts, they'd think I'd developed another disorder. When I arrive at therapy in a meltdown, Ethan has me sit quietly while he leads me through a meditation exercise, and then when I'm aware enough, we ask my inner world, "What's happening? Who is there?" And it's spooky—spooky!—because the parts respond. I begin to have conversations with them, but it takes a while to get to this point, because it turns out that I'm angry with a lot of my parts and attack whatever arises inside me. I'm mad at the exiles because they embody so much pain. Mad at the managers because they're always criticizing and shaming me. And mad at the firefighters, who think self-destruction is a way to stay safe.

21

Crossing the Mom Divide

Early that summer my mother's best friend, Sally, calls me. She says, "You're breaking your mother's heart," and begs me to call my mom. Sally is a seasoned guidance counselor and therefore well-meaning, but she's also hazy in her understanding of psychiatric disorders. "Sally says you can't possibly have BPD," my mother told me early on, as though her best friend's opinion was more weighty than any evidence I or a doctor could provide. I'm mistrustful of both of them. "Just call her," Sally begs. "Every time we talk, she cries about you."

There is only one way I'm going to reenter this mother-daughter gauntlet: We have to see a professional. So this is how, after twenty years of working on myself with therapists, I am finally joined by my mother. We will meet once a week with Janna, a couples counselor with a tasteful office in Cambridge. Janna has been my mother's therapist off and on for a few years, mainly in times of crisis. My mother uses therapy like an enema, whereas I use it like a feeding tube. I'm not sure where that puts us with Janna, but it's clear that we need her. We need someone who can dislodge us from the pain we cause each other.

Janna is my mother's age, wears big ethnic jewelry, and has a poker face similar to Ethan's when it comes to looking neutral. And she has a plan. My mother and I are to work on seeing each other's perspective, and to learn how to be together in a way that can accommodate both of our experiences (very dialectical...). We begin by describing, each in her own opinion, why we're in therapy now. And of course we have different reasons. My mother wants all the baggage dropped;

she wants to live in the present and doesn't want to focus on negative things like mental illness. She hopes I can learn to let go more and be less judgmental. In her mind, when that happens we can have a good relationship.

I listen with my heart pounding. *I'm* the one who's judgmental? "Mom, you're the one who told me I was always making myself look like a freak at school. You don't call that judgmental?" Oops... I'm already starting an argument.

My mother retorts, "You *did* make yourself look like a freak! Every day you'd come out of your room with some outlandish outfit, your eyebrows painted blue, wearing curtains, shaving your hair or dyeing it."

"I was expressing myself. It's called being creative."

"You were trying to get attention!"

Janna raises her hand and interrupts. She's going to need a foghorn before long. She suggests that we stick to stating our goals for therapy. I swallow hard and think about my first session with Ethan and our first goal: safety. That's pretty much what I want from my mother: to be able to be in her presence and feel accepted, not judged, not dictated to, not minimized, not shamed, and not treated like a burden and the cause of all her pain. I want to be able to be truthful about what I'm feeling. And I want her to understand that I have BPD and *learn how to help me with it.* How do I summarize that? "I want my mother to understand and accept who I am," I finally say. "All of me."

"I do accept you!" my mom interjects. "Have I *ever* told you to be a certain way? I've always said I just want you to be happy. Be anything you want!"

"Except a depressed, suicidal, drug-addicted mental patient. That's unacceptable to you."

"I don't think *any* parent wants that for their child."

"I'm not saying you should have wanted it. You just didn't want to recognize it or be around for that part."

"What was I supposed to do? Both you and your brother were completely out of control! I didn't ignore it. I found you therapists. I tried to get you help."

Janna is looking a bit flustered now. One of us should have warned her that we could go on like this indefinitely.

"Getting back to goals..." She pushes forward. "Can we agree that, as I suggested in the beginning, both of you try to find a way to communicate and understand each other that will honor each of your perspectives?"

Even as my mother and I nod hesitantly, I'm thinking, *But I'm the one who is right.*

Right about what? Are we trying to prove who's the bigger victim in our relationship? Who has been in more pain? Is that what this is about? We set another appointment and my mother and I leave the office. It's the first time we've been alone in many months. We stand awkwardly, watching the cars pass.

"So...," my mom says, "that was pretty hard, wasn't it?"

I nod, then burst into tears. I don't want to be in a fight with her. I wish to God I could let go of the past and not be so focused on this illness. "I want to work through this," I say as she hugs me.

"Me too." She starts crying. We are both such criers. Janna will have to keep the tissues, and her own sanity, in full supply.

My mom and I meet for therapy every Wednesday afternoon for the rest of the summer. Since Janna's office is down the street from a local meditation center, I linger around Central Square after therapy until I can go to the Center's evening meditation class and subject myself to forty-five minutes of torture. This place teaches a type of meditation called "Vipassana" or insight meditation. It's one of a number of meditation centers around Boston and Cambridge that I've been eyeballing ever since I left the DBT skills group, knowing that if I'm going to keep practicing mindfulness, the best bet is to find another community to do it in.

Linehan (1993a) makes a point of distinguishing meditation from mindfulness, but as you start to make mindfulness the foundation of your life, the idea of meditating becomes more compelling. As for the difference between the two, I think the answer depends on who you ask. Pure awareness, opening yourself to the present moment, nonjudgment, acceptance of what is—all are aspects of meditation practice as the instructors describe it. There doesn't seem to be much difference between that and the core mindfulness practice taught in the DBT skills group. On the other hand, this meditation involves a much more sustained effort: You sit for longer. You observe without describing. You get more leg cramps. I suspect the reason people meditate in groups is because it's hard to get up and turn on the TV with thirty people sitting around you.

The trick, the instructors say repeatedly, is to focus on your breath and watch the thoughts and feelings come and go; just observe and let them pass, just like in those DBT exercises—leaves floating down a stream, clouds passing through the sky. The breath is an added anchor, and a helpful one, because no matter what happens you can always go back to it. The instructors insist that eventually sitting meditation stops feeling like wrestling with porcupines. It is, indeed, intensely painful, even the posture. As I sit on a cushion, cross-legged and unmoving, all of the subtle aches and pains in my body flare under the magnifying glass of the stillness. So on those Wednesday evenings after the session with Janna and my mother, I sit in the meditation hall with thirty other silent people and watch as my mind revisits every word in the therapy conversation. I go into long, heated imaginary arguments in which Janna and my mother are submissively humbled by the force of my pain. All the while, I feel my lower back throbbing, my knees aching, and my neck muscles contracting.

Like a windup toy clattering in circles until it exhausts itself, the tension in my body and mind spins out in the space of doing nothing, and I have two choices: Jump up and leave the room, or stay seated and ride it out. On a cushion nearby, a large man snores. This I don't understand—how people can actually sleep in a sitting position. And there are so many of them! Here it's like adult nap time, only no one is allowed to lie down. If you open your eyes and look around, there's a sea of bobbling heads, people nodding off and then catching themselves before falling over. I'm waiting for the snoring man next to me to fall over into my lap, and that makes me even more tense.

If I'm lucky, I can pay attention to my breath for thirty seconds. It's another level of exposure, really. To be present to yourself at the most fundamental and basic level without running—and then staying there. Thirty seconds of pure awareness is a long time, especially after a lifetime of escaping yourself at all costs. When the meditation leader rings the bell after forty-five minutes, I raise my eyes and am amazed. It's just as they said in both DBT and IFS: If you pay attention and stay aware, things do change. It's subtle, to be sure. My body is still tight. Thoughts still streak past. Anxiety at being around so many people floats in my chest. And yet there is also looseness. Or call it slipperiness to the things that just an hour ago felt overwhelming. I can close my eyes and return to the image of Janna's office without the singe of anger. A freedom develops in this doing nothing.

Attachment to your version of reality is a terrible setup. It's this way for everyone, but especially for us borderlines, because we have such difficulty making room for the perspective of others. Extreme emotion automatically narrows attention. Cognitive filters, activated parts, core schemas, call them what you will—they make flexibility even more difficult. That's why DBT places so much emphasis on recognizing opposing truths and practicing skills like radical acceptance. You have to let go of absolutes and polarizations. No one ever shares your perspective entirely, even, or maybe especially, not your mother. For every incident I bring up from the past where I felt ignored or misunderstood, she comes back with a different version. I say she didn't take my problems seriously; she says she did, but she didn't know what to do. I say she treated my brother better than me; she says that my brother was more open to being loved. I say she always blamed me for being willful and difficult, as opposed to seeing me as mentally ill and desperate; she says that she couldn't see me as mentally ill and desperate because I was such a good artist, athlete, etc., etc. I say she ignored me in my times of deepest need; she says that those were times when she was compelled to take care of herself. Back and forth, back and forth. It's a tennis match and it's never love-love. But then again, it is. There's a bond between us that scares me with its intensity and polarity. I tell her that I never felt protected; she says that she didn't know the world could be so cruel.

As we go through our versions of reality, I try to concede to her point of view, but whenever I do it feels like I'm erased in the process. I know she was overworked and had a difficult time herself, yet I need her to know how I felt she failed me: how she always left me alone when I was in the most pain; how, when I came into her room hyperventilating because I thought I was dying, she treated it like a bad dream, saying, "Just go to bed and think good thoughts"; how she didn't say anything when my stepfather found me smoking pot and stabbed the joint out on my face; how she let me go from one hospital to another, one treatment to another, and never got involved; how, in her most trying moments, she declared I was ruining her life when I was just a kid and didn't have any control over the situation—or myself.

My mother listens and tries not to cry, but the tears gather and flood down her cheeks. I recount these neglects out of anger and hurt that until now I've never been able to express, and at the same time, I can feel her pain and helplessness. She says, "I did *everything* possible to take care of you and Ben. I raised you with love. I took that job at the school to give you a good future. I worked seven days a week so we could stop living on welfare. I sent you to summer camps and after-school programs. I threw birthday parties, went to your soccer games, bought you the clothes you wanted, and took you on trips. I have loved you in every way I could."

As I listen to her defense, I feel my heart breaking because there is nothing malicious; there is only her description of the pain and fear she felt as she watched me turn from an affectionate, happy child into someone who wore only black, hated herself, and was angry with the world. She says, "I watched you destroying your life and couldn't fix it. What else could I have done? Don't you understand that? You can't blame me for not doing the right things. No one helped *me*. I had to be the perfect teacher at a perfect school. I made all the money while your father didn't pay child support and your stepfather refused to work a full-time job. If you only knew how overwhelmed I was that whole time, how anxious and alone. I was hanging on by a thread myself!"

My mom and I are both crying, and Janna asks us to take some deep breaths.

"I just wanted a mother who would be there for me when I cried," I say, crying. "Why couldn't you have just been there for me? Why did I have be called 'bad' and 'rebellious' and 'attention seeking' and a 'burden'? Why couldn't you just understand that I was in unbearable pain?"

My mother shakes her head. "I knew you were in pain. That's what hurt the most. I couldn't sleep at night because both you and Ben and your lives were in my head. Everything went wrong and I didn't know how to fix it. Anything I said or did was because I felt so frustrated. I was just trying to cope…"

Janna leans in and asks my mother, "How *did* you cope when you experienced that kind of pain?"

My mother pauses and wipes her eyes. Tissues for all. "I suppose… I guess I just learned to live with it."

"But how *did* you live with it?" Janna presses.

"She left the country," I say. "Every vacation, every summer, anytime there was a break in the school schedule, she got on a plane and took off."

"It's an escape," my mother nods. "I admit to that. But it's kept me sane." She turns to me. "Kiera, you wouldn't even have had a mother if I hadn't learned how to take care of myself."

"What else did you do to take care of yourself?"

"I pretended," my mother says. Janna raises her eyebrows. "I mean, I just focused on other things, and that way I wouldn't get overwhelmed."

"They call that denial," I throw in.

"But you recognized that things were in trouble," Janna says.

"Of course I did! I just… I don't know… I knew I had to keep going on, so I'd turn the channel. Focus on positive things. I know that when you stew in problems, it only makes them worse, as does complaining."

I'm about to disagree, to say that it's only when you recognize and deal with problems that they get better, but Janna holds her hand up. "I'd like to suggest that you two have very different coping styles for getting through life. And that is why each of you feels like the other doesn't understand."

I think about that for a second. It is true. It's like we're from two different planets. She puts all of her pain into a box and walks away. And I'm like a pain magnet: Millions of metal filings—anger, hurt, fear, anxiety, hatred—fly at me from all sides and break through my skin, going straight into my bloodstream. The only solution I know is to erase myself in order to escape it. My mom's solution is erase the situation itself.

"Beth, you compartmentalize," Janna says. "It's a management technique. Everyone manages pain differently. You somehow learned that it was best to *not* talk about things, to shelve and maybe even forget them as a way to keep going on. If you were overwhelmed with Kiera's pain— with all of the troubles your children faced—then you had no choice but to do whatever you could to keep functioning. Unfortunately," Janna turns to me, "that wasn't what could help you, Kiera. Do you understand what I'm saying?"

I think I do. "That Mom's way of coping turned into a giant form of invalidation. She dealt with everything by ignoring it, because that's what worked for her."

"Exactly, but it didn't work for you." That's certainly true. I need people to understand and validate what I feel almost constantly, even when I'm in a good space.

"I never meant to ignore or dismiss you," my mom says. "I always focused on how strong and talented you were. Especially when you felt at your worst and didn't believe in yourself."

"But why can't you take my mental illnesses seriously? I feel like I've been set up, over and over. Like I'm a cripple without a wheelchair, and everyone keeps signing me up for marathons, then shaming me for not winning the race."

"I just can't see you as mentally ill."

I feel the rage returning. We're back at the beginning. "How can you say that after all I've been through?"

Janna turns to my mother. "This is a very serious issue. And I don't think it's in anyone's interest to disregard it."

"But you're doing so much better," my mother says to me. "How can you still say you're ill?"

I look at Janna pleadingly. I'd called her earlier, to see how capable she was of helping my mom understand BPD. She assured me she'd do her best. Now the moment has arrived. I wait.

"Beth," Janna says, "I'm not sure how much you know about borderline…"

"I read that book Kiera gave me!" she interjects. (Ah yes, *I Hate You, Don't Leave Me*. She also never mentioned it again.)

"Do you understand that, given Kiera's numerous diagnoses combined with BPD, she's very lucky to be alive?" My mom shakes her head. "One in ten people with BPD die by suicide. Factor a drug addiction into the equation and it's higher. Add depression and all the other issues, and the chances of survival are even less."

"Kiera is definitely a survivor," my mom declares.

"True. But you need to see how much she struggles—every day, sometimes every minute—and often with things that wouldn't affect you. Those of us without the disorder generally don't understand, but it's critical, I could say even lifesaving, that you recognize her different reality—her sensitivities and the kind of pain she has."

There's a long pause as my mom takes this in.

She nods hesitantly. "I just can't reconcile...how amazing Kiera is—the abilities she has—and this other thing. I don't see how she can be both."

"Think of it as being on the borderline," I quip.

"She's fragile in ways you might not be," Janna says, then turns to me. "But Kiera, your expectation that your mom be like you is also counterproductive. If you impose your own coping skills on her and don't recognize that she needs to escape or compartmentalize or do whatever she needs to do to take care of herself, then you're doing exactly what you accuse your mother of."

"Then it's like a mutual invalidation fest..."

"Fodder for another session." Janna smiles. I look at my mom. She's completely wiped out. Charged therapy sessions are hardly new to me, but I can already understand, based on this idea of different coping strategies, that sitting down and being this intensely vulnerable has drained the life out of her.

Out on the sidewalk, the shifting leaves dapple light over our faces. "This is so fucking heavy," I say. We take each other's hands. "Can we use your coping style now, Mom?"

"What would that be?" she asks.

"Let's go for some Thai food, see a movie, and not mention anything about our relationship for the rest of the night."

"Deal," she grins.

22

The Tipping Point

These days I always come back to the DBT stages and goals. They continue to be the closest thing to a road map I have for understanding what I'm going through and where I am. Ethan tells me that the road to recovery is always under construction, and it's obvious the stages generally don't occur in a neat, linear fashion. Sometimes several stages are occurring simultaneously, or you might skip over one for a while. It's not like a train that delivers you at a destination, though admittedly you do have to get on somewhere, and in that sense stage one is crucial, because it involves keeping yourself alive. Dr. Linehan says that establishing behavioral control and learning the DBT skills can take a year or more, and in general should be done prior to the stage two work of processing trauma and experiencing emotions (1993a). She also mentions that sometimes it's necessary to enter a different type of therapy at stage two, and she doesn't see a problem with that.

The recovery process itself is ever-changing and dialectical, bringing together opposing experiences and catalyzing new levels of growth even as it sometimes throws you back on your ass. I think I'm firmly in stage three now: I'm identifying and working on life goals, developing an enduring and loving relationship, creating meaningful work, and establishing a home that's not just an expensive suitcase (pending Taylor's help). And I'm also starting to feel the pull of stage four in terms of wanting more than just a life. I want an amazing life that isn't constantly tied to fear and need. I want to be free of the cognitive filters that insist the world is hostile and I am unlovable and alone.

I've come far enough to understand that my reality is deeply affected by these inner states, and I'm doing a much better job of managing how

I respond to and make sense of my experience. So in some sense, I've crossed the borderline. Isn't this what people want? To be loved, to have a secure and supportive job, to feel like you belong somewhere? I suspect that, at this point, some people with BPD decide that therapy is over. Their goals have been met, and a semblance of normalcy and stability have been achieved. But I'm not in that camp. Inside me, the parts pull me in numerous directions. I still don't know who I am, really, or where I belong without reference to Taylor. My six-year-old still can't climb out of the adult's bed. And I crave something, but what? Maybe it's the transcendence suggested by the fourth stage, or a sense of wholeness. Whatever it is, Ethan is the person who travels with me in the journey, and I'm not going to give him up just because I'm in better shape. In the three years we've been together, our sessions have decreased to once a week, but those fifty minutes are a precious respite where I'm able to breathe deeply and readjust my focus. More than anyone else, he has witnessed and is able to hold all of the pieces of me with an unconditional regard I only wish I could bottle and swig from all day long.

Recently Ethan has been teaching me the art of irreverence. I continue to get intensely caught up in perceived slights and annoyances, especially when I'm trying to do good things for people. Ethan suggests that when I get too embroiled in other people's behaviors, I just take a deep breath and say, "What the fuck."

"What the fuck": It works like magic for me. I've always found it so hard to let go in the face of perceived opposition. Now that I'm beginning to make forays into the "consumer" community of mental health, where other people with psychiatric disorders are beginning to create programs based on the concept of peer support, I need these kinds of tricks to help me stay balanced. It seems like every time I go to a meeting, I encounter someone who has been hospitalized for years on end or who is completely discombobulated from electroconvulsive therapy, who lectures me on the ways BPD is a tool of oppression. I'm full of arguments and vitriol in these encounters. You'd think that if any community would be a little helpful with the diagnosis, it would be other mental patients, but no. Or at least it feels that way. I end up exhausting myself trying to legitimize my diagnosis amidst psychiatric freedom fighters, and then I crawl back to Ethan, angry and demoralized. Of course, Ethan first wants to know why I have to join that community. My reply remains the same: I want to feel like I belong somewhere.

"But if the cost is too much, what can you do?"

I don't know. It's never clear to me when it's time to pull back and change direction. Linehan mentions that the borderline mind cannot easily let go of preconceptions (Linehan 1993a). Everyone wants life to be a certain way, but in our case, the emotional amplification can make the facts irrelevant, like a child screaming for a toy that no longer exists, unable to recognize that some desires are destined to remain unfulfilled. Ethan and I go over the fact that other people have their own limitations, and we examine how this conflicts with my attachment to what "should be." When I'm not in emotion mind, I can often see things from other perspectives. But even then, if I can't understand others' motivations, I'm incited. Why, for example, do people who are walking down the middle of a crowded sidewalk decide to suddenly stop? It's not like they don't know there are a hundred people behind them. So do they not care? If I kicked them or pushed them out of the way, not entirely gently, as I passed by, would it help?

"The truth is, you'll never know all the reasons people do the things they do," Ethan tells me. "That's when you can say to yourself, 'What the fuck.' At a certain point, you just have to walk away and let other people have their perspectives, their way of dealing. You can try radical acceptance, obviously. But sometimes it's just easier to throw up your hands and turn away. Let yourself be baffled and stop trying to make things work."

"What the fuck," I repeat. It's got a good cadence.

"That's the fourth state of mind in DBT," Ethan says. "It's called 'wiseass mind.'"

The desire for belonging and purpose continues to be a huge theme in my life, and the advocacy work is my main outlet for this, despite how exhausting it is and how often it triggers me. Ethan occasionally goes out on a limb and asks if advocacy is an effective way of satisfying this need to belong. As always, the answer is dialectical. I know that by publicly declaring that I have BPD, I automatically jeopardize my relationship with most people because of the stigma and the belief that it's dangerous to be in a relationship with a borderline. On the other hand, I'm still empowered by these efforts; in fact, advocacy is the only activity that brings me into contact with people who really understand

and validate me as a person with BPD. And while presenting at conferences, I've been meeting BPD clinicians and researchers, and many of them treat me as a colleague.

And these connections bring even more opportunities. The Borderline Personality Disorder Resource Center hires Bill Lichtenstein, a documentary producer, to create an educational film about BPD called *Back from the Edge*, and I'm one of the people featured in it. A residential treatment community in Pennsylvania called Project Transition invites me to collaborate with one of their medical directors, Loren Crabtree, on presentations about BPD. In half a year's time, I'm flying down to Philadelphia regularly to provide consultation services and train their staff, even their bus drivers, on BPD. Dr. Crabtree introduces me to every doctor and clinician as "Kiera, a consummate educator." Here my position as a person with the disorder is considered precious, a resource to be cultivated and nurtured. And when I'm just about ready to throw in the towel with the consumer community, Moe Armstrong, one of the leading advocates in mental health and the grandfather of psychiatric peer support, invites me to the table and champions the value of my contribution.

So yes, in many senses it feels worthwhile, but the balance is tipping too heavily in the direction of exhaustion, and I'm also starting to feel trapped. I don't want to be the borderline poster child forever. I hear my mother saying, again, "You need to get more outside yourself. Focus on something other than your problems!" It's not bad advice, even if she did always say it when I most needed validation. I've begun making life maps in my journal, diagramming all of the people, places, and activities that I have relationships with. I draw little houses, motorcycles, and stick figures and draw connections to show the networks that are evolving. Work leads to Raymond and Renee. Taylor leads to his friends, his family, and the motorcycle community. BPD leads to Listservs, consumer communities, and advocacy organizations. And I'm trying to expand outward even more. Taylor's mother belongs to an artist collective, and I venture there for weekly workshops until I feel too overwhelmed by the personalities and my own frustration with the creative process. My internal managers are so insistent on perfection that at the end of a session I destroy a clay sculpture I've spent two hours shaping. I try to make my own friends rather than relying on Taylor's circle. I'm getting to know a woman in my advanced DBT group, but friendships aren't allowed in our program, so it feels like we're having an affair, and this is exacerbated by my growing sense of possessiveness about her. Just as with Taylor, as soon as I feel like she's ignoring me, I get so angry that I want to destroy the relationship.

Somewhere in this period, I begin to understand that my progress and stability aren't just because of my management of my BPD symptoms. It's as much due to the environment, again confirming Linehan's idea that the disorder is created, and can be dismantled, in the context of relationships (1993a). Seemingly mundane aspects of life that so many people take for granted—having a job, a relationship, a place to live—are as critical to my recovery as learning the skills and being in treatment. They form a structure that keeps me from falling backward.

One of the most powerful experiences I have in understanding BPD recovery comes during my participation in a film project. Dr. Crabtree invites me to Project Transition, and the two of us join three borderline women who are in the residential program. As a group, we discuss the recovery process and where each of us stands. One woman is newly diagnosed and just entering the DBT program. She struggles with her behavior and pain constantly, a phase that Dr. Crabtree and I dub "surviving the dysregulation zone." The second woman has been in the Project Transition program for almost a year. She's in stages two and three, which Dr. Crabtree calls the place of emergence. She's starting to think about dating, going back to school, and getting her own apartment, and she struggles to enter each challenge without falling entirely back into stage one.

I can identify with all of the women, but I relate to the third most deeply. She's getting ready to leave the program after a couple of years of treatment, and, like me, she's on the cusp between stages three and four. We're both struggling to figure out how to cross that chasm from symptoms into normalcy, from patient to person. Both of us are reestablishing connections to the world and finding our place in it after decades of alienation, displacement, helplessness, and failure. At this point, our fragility isn't as obvious, but it's still there—and it's scary because there's an expectation that we're cured or at least over the hump. It's understandable. We all want to believe that BPD can be reversed. No one in recovery wants to think of this struggle as a lifetime condition, nor do our friends, our loved ones, or any of the people who believe in us. But what if it is? What if we will always be challenged and need a wide array of resources and support to keep our symptoms in check? Does that mean we're screwed?

As we discuss the future, it's clear to all of us that, whether you call it being in recovery, recovered, or in remission, with BPD the process isn't like mending a broken ankle. At every stage there's still more hard work to do, and we still need help. I recount how just dating Taylor triggered me so much that I thought I wasn't going to make it. And even now, when outwardly I seem so together, I still feel lost. I'm still living out of suitcases while staying at Taylor's, and I'm still terrible at handling stress. And when I'm triggered, I can go back to hating myself and seeing the world as hostile in an instant.

"Each new challenge," Dr. Crabtree comments, "brings with it another destabilization and potential loss. And so as you get 'better,' there's an ongoing need for more support, not less." We all nod at this. It's so very true. Success and progress would seem to be a good thing, but they can rip the ground away. This takes many forms: being discharged from a program; losing the empathy of others because they now believe we should be over it; and even—or maybe especially— invalidating and berating ourselves because we insist that we should be cured. If this last stage is real, with its promise of connection and mastery and all of the benefits of getting better, we need to have a different perspective on the process itself.

We decide that the last stage is about integration and examine how bridges and pathways might be created to get to this new place. At Project Transition, they consider clients to be lifelong members—not to stigmatize them as eternal mental health patients, but to acknowledge them as part of an enduring community that will always have a place for them. They can return to Project Transition whenever they need to, without shame. This creates a more porous interface between treatment and life, and this recognition—that integration can take years for some of us—allows us to inch backward and forward during these stages, or to slam into walls, and have a safety net either way.

If ever I doubted the benefits of getting a group of borderlines together, I am now a believer. At the end of the two days spent talking and filming at Project Transition, I go back to my life map to look for where I can keep creating pathways and communities to help my process of integration. More than ever, I'm realizing it takes a village to help a borderline. Treatment can give us the tools, and for those lucky enough to be at a program like Project Transition, professionals will be there to help with integration. Ultimately, however, we have to make this happen for ourselves.

But how? From the first session with Ethan, I've explained that I feel I don't belong anywhere. It's one of my deepest and most enduring feelings. That's why the 12-step community was so positive for me for a long time, and why being a Deadhead or a goth, or even just somebody's girlfriend, seems like a solution. Belonging is a primal need. But with BPD, it goes beyond this. To drink from the source of someone else's presence, no matter how sour it may eventually taste, creates a temporary sense of self. And in truth, I worry that I may be doing this even in my role as an advocate. I still don't understand or have much connection with myself beyond the roles and goals I set for myself.

Each week I go back to Ethan half triumphant and half exhausted from the latest conference, meeting, workshop, or training. I'm getting certified in anything related to peer support and have joined every organization I could contact. It's like a drug or sex binge. I come off of every run more depleted, even though my intention is to create more connection, to belong more deeply.

Ethan keeps asking, "Is this what you want?" We look at the pros and cons of my choices, weighing what I give out and what I receive. Which of my internal parts are involved? And how much of this effort is really connecting me to a supportive and nurturing community? No matter what the benefits, it's clear that the emotional reserve I've been building up these past few years is dwindling, and it takes longer and longer for me to recuperate from the conferences and presentations. I'm taking more days off from work simply to sleep. And despite my arsenal of skills, I'm becoming more reactive. I snap at a conference organizer. I accuse other consumer advocates of turning against me when they're trying to be supportive. My friend in the advanced DBT group finds a boyfriend, and it's so intolerable that I blow up in group and can't go back.

I'm devastated and ashamed. And depending on the moment, I'll go from thinking this woman is the biggest bitch in the world to thinking I'm entirely broken when it comes to making a single friend. Taylor tries to convince me it's not a big deal, I can make other friends, but this obviously doesn't console me. I'm not as upset about quitting the advanced DBT group, as my work with Ethan is now the meat and potatoes of my IFS therapy. Still, he suggests that I look for a different type of group therapy, but that isn't what I want. I need something else—something more than skills, therapy, or advocacy—but I don't know what. Even the mindfulness work is failing me. It's like food without taste; I get the nourishment, but something essential is lacking—something inside me, and in my connection to the world.

PART 5

Transformation
of Suffering

23

Taking Refuge

It's early fall, and I'm back haunting the third floor of the Harvard Coop, but this time not to hide in the bathroom or sift through the psychology section. I'm focusing in on Eastern religions, specifically Buddhism, because even though I don't think of myself as a Buddhist, more and more of my search for connection outside of the advocacy community is leading in that direction. The books I read, the places I go to practice mindfulness, everything points in the same direction: Buddhism.

And I'm confused. After all of my work to learn about BPD and DBT, now I'm a beginner again. The leap from dialectical behavior therapy to Buddhism wouldn't seem that far. After all, Dr. Linehan created a significant portion of the therapy out of her experience as a Zen Buddhist. Not only are some of the practices similar to those in Buddhism, many of the same principles underlie both: dialectics, interdependence, constant change, impermanence, understanding the nature of cause and effect. Yet it's still hard to understand exactly what Buddhism is. For a long time, I thought that if you sat and meditated and believed all is one, you pretty much qualified as a Buddhist—and I wasn't sure how much sense that made when I realized that was exactly what I used to do when tripping on acid. But now I find that equating DBT's mindfulness and acceptance practices with the core of Buddhism isn't accurate. It's just too broad. For example, yoga emphasizes awareness of the body and mind, as well as acceptance and nonjudgment, and the Christian and Jewish religions have traditions of contemplative practices and compassionate witnessing. So I must dig deeper. As with my exploration of BPD, DBT, and IFS, the route to change means diving into new information and culling out what's valuable and what makes sense for me.

The term "Buddhism" is incredibly broad, and it's easy to get lost in the many shapes it has taken. Since originating in India over two thousand five hundred years ago, it has spread into dozens of countries and most continents, and its practices and concepts have been molded by each culture it encounters. While this is part of what's so appealing about Buddhism, it's also frustrating. As a starting point, you really need to understand the original story of the man known as the Buddha and his life. In short, he was an Indian prince who was so deeply impacted by the pain he saw in the world that he resolved to find a way to be free of it. Abandoning his position and all material possessions, he studied with the great spiritual masters of his time but found that their path of asceticism and physical self-denial was as counterproductive as the opulent and indulgent life he'd left behind. So he sat down and meditated, determined to reach enlightenment or die. In the many days that followed, his meditation opened him to a level of wisdom that allowed him to clearly see the causes of suffering and how to be free of them.

In that moment, he became known as the Buddha, or "Awakened One." So the Buddha isn't a god or a divine being; it's simply a title given to one man, Siddhartha Gautama, who figured out how to liberate himself from all of the cognitive distortions and overwhelming negative emotions and behaviors that keep everyone trapped in pain and confusion. *Everyone*, not just people with psychiatric disorders. In this moment of profound insight, he'd gained "enlightenment," a word that, like "Buddhism," has many different connotations, but in essence means "awakened." But awakened to what? Some traditions would say this is an awakening to the true state of being. Others define it as liberation from all attachments. I discover that the qualities of an awakened person include omniscience, selflessness, and pure altruism—indeed, the perfect embodiment of compassion and wisdom.

I remember that when I entered DBT, the first worksheet Molly gave me described the goal of DBT skills training as reducing pain and misery by learning how to change emotions, behaviors, and thinking patterns. In the process, you develop the ability to create a life worth living. Back then that goal seemed impossible, but here I am. I *have* learned to reduce my pain and misery. I still suffer, but in many ways my suffering is similar to that of everyone else. Now I discover a new goal, if I want to take it on: To be a Buddhist is to aspire to freedom from suffering—not just for yourself, but for all creatures. The pathway to this worthwhile but seemingly impossible goal is simply to practice diligently until it happens.

And just as in DBT, the techniques for doing this involve working with your emotions, thoughts, and behaviors, but in this case for the purpose of eliminating misery altogether. The benefits are extended beyond yourself to all creatures great and small. I have to wonder if the decision to embark on this path is even a decision at all. Logically that kind of achievement seems absolutely impossible. And while I am doing much better, I still want to punch Taylor or burst into tears whenever he says something "wrong." I see that I care about people, but only to the extent that they satisfy me. Even in my advocacy efforts, I'm hooked on the effects I have on others, and when I encounter resistance, I don't feel empathy. I want vindication, and I want to be right.

When the Buddha taught, he cautioned his students to never take his word on faith, but to experience everything directly. Yet it appears equally important to have a guide and a community in this practice. Buddhism and DBT are similar in that both require a lot of support. In DBT you need a therapist, the skills, and a skills group, and the therapists themselves are part of a larger team in which they consult one another for guidance. In Buddhism you need a teacher, the teachings, and a community of other Buddhists, and, as in DBT, the teacher should be part of a community in the form of a direct lineage or tradition, informed by the guidance and wisdom of other teachers. The Buddhist term for this triad of support and guidance is the Three Jewels. The first jewel is the Buddha (and by extension, your teacher), who embodies perfect wisdom and provides an example of what can be accomplished. The second jewel is the *Dharma*—Buddha's teachings and the rich tradition of teachings that have sprung from them. The third jewel is *Sangha*, the community of practitioners and those who are actively following this path. Unlike DBT, you don't have to put yourself on a waiting list for a special program. It's up to you to find your path, and it's up to you to become enlightened.

I find that I want to take refuge in these three jewels, but I don't know how to access them. Yes, there are a zillion books, and in the Boston area alone, a dozen Buddhist communities. Some are pure transplants from other countries: Japanese Zen Buddhism, Chinese Mahayana Buddhism, Thai Theravada Buddhism, Tibetan Vajrayana Buddhism, and Vietnamese Buddhism. Then there are the Americanized offshoots that form another subset of communities and practices. However, all of the traditions have a common focus on the elimination of suffering. This goal is captured in the Four Noble Truths, which were the Buddha's first teachings after he achieved enlightenment: The first is that suffering is pervasive; the second is that there are causes for this suffering; the third is that this suffering can be stopped; and the fourth is that there is a true path to accomplish this. The details on how this is accomplished depend on which tradition you follow. For now I take the intellectual buffet approach. I read books by an American Buddhist nun in the Tibetan Vajrayana tradition, Pema Chödrön, who writes disarmingly about the need to open yourself to the pain inside you. I dip into D. T. Suzuki, the Zen Buddhist who insists that the less you think, the more you will know. I also digest a lot of Thich Nhat Hahn, the Vietnamese monk whose main practice is mindfulness applied to everyday living. (Dr. Linehan is a big fan of him.)

Meanwhile, in therapy I focus on more practical issues, like how to get Taylor to move the cats' litter box out of the kitchen, which drives me apeshit. There is no negotiation on this issue, it seems. Taylor insists it stays where it is. In response, a firefighter who occasionally comes out in the form of obsessive-compulsive behavior resorts to rearranging all of Taylor's kitchen cabinets, leaving him stunned and disoriented for weeks, unable to remember where to put the dishes.

I'm not doing well with the clash in our living styles—or the divergence in our directions. Taylor is still happy to stay at home, watch TV, tinker with motorcycles, and go out to play board games with his friends. I, on the other hand, am still deeply involved in my "Save the Borderlines" campaign, and between my growing passion for Buddhism, my job, and the constant advocacy work, Taylor and I tend to see each other only on the couch for our favorite TV shows and in bed. One thing hasn't changed: The bed remains the locus of many of my troubled and conflicting parts. I still don't open up to Taylor about difficult sex because, as always, I'm afraid of what will happen. I'm not faking orgasms—at least not yet. But the focus is always on his pleasure. And while that could be called a Buddhist practice of generosity, it really isn't productive. My understanding is that self-denial isn't the goal; self-liberation, and liberating others, is the aim. I have a growing sense that the way I'm handling this is trapping both of us in a cage I can't find the key for, in much the same way as his house traps us in a pile of chaos that he cannot clear out to make room for me, despite his best efforts.

They say that when the student is ready, the teacher will appear. In my case, it happens in late autumn, just after my mother and I have finished therapy and are on fairly good terms. One Friday afternoon on my way to Starbucks, I pass a flyer taped to the lamppost outside my office building. It has a picture of an Asian man in red robes sitting peacefully and staring at the camera in a way that makes me stop walking and stare back. His eyes have that Mona Lisa effect, as though he's looking at you from every angle. The flyer is for a weekend meditation retreat with a visiting Tibetan Buddhist teacher at a local divinity school, just two blocks from my work. I've passed by countless flyers like this: women in turbans who will teach you to reach bliss through breathing, men in robes who will teach you how to bring your mind and body into perfect alignment. I've always ignored them, but for some reason this one hooks me. As soon as I get back to the office, I sign up. Then after work I go to a Tibetan arts store and buy a fancy meditation cushion—sort of the equivalent of getting a new pair of shoes for a party.

The next morning I arrive at the divinity school and enter a hall that's been transformed into a Buddhist shrine, with an altar and an abundance of flowers, and a brocaded throne at the far end of the room. Large, colorful paintings of Buddhas hang on the walls. We stand next to our cushions and wait for the teacher, whose name is Shyalpa Rinpoche. (Rinpoche is an honorific term bestowed on teachers in Tibetan Buddhism; it literally means "precious one.") When he enters, he kneels and prostrates himself three times before the picture of the Buddhas on the shrine, then we do the same. As soon as Shyalpa Rinpoche sits down, I notice a change in the room. A charged intensity and something I can only describe as spiritual pheromones exude from him. He looks around the room, but not in a typical way. His gaze seems to be communicating with everyone. It's so subtle—the slightest nod to one person, a blink to another—yet when he sees me, I feel that he truly sees me. My heart pounds. My little "savior" antenna is buzzing. Maybe this is my teacher? Have I found one of the three jewels?

I've never been to a Tibetan Buddhist teaching before. This one begins with prayers to the lineage: Shyalpa Rinpoche's teachers and the tradition they've passed down. This is followed by short talks interspersed with sitting meditation practice. As always, I cringe at the idea of meditation. Then Rinpoche says that in any meditation practice, the most important thing is to have the right view, and that without this view, there is no meditation. This confuses me, because in practices like Zen meditation, the approach is to not hold on to anything—to have no view, and no ideas. And in vipassana, or insight meditation, the main form I've practiced, the key is to simply sit and return to the breath again and again: sit, sit, sit; breathe, breathe, breathe.

As though he's reading my mind, Rinpoche says, "Cows sit in a field and breathe all day. Does that make them Buddhists?"

Some people in the audience look at each other knowingly. Others, me included, look completely baffled. "So what is this view?" Rinpoche asks, then pauses and takes a delicate sip of water from an ornate mug at his side. "Impermanence. The view is understanding that everything that is born dies. Everything that arises dissolves. Nothing is exempt from this. Everything that is conditional is exhausted, from a leaf to a person to a universe." He stops speaking and lets this sink in. "This is not a Buddhist belief," he finally says. "We don't need to have faith in it. This fact of impermanence is self-evident. And when you know how impermanent life is, you will understand its preciousness: how at any moment, it can disappear; your own life can disappear. Each breath, if you think about it, may be your last. How can you guarantee you'll inhale again? Someday you won't. But all of us take that next inhale for granted. If you watch the breath, you see that it, too, is always coming and going. You can't hold on to it. Just try!" Everyone in the room waits for him to continue, but he's serious. "Try holding your breath." We look at each other, take deep breaths, and hold them. I last maybe a minute.

"We live in the illusion that things are permanent—that this body will always be here, this chair, this wife, this dog, this breath. Are they?" I shake my head along with the others, even as I know that deep down, I still believe in permanence. I'm feeling a bit like I did in CBT group when I discovered that so many of my thoughts were distorted and that I had core beliefs that colored everything I saw and felt. Here is yet another distortion, and this one is fundamental to the way we live. Wouldn't we be constant basket cases if we felt like anything—everything—could disappear at any moment?

A light goes on in my head. It occurs to me that while this is a condition that every human being lives with and finds difficult to accept, the borderline brain is even more at odds with this basic reality. With BPD, we are always suffering because of impermanence. Our grasping is intense and rigid, our attachments unyielding. Impermanence is our nightmare, even as it's the essence of life. No wonder Marsha Linehan emphasizes the principles of accepting reality (1993b). If reality is always changing, then we must not cling to it.

Now Rinpoche says, "There is nothing to grasp onto because things are always coming and going. If you understand this, you will eventually be able to also recognize the source of things and won't be caught up in the coming and going. You will ask yourself, 'Who or what is grasping? And where do all of these things arise from and dissolve into?'" He arranges his robes and takes another sip of water. The hall is silent. He smiles and the room brightens. He instructs us to mediate on impermanence.

We sit for half an hour, and for the first time ever in my meditation practice, I feel relaxed because by simply sitting and watching myself, I experience the impermanence inside me. It's not just about leaves floating down a stream and trying to accept the thoughts and feelings they represent. Until now, I've only understood awareness and mindfulness as self-help techniques for trying to feel better. Now it occurs to me that these practices open the door to a different way of viewing reality—a more accurate and sane way. The oddest thing is that this isn't some brilliant new idea. Everyone hears things like "Change is the only constant" and "This too shall pass." In her books on DBT, Dr. Linehan explains that continuous change is one of the basic principles of dialectics (1993a, 1993b). I've understood this on some level all along, but there's a difference between understanding and realization. I think I've just had a realization.

I sign up to talk with Rinpoche after lunch. When the time comes, I'm taken to a small back room decorated with more brocades and flowers. I introduce myself and he beams at me. It's like I'm a birthday present, but what's inside is a bundle of neuroses and struggles. I wonder if my need for a savior is about to play out again. With his shaved head and red robes, he looks like the monk he is. Even so, and especially because he's barely older than me, I find myself intensely attracted to him. He asks how I am. I know we're pressed for time, so I don't give a lot of backstory; I simply list the many psychiatric illnesses I've dealt with and the therapies I've tried and then explain that I now find myself drawn to Buddhism. I also say that even though I'm a lot better than I ever have been, I still struggle a lot.

Rinpoche nods. "We say that the Buddha is like a doctor, and the Dharma is the medicine. The people of the Sangha are like nurses, there to help you whenever you need it."

"But what is my sickness?"

"You are like everybody else. You suffer from afflictive emotions—from anger, desire, and ignorance. You believe in permanence when there is none; grasp at a solid self although there isn't one. You have yet to understand the infallibility of karma. But most of all, you do not recognize your true nature, the innate intelligence within: Buddha-nature."

"You mean that at the core of us, everyone is good?"

"Don't think in terms of good and bad," Rinpoche instructs. "What you are is primordially pure—absolute perfection. It's your innate nature. Buddha-nature does not come and go. It's like the sky, always there: an awareness and clarity that can be temporarily covered by clouds but is ever present. It's like the sun, never failing to shine. Do you understand that?"

"I do… But I don't believe it really, or feel it."

"Of course not," he smiles. "It must be discovered. It's like you're living in poverty, in a shack on a dirt mound, but under that dirt is the most precious diamond. A wish-fulfilling gem. You need to find it. It must be seized."

A gem that must be seized? I'm all about that—just give me an instruction manual for seizing!

"Right now," Rinpoche concludes, "you have the right motivation but need proper guidance. It's like you've been holding a very hot cup of tea and burning your fingers. Buddhist practice will give you a handle. Eventually you'll know exactly what is needed, at every moment, because you will have the clarity of your innate intelligence. Your compassion, too, can be infinite, because it won't be conditional. You will have true freedom."

"What is the practice?"

"If you are serious," Rinpoche says, "you should take refuge." I nod and my eyes start to brim with tears. It's just like the books on Buddhism described: the teacher, the teaching, the community—the three jewels.

The rest of the day passes in a haze of delight and confusion. I keep wanting to drag my cushion up to Rinpoche's throne and sit at his feet. Or maybe it's my duckling part, now imprinted again. I receive reading material on the refuge ceremony at the end of the first day, and I decide to go back to my own place rather than Taylor's so I can have total privacy and meditate on what's just happened, on what I want to do.

Taking refuge essentially means that you've decided to place your trust in the Buddha, his teachings, and his community—the three jewels—as the path to liberation from suffering. In the same way you can decide to trust a psychiatrist or type of therapy in order to relieve emotional pain, it's a form of committing yourself to receiving help and applying it to your life. In DBT you sign a contract to stay in skills group for a year, but this is different. By taking refuge, you declare your commitment to the path of Buddhism. There's nothing to sign, no money to fork over. And as Rinpoche explained later that afternoon, the Buddha never intended for there to be a formal religion with him as some kind of god. He was simply a man who discovered a way to free himself from pain and then devoted himself to teaching others the path to that awakened state. Taking refuge means acknowledging this—that we all are Buddhas, just in need of awakening. It also means committing ourselves to this goal.

This is what I want—deeply: to have a community and an ongoing practice beyond the hospitals and diagnoses. I understand how distorted my thinking still is, how emotion mind still drives me, how I still fundamentally lack compassion toward myself and others. I see the beginning of a path that promises to transform a borderline into a Buddha, and I'm willing—excited, really—to take refuge in that.

The next afternoon, four of us sit in front of Rinpoche and repeat after him: "I take refuge in the Buddha. I take refuge in the Dharma. I take refuge in the Sangha." He cuts a piece of hair from each person's head and gives each of us a Dharma name. Mine is Great Blissful Lotus, and I'm secretly pleased, as it's much sexier and more exciting than Defender of the Dharma, which another woman receives. He presents us with a length of cord that he's blessed, for protection, and gives each of us a piece of parchment paper with our Tibetan Buddhist names inscribed in calligraphy. I cry through the entire ceremony. It's a little embarrassing, because I can't stop. I cry through the afternoon meditations on karma and impermanence. And then, at end of the afternoon, a new emotion sets in: panic. I have no idea what to do now!

One of Rinpoche's students informs me that Rinpoche actually lives in Nepal and might not be back for another year. She sees how upset I am when I hear this and puts her arm around me. "There is nothing to worry about. Now Rinpoche is always with you." I nod and don't explain that I have a bit of trouble with separations and "internalizing" the presence of others.

The retreat ends with each of us paying thanks to Rinpoche and, in keeping with Tibetan tradition, offering him a white silk scarf. "Email me," he says, placing the scarf around my neck and smiling. This calms me down a bit. Thank god Buddhist Rinpoches have the Internet!

That evening I bring my meditation cushion and newly refuged self back to Taylor's. He's sitting on the couch with his laptop, watching a documentary on guns and the Civil War. "Hey! I missed you!" he says and jumps up to hug me. "How was the retreat?"

I sit down beside him. There's a swirling disorientation, like I'm coming off an LSD trip and now have no words to explain what happened: "It was...you know...like...wow..." I try to describe what happened, but it all comes out as adjectives: Amazing! Unbelievable! I show him my scroll and the new name.

"You're not going to shave your head and move to Tibet are you?" He looks genuinely worried. He knows how Kiki happens. I promise I won't. "Good," he says, "Because that's a long way to travel for some nookie." We settle down with the cats and the TV. A part of me is still in that hall, feeling another world open up to me. Another part is relieved to be back to the smells, sensations, and taste of Taylor's house and body. No one says a Buddhist can't have a boyfriend—or a husband. Two months later, Taylor proposes.

24

Reversals

It's like a fairy tale—what I've craved from the very beginning, what I believe will finally fulfill me. I have Taylor's undying devotion, a home we can share, and the promise that I'll never be alone again. Everyone is delighted. Raymond sends flowers. Gail and Renee take me out to lunch. My mother cries. Taylor's mother almost cries. I finally move completely into the house, where I discover that being at the center of Taylor's world does not include closet space.

There was immediate fallout after Rinpoche's sudden appearance and then absence. It was like a spiritual hit-and-run: I felt the ground lurch from under me even as I floated half off it on the fumes of his presence. Taylor, true to his word, doesn't seem the least bit jealous when I plaster pictures of Rinpoche all over my room. I need to keep the connection going, yet it feels very tenuous. I'm afraid to email him despite his encouragement because I now know that he has thousands of students all over the world. Plus, I really don't have anything to say except, "Please pay attention to me!" One of Rinpoche's longtime students gave me her email address at the end of the retreat, so I write her about my confusion and longing for a connection with Rinpoche. As the other student did during the retreat, she reassures me that if I think of Rinpoche, he will be with me.

"But I don't feel him," I say. I photocopy more pictures of Rinpoche and tape them to all of my notebooks and mirrors. I do prostrations at my altar and say the prayers, and still I don't feel anything. But I do feel Taylor. He holds me securely in his arms and rubs my shoulders when we watch TV. He sends me links to fifteen random and amusing Internet sites every day when I'm at work. No matter how strongly I'm pulled in the direction of a spiritual practice, I still find the concrete, visceral world of my relationship with Taylor most sheltering. From sharing French toast in the morning to lying side-by-side at night with our books and reading lights, it keeps me secured.

Eventually, I email Rinpoche for advice about the marriage (even though I've already said yes). He says, "You will know what to do," which is exactly what Ethan says. I buy an expensive wedding planner book and put it on the dining room table, where it instantly gets buried under the perpetual accrual of Taylor's detritus. It takes constant effort to prevent the house from sinking back into chaos; it's like a vortex I'm constantly pulling against. So it's the house I first start really complaining about to Ethan.

"I might be developing claustrophobia," I tell him.

"Or you could be anxious about the marriage."

"No, it's the house: the cat hair, having to put all my clothes in the attic, and the litter box back in the kitchen."

Ethan nods. "So, it's living with Taylor that is making you anxious."

"Well no, it's that…" I try to figure out what it is. Actually, I'm beginning to feel smothered—not by Taylor, who gives me all the space in the world when it comes to me doing what I want. It's something else. I've read that, for some borderlines, the flip side of abandonment fear is the fear of engulfment. It's another one of those "screwed if you do, screwed if you don't" situations. All you want is love and belonging, and your very existence depends on it. But when you get it, you have no existence except that love; there's still no you. And in relinquishing the last little holdouts where I was separate, I'm now covered with Taylor and cat hair. I just might be feeling engulfed.

Yet this is also new to me. I'm usually so busy figuring out how to keep whatever security I can. That Taylor is willing to commit his entire life to me and share everything not only scares me with its power, it also challenges core beliefs that continue to declare I'm an untouchable, unworthy of genuine love. Back when I examined the emergence process at Project Transition, Dr. Crabtree pointed out that every gain involves a loss. Even though successes are seemingly the building blocks of progress, they also upset the balance, and that makes you more vulnerable. I believe this is happening now.

And then there are all of my parts, each with its different needs and perspective. Where is the truth, and how do I determine what's right? I ask Ethan if there's a wise mind perspective, and he replies, "What does your Buddhist part want and see?" I hadn't thought of that before, asking the Buddhist part. That part is relatively new, and she's still smarting from not getting a bigger piece of Rinpoche, but she does have a voice. So what does she see? She sees that I'm still suffering, that even when I get what I want—a marriage proposal, a real home—I'm at war with something. The Buddhist wants me to go in a completely different direction and find the cause of this. She says that until I do this, all my efforts will only lead to more pain. And she's right, but as soon as I leave Ethan's office, I forget.

How do you shut up your Buddhist part? You focus obsessively on everything concrete, never allowing a pause in the ticker tape of thoughts running through your head, jumping from one activity to another, and numbing yourself with TV and sleep. In the daytime, this works pretty well, but at night I freak out. I wake up feeling like there's a cat smothering my face. Sometimes there is, but usually it's pure panic. For several constricting and seemingly endless minutes, I believe I'm about to make a giant mistake with this marriage, this house, and Taylor. I've gained a shell of security, but I've barely touched the seed within myself that is real and enduring—that primordial purity Rinpoche described. I lie there next to Taylor, his breath soothing me even as I'm realizing the horror of the situation. Then I fall asleep and am almost able to forget.

In the months that follow, I watch as my excitement about the marriage sours, and I feel paralyzed, unable to tell Taylor. I'm starting to cultivate a fantasy about what my life would be like if I were on my own. I'd have a little apartment close to work. I would practice meditation, become a vegetarian, go to night classes for grad school, and definitely wouldn't have any cats. My space would be uncluttered and my body completely my own. I'm also mentally compiling a list of our differences: our goals and priorities, food preferences, housekeeping styles, and even hygiene habits. Activities that initially kept us close, like sex and motorcycles, have fizzled out for me, and all we do together now is eat, sleep, and watch TV. But what isn't clear to me is whether these are valid reasons to break up or problems that we could simply keep working on.

My body appears to be deciding for me. First it's the feeling of claustrophobia—not being able to breathe in the space. Then there are those night panics. I wake up sweaty and anxious, feeling like I'm close to driving my car off a cliff. A horrible pit in my stomach develops whenever Taylor and I discuss our plans. And the house itself feels toxic. One night, when we're in bed and the cat hair has driven my allergic reactions to a height, I tell Taylor, "I'm going crazy in this house. I don't know if this will work." He hugs me closer and says, "Don't worry," already half asleep. "You get panicked. Everything is okay."

But it's not okay. It's like I'm giving birth to a monster. Taylor can't see it yet, but he will eventually; there's only so much time it can stay inside. Three nights later, I turn to him in bed again. He's got his arm around me and I can't look at his face, so I burrow into his shoulder.

"I have to cancel the engagement and move out," I say. No preface, no postscript. Taylor's arm tenses, and we lie there for a horrible moment, suspended in an intimacy that's been cleaved in half by a single sentence. This is exactly what I've feared Taylor would do to me, every minute, for years. How strange that now I'm the one who says the words.

Taylor gets up and goes into the other room. He doesn't talk to me the entire next day. I feel hollow and scared, and I don't want to face him either. I page Ethan, and he coaches me to stay grounded and focus on the things immediately in front of me, which I do. When I come home from work that night, Taylor is still in bed, and I begin to cry. I know what I've done and I wish I could take it all back, and yet I can't. This is what needs to happen. I knock on the bedroom door and he says, "I want you out of the house tonight."

"Okay," I cry.

"I want your things out of here in a week or I'm changing the locks."

I see him sit up through the partially open door, then he says, "You know what this means: It's over. You've ended it. You're not getting me back."

I say I know, and I pack my medications and some clothes. In the car, I drive instinctively toward my mother. On the way I call, and I'm sobbing so hard that she can't understand what I'm saying. "Just get here safely," she says.

When I pull up, she brings me into the house and lays me down on her bed. "I didn't know what else to do," I sob. She puts her arms around me and rocks me. "It's okay, it's okay, it's okay..." She holds me for what must be an hour. I finally fall asleep, the pillow wet with my tears.

"I still love him," I say when she wakes me up and brings me to my old bedroom.

"Sometimes love isn't enough." She pushes the hair out of my eyes and kisses me goodnight. "You're going to get through this."

Three days later I hire movers and move into a single bedroom apartment I find through a realtor. It's in an anonymous brick building in Waltham about a mile away from Taylor's house, far enough that I can't impulsively walk to his house in the middle of the night to beg for forgiveness, but close enough that I feel like I'm still grounded in the life we had. I feel completely lost as soon as I move in. All of my convictions about what I want and need evaporate in the desert of my sudden isolation. When I'm not at work, I'm in my new, clean, cat-free bedroom, curled up on my bed sleeping or crying. At work, people stop by and give me hugs. Gail checks in on me every hour. Raymond sends me more flowers. Since I was the one who ended it, I thought I'd be able to handle this better. My mother offers to pay my rent to offset the additional security deposit, and she buys me a TV with a DVD player so I'll have something to distract me when I'm at home alone. My father calls every night, and he's finally stopped suggesting I go to a meeting. He just wants to know how I am.

It takes a couple of weeks, but soon enough I begin to beg Taylor to give us another chance. He comes over and we talk. It's horribly painful and nothing gets resolved, but I'm adamant that we can work things out. Then a few days later I panic, remembering particular frustrations and difficulties in our relationship, so I email Taylor and declare that it's really over. Taylor says, quite justifiably, that he feels fucked with, especially as this happens over and over. But on the days when we're on the side of hope, we have sex. And I don't want to admit this, but I find it exciting: two bodies caught in this extreme tug-of-war, trapped within collisions and retreats. My passion is somehow tied to the knowledge that I'm losing Taylor. And just as my body revolted when immersed in his house, now it opens to him, trying to pull him back in. Taylor returns to me physically, but he's wrapped in ambivalence. I find his emotional distance more intolerable than the state of his house or any of our previous issues and differences—and that makes me want him even more.

Ethan and I discuss these attempts to win Taylor back, followed by sudden reversals that push him away. Ethan suggests that my difficulty with ambivalence—my own and Taylor's—propels these swings in perspective. Taylor isn't mine any more, and half the time I don't know if I even want him, but there's still a chance we could be together. We're in an indeterminate state, and I can't tolerate that. So the black-and-white thinking, the wild swings between idealization and devaluation, represent attempts to establish my position, and his. This happens so rapidly and subsumes my emotions so entirely that I will go from weeping and longing for him to an utter conviction that we must part forever, sometimes in the course of just a few hours. I genuinely try not to inflict these contradictory positions on Taylor. Yet it's inevitable. If he doesn't call me for a couple of days I'm desperate. Then, when I'm sitting on his couch in an attempt to make up, I only want to return to my clean, quiet apartment and be on my own.

It's obvious to me that this turmoil is drawing out my previous BPD symptoms. Like boils, they grow larger and more painful despite my years of therapy and training and what I've learned from Buddhism. It's all returning: the black-and-white thinking, an acute, consuming emptiness that makes being alone unbearable, and the desperate sex to avoid abandonment (that's my newest addition to the BPD criteria.). Five minutes after I walk into my new apartment, I feel like I'm trapped in a tomb, a lifeless place that centers around my bed, where I spend an inordinate amount of time crying or watching DVDs. It's the echo of so many other rooms where I've been forced to return to myself, only to discover that it's an impossibly painful destination.

When I cry in bed, I take to surrounding myself with all of my stuffed animals, as I discover the surges of pain pass more quickly when I do this. I've always had stuffed animals, but only now have I started talking to them. I look into the glass eyes in their plush faces and ask them to tell me I'm going to be okay. Moe the lion says, "You're going to get through this, Kiera." Luke the dog bobs his head in agreement and presses his face into my neck. Leon the bear says, "It's okay, it's okay, it's okay." Yes, I am a thirty-five-year-old woman, and yet I can only find comfort in having imaginary conversations with stuffed animals. That, and swaddling. I buy numerous plush blankets, and when I can't stop crying and the urge to cut feels overwhelming, I wrap myself inside them, naked, with only a small hole for me to breathe through. I lie there enclosed in softness, focusing on my breath and the sense of being held. Over and over, I repeat, "I accept this pain. I believe it will pass." Sometimes that gets me through.

If not, then I page Ethan. Just hearing his voice can bring me partway back from the brink. At some point, his phone coaching shifted from focusing on DBT skills to working with my parts. He'll ask if there's a part of myself that needs to be acknowledged. At first I don't know, then I grow fairly sure it's the little dark one—an exile who has surfaced in a big way now that I'm alone. She's a bit like Cousin Itt from *The Addams Family*: covered with hair, feral, only on the cusp of language. She is the part that creates that ache in my left palm and bangs her head against walls. Of all my parts, she is the most desperate for comfort and connection, and she's also the most angry and fearful. So she's usually locked up, because when she emerges her pain over-shadows everything else.

"What can you do to take care of the little dark one?" Ethan asks. I tell him I've been talking to my stuffed animals and even swaddling, but I'm still a mess. He suggests that I reassure this part directly and also ask her what she needs, rather than assuming. He reminds me that self-soothing doesn't necessarily allow my activated parts to have a voice, which is very important.

So I go back to my bed, and this time I try to maintain some dis-tance from the pain, looking at it as this part of me and not the whole. I imagine the small space where the little dark one is usually curled up, hair wild, rocking back and forth. She won't say anything, so I tell her that I'm going to take care of her. I promise her that. She remains silent. I ask if she can come out a bit and tell me what she needs. Again, I say that I'll do my best to give her what she needs. At first, she remains silent. Then (and this always freaks me out), I feel a small movement inside me and she speaks, in a whisper: "Juice."

"Juice?" I ask. There's a little nod in the darkness inside myself. I realize that she's thirsty. Is it me that's thirsty, or just this part? There must be more to this; she isn't crying because she's just thirsty. But maybe this is her way of testing whether I'm actually going to give her something she needs. So I go to the fridge and pour a glass of apple cider. It tastes like the fields behind my mother's house on autumn nights, punctuated with cold stars and warm scarves. The juice is so simple, the sweet liquid of childhood that returns every year carrying the orchards and sunsets. By the time I've finished the cider, my tears are gone. And I'm totally spooked, once again, that I have these parts and they actually communicate with me.

It's so hard not to perceive myself as totally relapsing. Though I'm not acting on the urges to hurt myself, my shopping habit is more impulsive that ever. One day I drive to the Burlington Mall to buy bras at Sears, and I end up charging a leather massage chair. My credit card statements show I've spent more in the past few months than I have in the previous ten years combined. Also, I have no patience or tolerance for minor aggravations, and my anger level surges at the smallest sense of invasion. I'm back to wanting to kick people who step in my way on the sidewalk and wanting to take an ax to the copy machine when it malfunctions. I want to do drastic things just to shift my focus away from the empty hell I'm returning to.

"It really feels like I'm back to square one," I tell Ethan. "How can I have done so much work and still get this messed up again?"

Ethan asks, "Do you think it's abnormal to feel alone and in pain when you're in the midst of a breakup?"

I say, "No, it's not abnormal... But it is bringing out all of my BPD symptoms."

"It might be just as valid to say that BPD symptoms come out temporarily in anyone who is in extreme pain or who's going through a terrible loss."

I hadn't thought about it that way, but it makes sense. Breakups devastate most people; maybe there would be something wrong with you if they didn't. And a lot of people lose their shit even more than I am right now. But what most of them don't have is twenty years of illness just waiting to be reactivated.

Ethan does his Socratic reality check, asking me if I'm really back at square one—back when we first met. He says, "I know it feels that way, but can you see any differences between then and now?"

Damn you, Ethan... He's right. All of my ducks are in a row: My bills are paid, I'm still going to work, I'm not harming myself (other than with my credit card habit), and I'm not alone. I have genuinely supportive relationships, especially with Gail. She midwifes me through my workdays. When she sees me sitting at my desk in tears, she gives me a hug. She sends me out of the office for walks and periodic airings and listens to my insane flip-flopping over Taylor without telling me what I should do. Over and over, she says, "You'll do what you know in your heart is right."

When I walk into work, there's a sense of coming home. I've never worked in one place for so long. Nor have I had such an enduring connection with a group of people that didn't involve sex or sitting in a circle in some support or therapy group. Being at my desk is the closest I can come to "sitting on the cushion" as a daily practice—and as a way of abiding myself. It's not meditation, but it's something. Each time I sit down, I must be with myself to a certain extent. Even with the distractions of the Internet and advocacy work, I have the space to be mindful, to observe myself from time to time. I'm not free-falling. I have to tell myself this repeatedly, as I make more maps of what I have in my life and who I'm connected to. Looking over them, I can see I'm not alone. My mother and father call me regularly. Even Taylor's mom checks in with me every couple of weeks. And Raymond takes me out to dinner on a regular basis, and despite my vegetarian aspirations, I still can't resist those fine cuts of meat.

One of my few pleasures these days is shopping at Whole Foods Market. Now that Taylor and I aren't trying to merge our diametrically opposed eating habits, I'm back to vegetables, grains, and organic fare, which I know will keep me healthy and help me get my weight back under control. When I was plagued by anxiety attacks, trips to Whole Foods were torture. Now, I can take some pleasure in lingering in the body care aisle and watching kids harass their parents for fruit roll-ups. One day as I'm eating sushi in the back dining area, I see a tall, thin figure standing at a checkout stand. I don't recognize him immediately because he's facing the register, but the familiarity of his gestures makes me think it's Bennet. I get up to take a closer look and, oh my god, it is! He sees me too, and comes over with his bag of groceries.

"What are you doing here?" I ask. It's like he's jumped universes. He's supposed to be in a different world, or at least a different town. Yet here he is, over four years later, looking exactly the same, down to the bright white sneakers and pointy sideburns. He says he's doing a carpentry job nearby, so he stopped in for some stuff for dinner.

We stand looking at each other for a moment.

"Listen…," I say, getting ready to apologize for being such a maniac in our relationship.

"No, it's okay," Bennet shakes his head. "We were both going through a rough time."

"I was really at my worst. You know you saved my life when you told me to go get more help."

Bennet smiles and says he's glad. He only wanted for me to be happy. I ask about Alexis—are they still living together?

"No, she moved out. Now she's involved with a group of Buddhists."

"Buddhists?" I echo. "What kind?"

"I think they're from Tibet. She's really heavy into it."

I tell him that's amazing, that I've become involved in Tibetan Buddhism too. (But I don't mention that I've kind of fallen off the enlightenment wagon.) Bennet digs around in his jacket pockets and writes Alexis's email address and phone number on an old receipt. Then we stand awkwardly. There's nothing more to say. It's obvious we're just crossing paths, so we hug and say good-bye.

Alexis. That name again. Her voice. Her heavy-lidded eyes. I'm ambivalent about contacting her, in part because I'm worried that she'll be more Buddhist than me. Not only have I stopped emailing Rinpoche and reciting my prayers, I'm still living the life I declared I wanted to be rid of. I'm still spending half of my nights at Taylor's house watching TV, eating meat, and having sex with him. Taylor asks, "How can I take your complaints seriously when the things you tell me upset you about our relationship are the very things you also want to do with me?"

I have no answer. I am so obviously fucked-up here that I can only say, "You're right. What do you want for dinner?"

It's early spring when I finally contact Alexis. I send her an email with a quick hello. She writes right away, excited to be in touch and eager to get together. She's still living in Lowell but spends most of her time with her Sangha in Somerville. We're amazed to discover that, although our routes were entirely different, we've ended up taking refuge in almost exactly the same type of Buddhism. The lineage of her Sangha and Rinpoche's share many of the same teachers and practices. However, her teacher and community are very close by, and they meet weekly.

I email and ask, "You have your own Tibetan monk right at home?" I'm so jealous. She tells me I should come to one of their practices, and I promise that I will. In the meantime, we get together for coffee. Although it's been many years since I've seen her, Alexis is the same: beautiful, strong, opinionated, quirky—and now a Buddhist. More than that, she's a *practicing* Buddhist. Going far beyond my meager efforts, not only did she take refuge, for the past three years she's been learning Tibetan, going on retreats, studying the texts, and meditating. And she has a Sangha for support in all of this.

She wants to know what I've been doing for the past five years.

"Remember how I was diagnosed with BPD while Bennet and I were dating?"

She has a vague memory of it.

"I got pretty sick after we broke up and landed in the hospital again. I don't know how much you knew, but I really thought you were destroying my life at one point."

"Really?! Little old me?"

"Well, more you *with* Bennet."

"Oh my god, it was so time to have my own life," she says.

I agree. Now that Bennet isn't in the picture, Alexis absolutely delights me. We spend hours in Starbucks, catching up. She says I'm lucky I didn't get married, because if I were a typical wife with children, I'd have no time to practice the Dharma. My god, she is hard core!

I admit that in spite of breaking off the engagement, I haven't let go of Taylor.

"You have to," she declares, with that same certainty as when she told me to apply for disability, and to never be ashamed of having a mental illness. She reiterates that I should come to her Sangha sometime, and once again I again promise I will. But every week when the time comes, I find an excuse not to drive to Somerville.

I'm not sure how long this indeterminate state with Taylor can last. He tells me he's dating other people, and I accept it begrudgingly. How can I make any claims on him when I can't decide from day to day if I want to stay with him? Yet we continue to sleep together. Then, one day I realize my period is late. I call Taylor three times, hoping he'll come to the store with me to get the test, but I don't hear back from him. Finally I go to the store by myself. Back home, I take the test, discover it's negative, and collapse in my bed. All day I had gone back and forth in my mind: Either we'll keep the baby and get married, or I'll get an abortion and turn my back on Taylor for good. Every five minutes it was a different answer.

I'm sweaty with all of the emotional reversals, and with anger at not having my calls returned. When I finally reach him late that evening, I discover that he's been home all day working on a motorcycle and didn't feel like answering the phone. I screech at him, "How could you avoid my calls all day?! I thought I was pregnant!"

"Well, you never said on your message it was an emergency."

I shriek that this must be the lamest excuse ever and start crying. Taylor drives over immediately. We sit on the couch and he holds me while I lament the entire situation. It's impossible to fix and impossible to let go of, but today we crossed a line. I can't keep doing this, to myself or him. I finally say, "This has to be over. Really. It's really, really over."

Taylor nods. "I figured this would eventually happen." We sit in silence for a while. When he gets up to leave, I have to hold myself back from pulling him down to the couch and kissing him. I'm such a mindfuck. I have to let him walk out the door. He has to stop letting me pull him back in. "I'm sorry," I say as he gets his coat. "I'm sorry, I'm sorry, I'm sorry." He leaves and I'm back to being alone in my little brick box. I make a cup of Sleepytime tea with milk and honey and cry to my stuffed animals—and sign up on Match.com.

25

Bad Buddhist

Sure, if I were Alexis, I probably would have headed straight to the Sangha and told them to chain me to the shrine room, force-feed me meditation practices, and do whatever it took to get me back to a place of balance and stability. But who wants that when you can log on to a dating site and start the insanity all over again?

It's been three years since I've even looked at the online dating scene, and some things have changed. The pictures, for instance: In the old days, one or two headshots sufficed. Now everyone is a documented adventurer or world traveler, crossing the finish line of a triathlon, planting a national flag on a mountain peak, or shaking hands with movie stars. The profile presentation has evolved into an art form. There are blogs where you can record your dating experiences, places to upload videos, keywords to help compatible people find you. The personal essays are as sophisticated and polished as something you'd write for grad school.

And on my first search for potential partners, after typing in specs like age and location, who do I find but Taylor, along with his picture and his words. I'm mortified. The idea of both of us returning to the source of our relationship and fishing for someone new really pains me. Taylor's profile also troubles me because it's almost the same, almost word for word, as what I read three years ago. It's incredible, actually, because it remains true; everything he says is still the same—what he likes, who he is, what he's doing. I, on the other hand, have changed a lot, and what I end up writing for my profile is nothing like my first. I describe myself this time as a mental health advocate and educator, a motorcycle rider, a

Buddhist, and a writer. Once again, even our online profiles reflect the divide between our natures: his deep stasis, my mercurial change.

My urge to quickly meet someone who might distract me from going back to Taylor prompts me to post pictures that are more provocative than before. I have a photo of me in racing leathers on the motorcycle, another of me wearing thigh-high boots and a corset, a third showing me in profile at sunset, and a fourth where I'm sitting in front of my Buddhist shrine. How's that for eclectic? I'm also more explicit in what I write. I emphasize my sensual nature, my love of touch, my "adventurousness." All in all, this newly packaged Kiera looks quite good, and the response is immediate. Hari, a handsome Indian man who rides a motorcycle, owns his own business, and is my age tells me I'm beautiful and intriguing. Like a snort of coke, his email hits my pleasure center and I'm happier than I've been in months. Two days later, I'm out on a date with him, and he's a spectacular man: well-built, freshly showered and shaved, dressed in that way that certain European men have—tailored yet also somehow rugby ready. He picks me up in a BMW and we go to a local Thai restaurant with golden Buddha statues, sequined elephants, bamboo plants, and framed pictures of dancing women. He takes my hand as soon as we're sipping our mango lassis and says I'm perfect. I demur and remind him that he hardly knows me. Ahh, but he can tell these things. He says he sees that I am kind and compassionate, creative and adventurous.

"Can you communicate?" he asks.

I say, "So far as I know, I'm pretty good at it."

He says that's critical to him. He asks if I'm independent. I say that I live alone and support myself (and cringe inwardly a bit at this, as I am more of a stray dog looking for a lap than an independent woman). I also say that I've been on my own since a young age, and that's definitely true. He says that he has as well, coming over to the States from India and working his way up in the business world.

He keeps taking my hand and stroking it between his. While his hands are soft and his touch is soothing, his eyes burn. There are two forces in him, as there are in me: gentle and yet forceful, aloof and yet desperate. We savor the curries and give each other short rundowns of our previous relationships. I explain that I was deeply in love with a man who was so different from me that I ended up having to break off our engagement when I realized it would never work out in the long term. Hari describes being involved with a woman who was very intelligent and passionate but had a lot of trouble with him being away on business trips.

He looks at me. "How would *you* handle it if I had to go away for weeks at a time, or suddenly take off without warning?"

Oh dear. How do I feel about absences and being left? Bad first-date question for a borderline. I know I secured Taylor's constant presence by camping at his house for years. Since he didn't go anywhere, I could keep him close. "I guess I'm not happy when I'm dating someone and they're always traveling," I tell Hari.

"The reason I'm asking," he lowers his voice, "is that my last girlfriend had a very difficult time with it. She'd call and beg me to come home when I was in the middle of important work overseas. She'd be so upset that when I got home, I had to spend days trying to convince her that I still loved her." He shakes his head in bewilderment. "You can't imagine what happened if I didn't return her phone call right away."

"I think I have an idea," I say quietly. His ex sounds all too familiar to me—BPD familiar. How do I break it to him? And if I tell him, how do I then tell him about me? *Oh, by the way, your psycho ex-girlfriend? I've got what she's got. But don't worry, I'm better. Just don't ask my ex. He might tell you something else...*

Hari wrings his hands. "One day, I called to say I'd be late coming home. Then my plane was delayed, and then it got stuck on the runway. When I got home, she wouldn't come out of the bathroom. I ended up sitting on the bed for an hour trying to get her to come out, and when she finally did, her arms were covered with blood." He looks up at the ceiling and breathes deeply. "Then she said, 'Look what you made me do.'"

I take Hari's hand. "There's a reason she did this, but it's not about you."

"I don't understand."

"She probably has borderline personality disorder." I run through the symptoms with him and he nods at each. She's nine for nine, alright.

"Do you know her?" Hari looks baffled.

"Well...in a sense." Here is a moment when being a borderline "in recovery," as I now construct myself, can make for confusion. If I tell him that his ex has BPD and that I also have it, he's going to run for the hills. If I don't say anything and we get involved, it's a setup for both of us, because I'm still like his ex, just more in control of myself and more aware of what I struggle with.

I take a deep breath. "This is probably going to freak you out, but I know what happened with her because I have the same problem, only I've learned how to manage a lot of my symptoms."

Hari remains still for a moment, then sits back in his chair. It's like he's backing away from me, but the chair is as far as he can get. I hurry to add that I'm not like his ex in many ways, that I've gotten treatment for BPD.

"Is it gone?" he asks. "Are you normal now?"

I think about everything that's gone on in the past few months and know, deep down, that I'm not cured. I still have this thing, even as I also believe that I don't. It's that dialectic Ethan first saw within me. I both have and do not have BPD.

"No, I still deal with it," I finally say. "Just better than most people."

"What if I never called you again?" Hari asks. I'm sure he's afraid that if he says the wrong thing, I'm going to retreat to the bathroom with my cutlery. I assure him that I can live with it. I don't hurt myself anymore, and I try mightily not to hurt anyone else, either.

"You are so beautiful," he says. "I don't know what to do. I would like to see you again, but only if you can assure me that this won't happen. I can't go through another experience like that. It...." He can't finish the sentence.

"I know," I say. "I don't want to go back there either."

When Hari drops me off at my place, he kisses me at the door and we hold each other. I'm thinking that it was a good first date, and I can't believe I actually outed myself without driving the person away or going into too many gory details. It probably wasn't a good idea to kiss, however, because after a long hug Hari asks if I have time for a cup of tea. I agree that it would be nice to relax together for a while—which leads to more kissing in my apartment and then a tussle on my couch when I realize he's going for my underwear. I pull back. "Let's slow down."

Hari asks if I've ever been with a dark-skinned man before. I don't answer, since he's probably the eleventh ethnicity I've locked bodies with. He begins to stroke my legs, and I feel myself weakening again in the hold of his muscled arms and deep kisses. Without warning, he bends down.

"Wait," I say.

"I just want to taste you."

"Really, wait." I try to pull his head up, but he's planted himself between my thighs.

Now there are two battles going on: My body is responding to a lover and I want him to keep going, especially because my clitoris is having feelings that it hasn't had in a long time. But I'm also no longer feeling safe. What really disturbs me is that this conflict and my arousal are simultaneous. I'm starting to get off on the struggle. While Hari tries to reach my most delicate point, I alternately lift my head and say, "I don't think this is a good idea," and then fall back, writhing.

"Enough," I finally declare. I roll over and stand up.

"It seems to me you were enjoying that."

I pick up his coat from the kitchen chair and hold it out. "I think you should leave now." He takes it and pulls out his car keys. And only at this minute do I realize that I don't know his last name, what company he owns, or anything about him, really. He's just a handsome man who complimented me, and I took him home because I'm lonely.

Ethan and I discuss the episode at our next session. He wants to know what I feel now. It's totally cliché, but I feel guilty and ashamed. If I hadn't taken Hari home, hadn't been so desperate for attention, I could have prevented this whole thing. Ethan reminds me that I'm not entirely capable of controlling the environment and that I did the best I could.

"But that's not the end of it. I was freaked out *and* aroused. I resisted him, but that made me more wet. And after he left" (how I hate telling Ethan these things), "afterward, I, you know, was able to get myself off." I don't admit that I also fantasized about Hari fucking me.

Ethan is nonplussed. "Why wouldn't you be? He made you feel good on some level, even if you ultimately had different goals."

"Well… But…"

"It's possible to have contradictory feelings at the same time, just as it is to have opposing viewpoints. Think again of the dialectic. You want and you don't want. Both are true."

We sit in silence and I feel shame bubbling up. Revealing my sex life to Ethan is difficult. When I tell him these things, I'm constantly worried that he's thinking the worst of me. So far my sex life has been focused on Taylor and our issues; Ethan hasn't witnessed me freelancing full force, and hasn't seen how quickly I can get into trouble. When I tell him how I worry that he may be judging me, he asks if he's ever given me any reason to think he's negatively judging me. I admit that, for all these years, he hasn't. But here's the difficulty with validation and acceptance: People can say anything, but what goes on in their hearts and minds is ultimately unknowable, as is any state of another person's mind. How do you confirm love or devotion? In exposing myself to Ethan, I'm always looking for some undercurrent that will reflect back how fucked-up I am. I wonder if that's why he still so rarely uses the word "borderline," to avoid adding to my arsenal of self-flagellation. After we review my date with Hari, Ethan asks me, just as he did years earlier, what I want from a man, a partner, or even a first date. And again, this intense conflict arises within me: I want someone gentle and strong to win me over, slowly and skillfully, and to not lose myself along the way. And yet I also want to be taken, broken open and entered, so that in the end I am no longer myself but lost in someone else. How do you resolve that dialectic?

⚜

Sometimes it feels like this must be a psychiatric experiment: How long can the borderline do online dating without losing her little mind? The process is grueling, the results demoralizing. I am hooked as quickly as I was the last time, up until I met Taylor. In an hour, my entire life shrinks, my fate hanging on an email exchange—from a stranger! With Taylor, at least, I feared rejection from a concrete, complex human I had a real relationship with. Now my attachments are fixated on chimeras, ghosts on a screen, and I'm being tortured by my own projections. There's no way I can convince myself that these limited exchanges and superficial dates justify the life-and-death gravity I'm feeling, and yet those feelings persist. I'm strung out on Internet dating, and I haven't even gotten laid. Men who email me intensely for days disappear without a trace. I go on a date with a cute Buddhist guy and he baits me with the hope of sex, then plays cat and mouse for two weeks until I want to stalk him and have my way with him in a dark alley. Should I even be playing with this stuff? I tell my mom about my frustrations, and, not for the first time, she suggests that I join the Appalachian Hiking Club.

(Which, I hear from one of my coworkers, is glutted with single women hiking Mt. Monadnock like packs of hungry she-wolves. Apparently, men just go to bars when they get lonely. Women go to lectures and join hiking clubs.)

At least once a day, the longing for Taylor washes over me like a tide, leaving pieces of my need stranded on the shoreline and exposed. I gather the detritus and heave it all back into the Internet, hoping something might get hooked. If it weren't for Alexis, I'd have no more ties to my Buddhist practice. When she observes how lost I'm becoming, she once again tells me to come to her Sangha. Actually, she tells me to cut the shit, then tells me to come to her Sangha—direct as always, but it doesn't penetrate.

I spend close to a month having chaste dates with a divorced man. As it turns out, his ex-wife has BPD. (Are they finding me, or am I finding them?) Then he ends it, explaining I remind him too much of his ex. For a couple of weeks, I see a man with OCD, and then I spend a couple more weeks dating a man with an anxiety disorder. It's like I'm forming my own little mental health support group. So far I haven't slept with anyone—not until Tony. Like Taylor, he rides a motorcycle and is a computer geek, but that's where the resemblances end. In fact, he's so completely inappropriate that I can't tell Alexis about him because she'd scream at me. Not only does he ride his motorcycle, with me on it, through freeway traffic at 130 miles per hour, he also drinks daily and actually makes a pot deal in the middle of our second date. I sleep with him that night, numb and clinging to him like a child. When he doesn't contact me for another date, I'm devastated. This is such insanity. It's like I've been working on a broken car for years, and now that I've finally gotten all of the parts working, the transmission goes.

"You're grasping," Alexis tells me. "You're caught in the vicious cycle of samsara. Put all of your sexual energy into Dharma practice and you'll be like a rocket—you'll shoot toward enlightenment in no time."

But what does that mean? I've lost sight of how Buddhism can relieve my suffering. I can't see beyond the feelings that sweep me up from minute to minute: hope, frustration, despair, desire, anger. I call or email Alexis every day now so that someone knows what's going on, because I'm starting to scare myself. I even start sitting in front of my shrine more regularly, trying to connect my mind to Rinpoche's, way out in Nepal. Many of my parts are clamoring that I need to put the brakes on this sexual searching, but every day while I'm at work, every night at home, I sit at the shrine of the computer, hypnotized by the collective mirage of need.

Amidst this chaos, spring has sprung once again, replete with flowers in the manicured Cambridge gardens and students in shorts. I go to work, answer the phones, and try not to be a bad Buddhist. But I am, fever-ishly checking my emails and scanning profiles. Phone calls, dates, and heartbreak. I'm exhausted. It's like I've been in one of those survival TV shows for too long, running obstacle courses, trying to make fire from horsehair and three donuts, except here my endurance is mea-sured not in physical stamina but in my emotional capacity to want, to have, and to lose—intensely and repeatedly. It's a gauntlet of desire and rejection, possibilities and refusals. It is, as Buddhism says, the essence of "Samsara"—the endless cycle of grasping that keeps us bound in a state of suffering.

How many days of my life have I spent focusing on the attention of men, no matter how questionable that attention may be? I've devoted endless hours to craving touch, reeling from its reverberations, gnawing on its absence, and chasing after it again. It's true that I'm not as dev-astated by all of this as I used to be. I have to keep reminding myself of this. Whatever is happening with my loneliness and sexuality now is emerging because I'm somehow ready to be exposed and to resolve it. Even in this insanity there is a process: I go under and feel like I'm drowning, but now I can open my eyes underwater. I can see the distor-tions when I'm immersed. As in drowning, a moment underwater can feel like an eternity, with no hope for escape. But I continue to find the strength to rise up through the water and eventually climb out and get back on my feet.

All of this insight is great, but it doesn't take away my Match account. In fact, I start joining other sites when I realize there are more options out there: Chemistry.com, eHarmony, Yahoo! Personals, and Nerve.com. I don't mention this to Ethan; I know it's excessive, as is the time I spend creating and revising my profiles. I have five now and each is unique—you might even say, unrecognizable from the others. I don't want people to see that I'm so desperate that I've signed up on every dating site on the Internet, so I use different pictures for each and emphasize different aspects of myself. A little more artsy and edgy here, a little more stable and conservative there. It's all me, I reason, depending on the day. And I've never been short on contradictions: The Buddhist desires to be free of all this attachment. The fertile woman wants to get fucked. The younger parts want to be nurtured. The borderline wants security at any cost.

On Nerve, the raciest of the dating sites, I receive an email from Larry, an older man with a boilerplate ad: likes long walks, the ocean, and movies. He says he's a doctor, and there are pictures of him on a boat, on a horse, and standing next to his Mercedes, which I find really tacky. There's no reason to respond to him except that he writes, as an introduction, "I think your arms are really sexy." This stumps me. I look at my Nerve profile. I only put up one picture, and I'm just sitting at my desk in jeans and a tank top. I've been working out, but not that much. I write back and ask why. He replies, "Your arms—covered with hair—the most beautiful quality a woman can have."

I've never met a hair fetishist, but I'm about to. I tell Alexis about him when we meet at Starbucks for coffee.

"He has a hair fetish?!"

"Maybe that's a good thing. I'm tired of shaving half my body just to feel normal."

"Okay, listen," Alexis says. "Just because he gets off on body hair doesn't mean you should go on a date with him."

"But do you know how rare these men are?"

"Go to Germany!" Alexis throws her napkin at me. "I thought you said you wanted a relationship."

"Well… maybe it could lead to one."

"That's not the way things work."

How is it that, after all of the emotional grief I suffered due to Alexis, now she's giving me relationship advice?

I bring up the subject with Ethan at our next session. I've given this man my phone number now, and half regret it. Ethan tells me I don't have to do anything. He suggests that if it doesn't feel right, I should just put the date off and wait a couple of days. Put off a date with a mysterious man who in his latest email said he'd like to worship my body with his mouth? As I drive away from my session, my cell phone rings and I answer it without thinking. A deep, resonant voice asks for me. It's him—hair fetish man. Before I can figure out what I want or what to say, he asks, as though we've known each other for years, what I prefer: a tongue right on my clit, or being licked up and down along the sides? I almost go off the road.

I tell him that's a bit too private to discuss with him, as though I'm offended. Yet I'm not. A man who likes hair and wants that kind of information definitely has my interest. Maybe it doesn't have to be a long-term thing. Everyone deserves to have every inch of their body worshipped. That's why, two days later, I end up driving an hour south to meet Larry at his house. He says he has a pool and that he'll make us brunch. And he begs me not to shave.

I know this is a hookup. From the time I get into my car all showered and unshaved to when I pull up in front of a large colonial in a suburb I've never visited, it's just lust that's bringing me here—pure desire. The man who answers the door is shirtless and overly tanned, and handsome but reeking of a cologne that immediately causes my eyes to tear up. He extends his hand in greeting, and when I reach out to shake it he pulls me to his chest and tilts my head back to kiss the length of my neck. We step into the foyer and he murmurs, "I've been waiting all day for this." I'd tell him it's only eleven in the morning, but I can't because he's kissing me passionately. Too passionately. I'm reminded of Hari's forcefulness, and once again those conflicting desires rise up. He pulls me toward an open living room, and I barely have time to look around. All of this is happening too fast, and as I realize that, all of the lust that propelled me to this point evaporates. It only takes a second. Now I'm completely dissociated, and completely outside the embrace.

How do I tell him to stop? It would seem so easy; just say something. Yet I can't. He undresses me in the living room. And yes, he is in awe of my hairiness. If only I could say the words "I have to leave." He pulls me up again and leads me upstairs, to a bedroom with mirrors on the ceiling. I am not joking. For the next two hours I watch myself get fucked and worshipped like I'm the star of a porn movie, covered in saliva and lubricant, only I'm upside down and numb. As soon as I understand that I've become choiceless again, it's like an actress takes over. I pretend to like it, and this terrifies me even more. I'm playing along with his passion, even as it feels traumatizing. I still can't tell him to stop, and it's only when he dozes off after his third orgasm that I get up, pull on my clothes, and say, "I have to leave."

"You've got to stop this," Alexis barks when I tell her. "He could have killed you."

"I know, I know."

"Take all of those ads off-line."

"But I don't want to!"

"Take them off before someone chops your body up and throws it in the woods and I have to go looking for it."

Until now, it hadn't occurred to me that I'm playing with fire, especially since I don't know how to say no—even when I really, really, really don't want to have sex.

"You know how fucked up that was, right?"

I do.

I admit the whole thing to Ethan, who listens to the story without any visible reaction. I tell him I want to go into a monastery.

"Do you think that if you go there, you won't have sex with anyone?"

Probably not. I'd probably be trying to seduce the monks. Ethan wants to know which of my parts were involved in this experience with Larry. What prevented me from taking care of myself? I go back over the sequence. At the door's threshold, when he pulled me to him, there was a rift: My younger parts got scared, and my older parts wanted to get laid.

"So you didn't pay attention to what the scared parts were feeling?"

"Worse than that, Ethan. I lost touch with the adult who is capable of saying no to sex. I became the child who lets an adult do anything to her—the part that doesn't have the concept of boundaries and rights."

I start to cry. How can I be so driven by the need for sex and connection and have so little ability to protect myself? I'm the lamb being led to slaughter, but I'm the one leading me. With Taylor, this conflict was somewhat contained. He took care of me, protected me, so that the young parts and adult parts could coexist on some level, even if they got confused in bed.

"Who inside you was in charge when you were at Larry's house?" Ethan asks.

It was the six-year-old. I let a man have sex with my six-year-old. I suddenly realize that she was never taught to say no, and that I have to protect her.

"I'm being a bad Buddhist," I tell Alexis during our weekly Saturday chai at Starbucks. "I can't meditate, I'm chasing after pleasure and avoiding pain, and I can't even get myself over to your Sangha."

"You are *not* being a bad Buddhist, silly. There's no such thing."

"But why can't I practice?"

Alexis finishes her chai in a big swig. "They say that the greater the purification, the greater the obstacle."

"What does that mean?"

"That sometimes you have to go through a lot of shit to get to the diamond. Come with me to the open house this afternoon. At least get some of the energy from the Sangha." The community recently rented half of a large house in the suburbs outside Boston, so they now have an actual meditation center where the Lama lives and gives teachings and people come together to practice.

I feel that same resistance I've always had about going to meditation practices, but with Alexis, even her requests have an inherent command.

Fine. I'll go. But just to the open house. And they'd better not make me meditate.

26

Vajrayana

There are times when impulsivity leads to buying massage chairs, cutting off all your long curly hair, sleeping with strangers, or quitting school. Not having a sense of the consequences has its drawbacks. The flip side is that, if you aren't held in place by boundaries, you can move in ways other people would rarely dare. Sensibility, reason, and planning don't leave much space for intuitive and spontaneous action—like when you walk into a big house filled with Buddhas and Tibetan monks and realize that this is the place you need to be. Especially when this is followed by forking over your next month's rent to a woman you once believed was destroying your life.

I recognize the house instantly because of all the colorful Tibetan prayer flags strung from its trees and awnings like party streamers. On the walkway and porch steps, people sit with plates of food. I still hate crowds, even those full of Buddhists, so I'm surprised at the calm spaciousness I feel once I step inside the house. Much of the first floor is taken up by a large meditation hall and an elaborate shrine room. Between the tall ceilings and hardwood floors, minutely detailed paintings of Buddhas line the walls and exquisite bronze statues sit on pedestals and mantels, surrounded by flowers and offerings. Alexis shouts out to me from behind a buffet table, and as I approach her, I scope out the scene. I don't believe it. There are *no* hot Buddhist men.

"Why are there no cute men here?" I immediately ask Alexis.

"Horrible, isn't it?" She leads me through the other rooms on the first floor: dining room, sun porch, shrine room, pantries. "It's an epidemic. Guys seem to go for martial arts and only wise up when their bodies start failing them."

Currently, three people plus the resident teacher, Lama Sonam, are living at the center, and although Alexis still lives in Lowell, she spends almost every day there.

Alexis pokes me and says, "Hey, there's another room for rent. But you'd never survive."

"Why?"

"Well, for one thing, there's no *sex* in this house." Seriously? Why would anyone live in a house where you can't have sex? On second thought, I can think of a few very good reasons why.

When I ask Alexis to show me the room, she says, "But do you really think you can live in a place without sex? Or meat? Lama Sonam keeps all of the monks' vows. Living here is like being in a monastery— just without, you know, the other stuff."

"Can I have sex and meat outside the house?"

Alexis pats me on the head. "You can do whatever you want outside the center, carnal Kiera. You just have to be a good girl in here."

I think I can handle the no-sex rule. It's a good thing. It will help me make sound decisions and provide some outside structure. We borderlines need that. Yet there's a problem: I start looking more closely at the Buddhist paintings on the walls, and I discover many are of naked couples—having *sex*. I point one out to Alexis and suggest that maybe it's not a good idea to ban sex and then put pornographic posters all over the place.

She swats me on the head. "Those images," she says, "represent the most profound teachings in all of Buddhism." I look more closely. Sex as something profound? Maybe they *can* help me here. "Those aren't ordinary people, Kiera." We stand in front of a large painting of two bodies clasped together, a man sitting cross-legged, and a woman straddling him so they're belly to belly, groin to groin. Both look pretty happy. "Don't think of them as people; they're images of *enlightened qualities*. The male symbolizes compassion and skillful means, and the female symbolizes wisdom and insight. The merging of those qualities represents enlightenment."

She leads me around the shrine room. "You can't be literal here. All of this," she says, sweeping her hand around the room, "*all* of this is symbolic. These images, these statues, and the practices are teaching devices, ways to train your mind to see differently and to cultivate positive qualities." I look around and it's true. Everywhere I look, there are symbols, ritual objects, instruments, and sculptures. And unlike the other places where I've seen Buddhist images, here there are both male and female Buddhas, along with Buddhas with thousands of arms, naked women dancing on piles of skulls, and images that look like demons—red creatures with fire coming out of their heads. But before I can ask more questions, Alexis is dragged off to help prepare more tofu casserole. It's a good thing they don't have pictures of steak tips and chicken wings on the walls. I can only take so much temptation.

Later, Alexis introduces me to the other residents: Marianne, an operating room nurse in her fifties; Sophie, a beautiful artist in her early twenties; and Andrew, a young man who packed up everything he owned in Florida to move up here and help establish this meditation center.

And then there's Lama Sonam, the Tibetan monk and teacher, with his maroon robes and shaved head. When Alexis introduces me, she says, "Kiera wants to move in, and I think she'd be perfect here."

Lama Sonam smiles and takes my hand. "This is a good place to be."

"Actually, it's where she has to be," Alexis says, and I glare at her. I don't want my vices displayed quite just yet.

Lama Sonam nods. Maybe he knows more than he's letting on? I thank him, and he gives me a welcoming hug. Apparently, whether I like it or not, I'm moving in.

Before we leave the open house, I've written the check.

"I may have done either the stupidest thing in my life or the wisest," I say to my mom on the phone that night.

"Oh god, please don't tell me you've shaved your head again."

I find it oddly amusing that my mom thinks of my hair first, among all of my numerous misguided actions, from accidentally burning down my school's old boathouse to getting arrested and put in jail.

"I'm moving to a Buddhist meditation center."

"How wonderful!" she declares. She says she's never liked the idea of me living in that brick box in Waltham all by myself. I agree; it hasn't been much fun there. But she wants to know if I'll have to do "certain things" to live at the center. Are there expectations? I explain about having certain rules when I'm at the center, in keeping with its status as a holy place.

"But you don't have to be a monk, or is it a nun, do you?"

"No, Mom, everyone there is normal." At least, I think they are.

Raymond is more worried about this move and asks, "Are you sure they won't make you take some kind of Kool-Aid?" I don't think so, but the truth is, I don't know. It's all an experiment. I want to be a Buddhist, and this is where I'm landing. It can't be any worse than living alone and man-hunting around the clock.

My father says, "This is the best thing you could ever do."

That surprises me, and I ask him why.

"Because you don't do well alone," he says. "Even I know that. And of all the places to be, a group of Buddhists is probably as good as it gets. At least you won't have to worry so much about the dishes getting done."

I tell everyone I know that I'm going to be "on retreat" indefinitely at the Drikung Meditation Center. This sounds a lot better than saying that my life is completely out of control again and I'm back in the dysregulation zone. Ethan continues to remind me that I'm not, but wherever I am, it's a shaky place. And I have to admit that this makes me wonder how much of my mastery over my BPD symptoms is due to hard work, and how much is because, until relatively recently, I was held securely by Taylor and the DBT groups.

Current research is claiming that up to 88 percent of people with BPD eventually go into remission (Zanarini et al. 2006). But maybe I'm one of the 12 percent who will continue to struggle; maybe I'll spend the rest of my life on the borderline between neurotic and psychotic. No. I can't look at it that way. "Remission" doesn't mean recovery, just that you have less than five of the symptoms on the official DSM list. Nor does it recognize the cyclical and complex nature of our progress. The whole point of moving to the Buddhist center is so I can stop thinking of myself only in terms of a diagnosis, with symptoms, criteria, and percentages. I'm making this move so I can deal with the BPD symptoms on a spiritual level, and as part of a daily practice with other people.

I think it's a good path, yet if it weren't for BPD, I never would have arrived here. And then there's Alexis, the woman I once believed was my nemesis and the catalyst of my destruction. Now she's opened the door to a place perfectly suited for me, one without saviors, but full of Buddhas in the making.

I imagine that moving into a meditation center will be like diving into a spring-fed pool. I'll float in the clear, calm waters of the house, where once a day people gather to sit on cushions and breathe deeply, and to cluster around sacred texts, studying and sharing deep spiritual revelations. I expect it to be a more colorful and homey version of the other Buddhist gathering places I've visited: regulated, formal, and, above all, quiet and peaceful. So I'm not expecting that monks will clang cymbals, bang drums, and perform rituals that transform grape juice into the nectar of wisdom in a cup shaped like a human skull. I'm unprepared for people to appear at odd hours to get blessings from Lama Sonam and make offerings to the Buddhas on certain days of the moon cycle. But I don't complain, as the shrine room is a virtual pantry full of fresh fruit and tasty niblets delivered by the faithful.

It is both humbling and frustrating to discover how little I know about Tibetan Buddhism as a living practice, beyond my occasional reading and the retreat I attended with Rinpoche. So far, all of my training and experience with Buddhism has boiled down to "sit your ass down and breathe" and intellectually grappling with concepts such as impermanence, Buddha-nature, and refuge. The atmosphere and events at the Drikung Meditation Center are entirely beyond my grasp.

Finally, I force myself to sit through my first group practice, and it doesn't involve meditation as I know it. Instead, we chant mantras and prayers in Tibetan and visualize Buddhas dissolving into the crowns of our heads.

"I don't understand," I say to Marianne, on the verge of tears, my head hurting from trying to read the phonetic translations of Tibetan prayers.

"It's *Vajrayana* Buddhism," Marianne tells me. "It takes a while." She smiles and tells me not to worry. "Some things need to be experienced in nonconceptual ways, and this kind of practice will do that."

I turn to Alexis, who is stacking up cushions, for clarification. "Does that mean I don't need to understand what I'm doing? I thought the Buddha said that we should never do anything on blind faith."

"Each tradition has its own focus, and its own practices to bring you to enlightenment," Alexis says. "Ours is part of the Tibetan Kagyu lineage, which emphasizes physical practices like praying, chanting, and visualizations. Other lineages have a different focus, like studying texts or certain kinds of yoga. It's all about what works for you."

I'm torn between resistance and longing. I've already complained to Alexis ad nauseam about how tired I am of just sitting and breathing—that I want more than a mindfulness practice; I want the three jewels—the Buddha, Dharma, and Sangha. I want to get to the root of this antagonism I have toward myself and the world and change it. However, now that I'm in the maw of the Tibetan Buddhism of the Drikung Kagyu lineage, I'm not so sure. My once-clear ideas about how Buddhism relates to my recovery, therapy, and skills grow fuzzy, and I'm trying to keep the threads connected. I know that the cognitive behavior therapy triangle of thoughts, feelings, and behaviors I learned back at MAP had its origins not in psychology but over two thousand five hundred years earlier, when the Buddha taught his first students that "all that we are is the result of what we have thought. The mind is everything. What we think, we become" (Cook 2007, 346). Buddhism describes the causes of suffering as rooted in the "three poisons"—attachment, aversion, and ignorance—and from my years in therapy I've learned that my attachments, self-hatred, and cognitive distortions are among the greatest causes of my distress. The connections and similarities can be made into neat little charts, and I've done that. So why, why do I want to run away from this new type of Buddhism?

Part of the reason obviously involves broken expectations—attachment again, this time to the way I'd come to think of Buddhism. I had a very concrete vision of what would happen when I moved to the center. I wanted a lotus pond, and what I got is a three ring circus of Tibetan Vajrayana Buddhism, where I'm scampering from ring to ring, dodging clowns and trumpet players. People at work keep asking me what living at the center is like: Am I relaxed? Getting my meditation groove on? And I'm asking questions, too: If I complain about it, does that mean I'm still being a "bad Buddhist"? Should I admit that I spend most evenings holed up in my room cruising online dating sites because I'm afraid that if I go downstairs, Alexis will rope me into a practice and I'll be stuck chanting for the next hour?

When I try to explain to Alexis, she says, "Talk to Lama Sonam." But for some reason I have trouble doing this. Here I am, just where I thought I wanted to be: living with a monk raised and trained in a Tibetan monastery. He crossed the Himalayas three times and was imprisoned twice by the Chinese, and he's determined to bring the teachings to people like me. Yet when I stand in the kitchen with him making tea, I'm tongue-tied, probably because I don't want to sound like an idiot.

So I approach Marianne instead. One evening at the kitchen table, I ask, "Can you tell me what the essence of this Vajrayana practice is? I know Buddhism is about being liberated from suffering. But how do the practices here do that? I'm totally lost."

Marianne nods sympathetically. "Really, it's just about transformation."

"How?"

"Well, as humans, we're mired in past karma and have all sorts of obscurations—emotional, mental... We practice in order to transform all of that, and to do the same for all other beings."

Marianne points to a picture of a four-armed Buddha sitting cross-legged, two palms pressed together and the other two holding a lotus and a crystal necklace. "That's Chenrezig, Buddha of Compassion. When we do Chenrezig practice, we visualize every being in the universe as this embodiment of compassion. The mantra we say is the expression of compassion. When we imagine ourselves as Chenrezig, we dissolve all of the emotional afflictions and mental obscurations to become pure enlightened awareness itself." She smiles at me. "It's sort of the fast track to liberation."

One day, I finally get my nerve up to approach Lama Sonam and ask him what advantages this type of Buddhism has over, say, Zen or insight meditation. I describe how confusing it all is and that, while I'm still holding on to Shyalpa Rinpoche's insistence that the view is the most important thing, I'm not finding any clear view at all here.

Lama Sonam sits down at the kitchen table and waits until I've exhausted my thinly veiled complaints.

"In the past," he says, "these techniques weren't as necessary. People's minds were more tamed. It was easier to practice, and easier to accomplish realization. But things are different now. This is an age of decline. All of humanity has slipped down, including spiritual masters. Everyone is so-so."

"So?"

"So you need skillful means, forceful means, for uprooting igno-rance and desire. For transforming aggression. The Vajrayana is pow-erful. Through it, enlightenment is accomplished quickly through the skillful means."

"So the practices here are the answer?"

Lama Sonam furrows his brow. "The answer? What is the question?"

"How I'm supposed to do things."

He looks at me tenderly but possibly with growing concern. His English isn't the best and my confusion is vast.

"You're here," he smiles. "In the community, with others. Surrounded by the Dharma. Learning. How many have this precious opportunity?" He pauses, then says, "The main thing is to be kind."

His eyes flash at me—just for that one sentence. It's like a flashbulb goes off behind his eyes and there's an illuminated moment. Kindness, seemingly such a benign concept, is really a huge step beyond mind-fulness and acceptance. Lama Sonam and I stare at the picture of Chenrezig, embodiment of compassion, and once again I have that same feeling as when I first walked into the Drikung Meditation Center: I might not understand everything, but I am on the right path.

❖

On the second floor of the house, we have a library full of books on Vajrayana Buddhism. All of these, without exception, describe what it is and all of the wild ways it teaches people to achieve an awakened state. And just like DBT and CBT, it comes with a toolbox full of skills and techniques to achieve its purpose. Mindfulness and medi-tation are among the tools, but Vajrayana practice uses more intense techniques—you could even say confrontational. Call it desperate mea-sures for desperate times. Marianne used the word "transforming," and Lama Sonam talked about "uprooting." Whatever words you use, it's a far cry from simple techniques of acceptance and nonjudgment.

As I burrow through the center's books, the intensity of the approach comes out in the language itself: eradicating negative thoughts and cultivating positive ones; purifying negative behaviors and engaging in beneficial ones. This type of practice doesn't mean simply letting emotions come and go, like leaves on a stream or clouds in the sky; it aims to eliminate all disturbing emotions. You don't just let peacefulness come into you; you generate it through specific attitudes of compassion and loving-kindness. You don't just try to be selfless; you visualize offering up your body and everything you possess for the benefit of others. In one practice, you literally breathe in the pain of others and exhale all of your goodness for their needs. This type of Buddhism actually sounds a lot like the DBT skills for change, which are usually described as cognitive behavioral.

Indeed, the whole gist of this approach is aimed at transforming the mind, and I finally start to understand why Marianne, Alexis, and the others sit around visualizing and praying to Chenrezig—not because they think the four-armed Buddha is a god; they're using the image and its enlightened quality as a way to train their own minds in compassion. With Vajrayana, the practice is considered to go so far as to imbue all beings throughout time and space with compassion, in the process transforming the mind from narrow, clinging, and self-obsessed to spacious, generous, and selfless.

This sounds like a noble thing to want, but I continue to wonder: If you take away the self (which, of course, I've been furiously trying to build, given it's so damn unstable), then what can you rely on? What do you have if you don't identify with your thoughts, emotions, or any other aspects of yourself? Buddhism says that everything tangible and concrete is ultimately empty because it's impermanent. So what is enduring? I can hear Shyalpa Rinpoche's voice clearly: Buddha-nature. It's impossible to destroy Buddha-nature because it has never been born. It's simply what we are: primordial purity, innate intelligence, the awakened mind—that diamond under the dirt. Learning all of this rouses me a bit, and I start to at least think about going downstairs to practice. Right now, in my room, I can hear the Buddhists chanting and their bells ringing, followed by silence as the world is transformed into battalions of light and kindness. It makes a great counterpoint to the click of my mouse as I scan the profiles on my newest online dating find, Fling.com: "the hottest place to hook up."

27

The Meat Man

By now, you surely know that it's only a matter of time before I get into trouble. Just because I can't have sex in the house doesn't mean I'm going to give up men. The desire realm (as conceptualized in Buddhism) has its hold on me, and it's going to take more than a few mantras and a zap from Lama Sonam for me to break free. And if I simply moved in here and changed everything, perhaps I wouldn't be practicing genuine Vajrayana. In this tradition, everything is fodder for transformation. If someone throws a brick at you, it's an opportunity to practice compassion—to realize that the other person is generating bad karma and therefore doing more harm to himself or herself than to you, or so the reasoning goes. And besides, the only way to reach enlightenment is to purify your own karma and cultivate positive qualities. So that brick hits a lot of targets at once. The trick is to be able to use every situation with that kind of skillful means.

So when I meet Matthew that summer, after living at the center for a couple of months, it simply brings to the surface the passion play of the dualism and conflict happening within myself. People gather for meditation practice, and where is Kiera? About to sneak out with her motorcycle helmet and her high heels in a bag to meet a man who not only drinks and smokes pot on a daily basis but is a diehard atheist. He's also a computer programmer, amateur pilot, and motorcyclist, and he plays guitar in a band. Okay, so it's a country-western band, but I'm not too choosy at the moment. Given that he's also the father of two young boys and one court battle shy of divorce after twenty years of marriage, you could even say he's virgin territory for me. Altogether, he pushes a ton of my buttons: bad boy, father, adventurer. How can I not go out with him?

As I'm trying to sneak out for our first date, Alexis suddenly appears in the doorway and says, "Don't do it." I pretend I don't know what she's talking about even as Matthew is revving his motorcycle under the prayer flags.

"It's just a date," I insist.

"Yeah, right, and when has it ever been 'just a date'?"

As I make a break for it and pull my helmet on, Alexis steps outside, followed by Lama Sonam. Reluctantly, I turn and introduce them. Alexis eyeballs me with that "you're an idiot but I love you" look that I'm growing so fond of, then turns to Matthew and says, "Bring her home safe."

Once we're over at Matthew's place, he asks, "What are they, your parents?" I tell him that I need a lot of nurturing. "You don't think it's kind of weird that you live in a house where people have to check out your dates—not to mention the whole religion vibe? Doesn't it spook you to be around all those statues?" He shudders. "It reminds me of the Catholic Church, but worse... It's like a cult."

"For your information, there is no God in Buddhism. And there's also no form of punishment, only karma. No one's forcing anyone to believe anything. The Buddha is just a guy who figured out how to be free from all the crap we suffer from every day."

Matthew shrugs and goes to his fridge. "Can you stop your self-denial for a short while and have some good food?" I have no problem with that. Nor with the way his hands come to rest on my hips after we hug each other, or how he kisses.

"Please tell me you didn't sleep with him," Alexis cries when she sees me.

"I didn't...yet."

"You know what's going to happen, right? If you sleep with him? If you make yourself vulnerable?"

I nod. I've told Alexis everything about BPD. I even explained my different parts, which means she now cares about them.

"It's your six-year-old, isn't it? She wants to be taken care of and he's this newly divorced daddy." I nod again.

"Let the Dharma take care of you, Kiera! Let the community here meet your needs. He's not going to do anything positive for you."

I know, I know. But it's like telling an alcoholic not to take a drink just as the bottle is opened. Alexis shakes her head. "Let me know when it's over," she says, "and I'll help you put yourself back together."

I wish I could say that the same things aren't happening again. But they are. Once Matthew and I have sex, within a week I'm spending half of my nights there. As much as he needs someone to replace his recently departed wife and two boys, I need someone to contain and regulate me, and I don't seem to be able to let the Sangha do it. For one, the Sangha doesn't offer regular morning sex. And no one from the Sangha emails me at work to ask what I'd like for dinner: glazed duck, slow-cooked ribs, pan-seared scallops, asparagus, gnocchi? When I show up at Matthew's, he'll be downstairs, wearing an apron, laying out a cheese board with unusual chèvres and bries, and arranging grapes in a bowl. After dinner, he turns on the TV and puts one arm around me, the other hand wrapped around a beer. We go through the same rituals every day: each night brushing our teeth and flossing as we stand side-by-side at the double sinks in the bathroom, and fucking in the morning. He's baffled that he can't bring me to orgasm the way he could with his wife, and I do the usual "it's the medication" thing, though I know at this point it's much deeper than that. I briefly consider enlisting him in trying to figure out alternative methods, but Matthew isn't a fixer. He shrugs and says okay, and from then on my pleasure is in my own hands, so to speak. Afterward we shower together, soaping each other's backs. He makes me eggs any way I request and hands me a travel mug of coffee for the drive to work.

In no time I am completely miserable, but I'm so tightly tucked into this arrangement that I can't find my legs to walk out. I'm miserable because Matthew and I are like oil and water. He's the anti-Kiera, or maybe I'm the anti-Matthew. He doesn't talk about feelings, he hates religion, and he has no interest in mental illness or anything I've survived. When I start a conversation about politics, he gets an amused look, like "Aw, isn't she cute? She's trying to be smart." And then he ends the conversation with some definitive statement that I can't rebut. Plus, there's the unfortunate fact that he's in a country-western band. But none of that matters when I'm in his arms—or when he's feeding me pan-seared scallops.

The most surreal aspect is how I'm vacillating between two worlds, bouncing back and forth between two lives, two perspectives, two identities. The Buddhists say that we're all trapped in dualism, and that seems especially applicable to me, here, now. There is the world according to Matthew, and the world according to Buddhism, and I have one of my feet in each. In Matthew's world, things have no meaning other than what you give them, or they happen randomly and often unfairly, and actions have no consequences as long as you cover your tracks. Quality of life is measured by how high you can get and for how long, whether on music, wine, good food, or pot. In his world, nothing trumps a good lamb stew and back-to-back episodes of *South Park*.

Meanwhile, in the world according to Buddhism, there is absolutely no randomness or unfairness; everything exists because of cause and effect—the law of karma. Buddhism says there *is* a true reality, and that we just can't see it because it's obscured by our own ignorance and negative emotions. The success of a life is determined by the positive inner qualities you cultivate and the amount of merit you generate through generosity and selflessness.

And the world according to Kiera? It entirely depends on where I sleep at night, and this flip-flopping of perspectives exhausts me. I want to solidify my position, yet neither situation holds me securely. In fact, it feels like each drives me toward its opposite. Matthew's nurturing style is sporadic and interspersed with wildly insensitive comments and outright dismissiveness, which upsets me enough that sometimes I drive home in tears. Then, when I'm settled back into the inwardly focused and ascetic world of the Sangha, I feel itchy and trapped in a different way. I want more stimulation, physical touch, and a motorcycle or a man between my legs.

If I were looking at my relationship with Matthew from the perspective of my "disorder," I'd probably still be thinking in terms of relapse or being symptomatic, and I'd be inclined to believe that I'm not making progress on my core problems. But from the Vajrayana perspective, my behavior doesn't create such a gloomy picture. Not that it's pretty, but that's what's so powerful about the practice: recognizing how even poison is a form of medicine when used the right way. I realize that perhaps Ethan has always been taking this approach with me.

When I tell Ethan about this latest affair, he wants to know what's happening with my parts. We establish that the young parts appreciate Matthew. He cuddles them, feeds them, and gets them up in the morning. The older parts enjoy his male attention, being touched and fucked. But other parts are unhappy. Kiera the Buddhist wants him to stop bashing her worldview. Kiera the intellectual would like to have some deep conversation. Kiera the ManRay chick would give anything to ditch the country music and wear a corset. And more than anything, I want to be loved—not just plugged into someone else's self-serving needs (which, of course, is exactly what I'm doing to Matthew as well). I want too many conflicting things, and this time there's no synthesis to the dialectic, only more polarization: I want freedom from desire. I want sex. I want to do no harm. I want a big fat steak.

This goes on for another month, and whenever I come home from work to pick up my overnight bag, Alexis has just one thing to say: "Dump the jerk."

One of the benefits of being part of a Buddhist lineage is that you have the opportunity to work with many teachers. The Drikung lineage has monasteries in Nepal, India, and Tibet, and many of the Lamas and Rinpoches periodically travel to the United States to visit and teach, which is what Ontul Rinpoche will be doing at our center toward the end of summer. I had planned on blowing off the teachings by Ontul Rinpoche, a visiting Buddhist master, until I heard they would focus on *bodhicitta* (literally "awakening mind" or "altruistic mind"), a practice of compassion that seeks to attain liberation in order to benefit all beings and free them from their suffering. The specific practice Ontul Rinpoche leads us through, called *tonglen*, involves exchanging yourself for others on a mental level. You willingly give your happiness to others and take the suffering and hardships of all others onto yourself. This sounds awfully masochistic at face value, and it also means you have to believe that there is enough goodness inside you to be helpful to others.

While he leads us through an exercise where we imagine breathing in darkness and exhaling light, I'm struck by the poverty of my inner resources. I'm still trying to suck in all the love and light I can get from others—preferably from someone with a penis. By the time

Ontul Rinpoche has us inhaling the black vapors of the world's pain and exhaling the white light of happiness, sending it out to others, I finally get it. Tonglen, bodhicitta, transforming the mind—all boil down to one critical factor for me: I'm not able to tap into compassion for others because I lack it for myself. This is my core problem right now. I'm not a codependent woman who loves too much, or a recovering alcoholic borderline, or a fuck-up. I'm a woman who cannot abide herself. Here I am, living at one of the most special places in the world, with the opportunity to get support and guidance on every level, and I'm sleeping with a man who has just started calling me his "fat, stinky girlfriend."

I request an interview with Ontul Rinpoche, and when I sit down with him the next day, I ask how I'm supposed to exchange myself for others and have compassion when I don't have this for myself.

He stares at me for a long time before answering: "Despite our goal of becoming selfless, self-love is essential. And it's critical in the beginning. Self-love is you extending compassion to yourself as you would do for any other sentient beings. Bodhicitta is inexhaustible. It flows wherever it is needed. If you hate yourself, you are cutting off the root of bodhicitta."

He asks if I understand the concept of karma and what happens when I harm others.

I nod. I've studied this as a Buddhist, and DBT and CBT have reinforced this basic law of the universe: that every cause generates an effect, and harmful actions, even if they temporarily provide relief, always result in more pain.

"So if you harm yourself, if you hate yourself, it's the same as doing it to another. Self and other are the same; the karma is the same."

Late afternoon light begins to flood the room as I try to process all of this. Then it strikes me. "Rinpoche, is killing yourself the same as murdering someone else?"

He doesn't pause to think. "Yes."

"Even if it's your choice?"

He shakes his head. "If you understand that killing in any form results in great suffering, why would you choose to kill yourself? It's like scratching an itch with a sword. Karmically speaking, there is no relief after death for those who kill, even those who kill themselves. They have to experience the consequences, as with every action, beneficial or harmful."

I show him my arms and say, "This is what I used to do to myself. I don't do it anymore, but I find other ways to hurt myself. I don't know how to get to bodhicitta. I've taken refuge. I try to do Chenrezig practice. I'm practicing transforming my mind by viewing people who harm me as my teachers. It's that source of goodness and purity I can't get to. Even though I'm living here, I still can't find it."

Ontul Rinpoche leans toward me. "But you have. It's always here. You're learning now."

I'm about to ask him how to do that, and then I catch myself. It's what he's been teaching for the past two days, what all of this path is about.

That night I don't go to Matthew's. I hole up in my room. Below me, rambunctious Buddhists sit in the kitchen, drinking chai and eating cookies. The Tibetan Lamas are on the floor above, doing whatever they do after a long day of teaching and trying to advise confused people like me—probably watching reality TV and laughing their asses off. I lie on my rug and breathe, and try to allow the intensity of the day to settle. I feel a little off-kilter, but realize that it's more like a shift—more like a realization or the revision of a problematic belief I've harbored despite all of my recovery. In the back of my mind, somewhere to the left of where the little dark one hides, is the firefighter of last resort. She's got a full bottle of pills hiding in her sock drawer, a package of razor blades in the bathroom, and a suicide plan up her sleeve, like a secret agent carrying a cyanide capsule in case the enemy captures her. I've still been holding on to killing myself as a legitimate option. And while it's unthinkable that I would pour a bottle of pills down someone else's throat or slice another person's flesh with a razor blade, the relationship I have with myself allows this option to exist for me. In some ways, coming to terms with myself and working toward recovery has been like saying "I love you" to someone but keeping a loaded gun hidden in your back pocket, just in case that person pisses you off enough.

The concept of karma has seemed so secondary to things like compassion and wisdom that I've paid little attention to it. But now that I do, I realize that, for someone who has been operating most of her life under the blindness of overwhelming emotions and impulses, it's like being given a new set of eyes. When I first moved to the center, Lama Sonam gave me a little folded card with a picture of the Buddha. On one flap it reads:

Do not commit any harmful action.
Perfectly engage in virtue.
Completely subdue your mind.
This is the teaching of the Buddha.

On the other flap is the refuge prayer, which he suggested I recite every day, morning and night. I haven't exactly adhered to that schedule, but now I decide I will. So even though I live in a house filled with precious Tibetan manuscripts, paintings of enlightened beings, and consecrated statues, I sit down with my little card. I feel like a preschooler staring at the alphabet as I recite the prayer:

In the Buddha, the Dharma, and Sangha most excellent,
I take refuge until enlightenment is reached.
By the merit of generosity and other good deeds,
may I attain Buddhahood for the sake of all sentient beings.

Then I hunker down in my bedroom and resist the urge to drive to Matthew's. I decide to take another step, and join other members of my Sangha at the kitchen table. I explain what's going on and say that it's like being in the movie *The Matrix*: I've decided to take the red pill, the one that strips you of illusion, so you can never go back to the bliss of ignorance.

My housemate Sophie asks, "Have you ever found that your ignorance was blissful?"

28

Mirror of True Nature

As fall arrives, the Drikung Meditation Center is showered in bright maple leaves. Prayer flags flap in the wind. Besides my work at the office, I have nothing to do but be a Buddhist. I've quit all of my advocacy work, and Matthew dumped me as soon as his divorce was finalized. And even though that's what I'd wanted for quite some time, I still spent two weeks crying nonstop. The devastation is the same as always, despite my awareness that this was both necessary and inevitable. I feel both bereft and liberated, lost and found—and this time it isn't all about a guy. It's been almost six years since I discovered I have BPD. A lot has happened, not only to me, but to the diagnosis itself. New technology has shown that BPD has biological underpinnings, and more research is revealing hereditary components (Lis et al. 2007). Treatments other than DBT are being developed. I'm interested in all of this, but not the way I used to be. My concern is no longer what BPD is or whether I have it. My focus, and where I'm headed, is answering the question of how we finally transcend the illness and yet keep traveling along with our borderline nature—our intense, wildly loving, painfully clinging, impulsive selves. How do we internalize an image like the compassion of Chenrezig rather than grasping for some other person to fulfill us? How does the example of an awakened being take hold enough to inspire and motivate us toward new levels of mindfulness, where we can actually see reality and not be blindly caught up in those three poisons of attachment, aversion, and ignorance?

Right now Buddhism is my answer. The more I immerse myself in it, the more it normalizes every aspect of my suffering and connects me to others. It's slowly teaching me to work with the craziness in my head, no matter what side of the borderline I'm on. When I say Buddhism is teaching me, I mean more than intellectually. I'm surrounded by people who have lived and practiced the Dharma for years. The practices themselves are alive, not just a collection of images or rituals or books. Within this world, BPD isn't an aberration; it's simply a name for an experience I and many others have, where we live at the farthest end of the continuum of pain. The borderline symptoms are the core element of what Buddhism describes as *dukkha* (suffering): endless grasping, all-consuming intolerance, and complete ignorance of how our actions keep us trapped in this endless cycle.

Buddhism holds that all beings are deluded, that we all want happiness but don't know how to create the right conditions for it. So what are the conditions? For me, it's being here, at the center. Some people might not need this total immersion, but I do. A lot of people aren't able to get all of this in one place and will have to build up their village person by person, here and there. Some people might view my immersion at the center, indeed my growing identity as a Buddhist, as another borderline trait: shaping myself to the circumstances that I hope will redeem me. That's understandable, but ultimately ironic, as I'm taking refuge in a practice that has no saviors. I'm adopting the identity of a Buddhist with the goal of dissolving my attachments to a solid self. Some might see my life today as a failure to reach true independence as it's defined in our culture. But this is what I need, and more. I'm like a baby; I have to go through the mirroring stage again so that others can reflect back at me the innate nature I have but never knew existed. You can do a lot of other things—say prayers of aspiration, read books, be mindful of all that happens, do deep breathing exercises, clear your chakras, feed the hungry, receive teachings—and yet all the effort in the world to generate an awakened mind is futile without that mirror: the person who can see the Buddha within you. For a long time, I thought that the eyes of a lover were what could reflect that back at me, so I clung to my lovers with my life hanging on their every word and perception. I have these mirrors all around me now, and they embody a different form of love entirely. The difficulty is in keeping my eyes open and allowing this new vision to take hold.

For the rest of fall and winter and into spring, I cocoon at the center. I'm a bodhicitta seedling that's in need of serious water and light. I plant myself in the midst of my Sangha and whine a lot. Lama Sonam and I take walks around the pond, and I tell him how much I crave a lover and how difficult it is to be with myself.

"Of the three poisons that obstruct the mind's clarity," he says, "attachment is the most difficult of the afflictions. You have to be constantly vigilant, or it will take over your mind."

"Will I ever be able to love someone without attachment? And also have sex?"

He smiles. "One thing at a time. First, practice. Then, see what happens."

Alexis is more practical. "I'm not going to let any man near you," she says. And she means it. I have to sneak out of the house and lurk around Starbucks just to catch sight of FILFs (fathers I'd like to fuck). Every time I want physical love or touch, I go down to the shrine room to do prostrations and recite refuge prayers, taking refuge in the Buddha, the Dharma, and the Sangha. Or I find Alexis and climb into her lap. She's like a reset button, a touchstone. She won't sleep with me, but she promises that if she were bisexual, I'd be at the top of her list.

I still find it impossible to sit through an entire meditation practice, and sometimes I avoid going for weeks. At first I'm afraid I might be kicked out for not doing the practices, so I hide in my room. Sometimes there's a timid knock on the door, and it will be Marianne or Sophie, with a cup of tea, coming to check in on me when I've been hiding for too long. I understand that my absence and the guilt around it are my own, yet I still find myself projecting it onto the others. For a while, I think they don't consider me a real Buddhist. But what is a real Buddhist? I don't know if even the Buddha could answer that question.

I do know that as the winter progresses, a shift in my understanding occurs, the same way it did in DBT. After being exposed to so many confusing words and ideas and practices, a foundation of understanding appears. And while putting myself in this hotbed of compassion doesn't immediately dissolve my anger, self-hatred, and self-absorption, it does shape me and orient me toward a new way of seeing things. I'm getting the mind training I so badly wanted, and I have to admit that it's vaguely annoying, like when Marianne puts signs in the kitchen that read, "Please do not cook or bring meat into this house. We do not eat our sentient mother beings." Sometimes it feels like I'm basically being brainwashed into thinking of others every time I do something for myself. When bugs come into the house, we form a rescue brigade and take them back out. But it works both ways, and when I arrive home in pain, crying, and in need of care, I don't have to hide or pretend. In fact, needing compassion from others gives them the opportunity to share it. It's win-win, except when it comes to sharing the last pint of Ben & Jerry's ice cream. In the realm of desserts, the afflictions are deeply rooted.

In early spring, ten gigantic wooden crates arrive from Nepal. Together they hold a statue Lama Sonam commissioned for the center. When put together, the ten-foot-high statue of a golden Buddha shines with jeweled ornaments, brocade, and silk. It's a replica of the most famous statue in Tibet, the Jowo Rinpoche, kept in Lhasa. For Tibetans, just seeing the statue brings them one step closer to enlightenment. Some make pilgrimages to the Jowo over hundreds of miles, doing a prostration every step of the way, each prostration affirming the three jewels: the reality of Buddha's accomplishment, the truth of his teachings, and the community of those who practice.

Lama Sonam made two journeys across the Himalayas just to get out of Tibet, and both times he was caught, put into prison, and beaten. Yet this has never stopped him from practicing and teaching us a core tenet of Buddhism—that no matter how much suffering you endure, it ultimately can be transformed into a greater good. So when I sit in front of the statue, I think about how many footsteps it took for him to arrive here—and Alexis, and myself. I think of that endurance and how the transformation of suffering is never over. For me, it's no longer a question of arriving, or of having to escape. These days, when people ask if I've recovered from BPD, I don't say yes. Despite my current sense that the symptoms have shifted back over the border into the normal range of human suffering, I am aware of the potential for its reemergence—not as a pathology that needs to be cured, but a set of problems that make my life feel unbearable. And yet without a name for it, I never would have been able to learn how to transcend it. Indeed, without BPD, I wouldn't have had the same opportunity to awaken.

So while it's undeniable that BPD destroys people, it can also open us to an entirely new way of relating to ourselves and the world—both for those of us who have it, and for those who know us. Look at my mother, whose capacity for being present to pain grows daily as we are finally able to share it with each other, and my father, who listens to me now with the attention of a doting parent and offers insights because he is capable of understanding me beyond his own definitions. BPD has been our teacher. Maybe not in the prescribed ways of family therapy or self-help books, but the journey itself and the bonds between us have accomplished the seemingly impossible: We are there for each other.

Am I recovered? I no longer struggle with the urge to hurt or kill myself, but other symptoms persist: my impulsivity, my sensitivity, my shifting moods, and my inherent fragility when I'm under stress or begin to feel connected to someone. I still have difficulty being alone, a deep need for security, and a gnawing dissatisfaction with what is. Is recovery the absence of symptoms, the eradication of pain? If so, then I'm not in recovery. Then again, those things that are often touted as "real" signs of progress—like having a solid sense of self or being independent—can actually be seen as illusions. As I and the other women established back at Project Transition with Dr. Crabtree, we need a different way of formulating our emergence and integration. We have to create communities and a language that can accommodate the borderline nature and experience. That is a task many of us are just now beginning.

Tonight, as people show up for the Wednesday evening meditation practice, I don't look anything like an enlightened being. I've taken a mental health day from work and have been sleeping most of the day. I come downstairs after a shower, wearing a green mud mask, totally forgetting that the center is in use and accidentally disrupting a practice. I forage the fridge for food and wish I could cook up a nice big steak. Then I check out the men who are meditating. Hmm… The windows are partially open and there's the scent of warm dirt conspiring with the flower bulbs to raise petals into the air. Soon I'll probably be rising up again too, testing the air, uncurling, and sensing.

I know my six-year-old has more to say. And Kiki is still with me, putting on costumes and changing her accents. I decide that from now on I'll give her many masks to play with and more exciting roles to explore, and that I'll never call her a fake. This part of me, so capable of shifting and remaking herself, is a precious tool of the Vajrayana, as is this body, the vehicle carrying an energy I barely know how to direct.

There are many uncertainties regarding BPD recovery, but by now I'm quite sure that I'll never look for another savior to deliver me to myself. If any training of my mind has taken hold, it's to turn toward the teachings and the relationships that keep me on the path.

Ironically, the word "borderline" has become the most perfect expression of my experience—the experience of being in two places at once: disordered and perfect. The Buddha and the borderline are not separate—without one, the other could not emerge. How I approach these opposing forces continues to be the key, together with help and support from people in my life: Ethan, sitting across from me and channeling Socrates; Alexis, who tells me one evening that she's having a borderline moment, and could I please reassure her that I love her; the Drikung Sangha; the coworkers in my office, where I'm now known as the office goddess who lives in an ashram.

The path to discovering Buddha-nature is found within suffering and our relationship to it, not by escaping it. And BPD has become my teacher. I no longer want to deny it or disassociate myself from it. Neither do I identify myself with it. My work now is to allow the bright seed within me to crack its sheath and grow, no longer ashamed and hiding. Turning toward you, Buddhas-to-be, I will try to mirror your true nature and share your pain.

Acknowledgments

This book could never have been written without the incredible dedication, kindness, and generosity of so many people. My deepest thanks to my editors Catharine Sutker, Heather Mitchener, and Jess Beebe, and all those at New Harbinger who believed in the vision of this book and brought it to fruition, and to Jasmine Star, copyeditor extraordinaire, for the clarity and grace she gave my writing despite my howls of protest, and for her dedication and gentle hand along the way.

I am also grateful for the friendship, encouragement, and collaboration of so many extraordinary clinicians, in particular Dr. Blaise Aguirre, Dr. Seth Axelrod, Dr. Loren Crabtree, and Dr. Roy Krawitz. Thanks as well to the New England Personality Disorder Association (NEPDA), the National Education Alliance for Borderline Personality Disorder (NEABPD), the NAMI Greater Boston Consumer Advocacy Network (NAMI GB CAN), and the Transformation Center (and especially Howard Trachtman and Moe Armstrong), for all your support and guidance.

To Dr. Matthew Leeds and Dr. Martha Sweezy, thank you for teaching me the DBT skills and IFS techniques and providing me and countless others with the tools to rebuild our lives, and to Dr. Marsha Linehan, the founder of DBT, my deepest appreciation and admiration for all that you've done in bringing compassion and skillful means to the BPD diagnosis.

To Richard Tabors, Gail Hickey, and the TCA gang, thank you for raising me from a fledgling receptionist into an office goddess, and for formalizing my position as artist-in-residence by providing me with the perfect "office suite with a view" for writing the first half of this book. To the GMA team, who allowed me to be the only reception-ist in Boston with a corner office, and who did everything possible to keep me on the path to completion, from disabling my online dating accounts, to sending me cards when I ran off to "write on retreat," to filling the copy machine paper while I was too busy revising a paragraph for three hours. I could not have asked for more supportive coworkers and employers. Now that this book is done, I promise I'll make more smoothies.

To Will Turano and the Turano family, thank you for your uncon-ditional love. To Colleen Favier, who still checks the *New Yorker* looking for my poems, for your unwavering faith in my talent, and to Jan Waldron, my writing teacher and inspiration, for teaching me that a memoir's power is equal to its honesty.

Thanks to my friends who arrived at the exact perfect moments: Charlene, Lana, and Lola Dickson, with your homemade chai and puppy love; Peter Munoz-Bennet, whose check-ins and car rides kept me on track; and Chris Martiniano, for seeing me through the longest nights with song, poetry, and pixilated presents. And to the Starbucks crew at the Kendall Marriott—Barbara, Cisco, Dragana, Marta, and Sandra—thank you for giving me life and smiles each morning."

To my dear readers Shannon Lemay-Finn and Zach Larson, my gratitude for lending your talents as writers and editors to this book from beginning to end, and especially to Rosanna Alfaro, who has cheered me on since I was a wee girl at Groton and declared even then that this day would come. To Scott Edelstein, my agent, guide, and reality-checker; without your help I'd surely be sitting in a corner, clutching a handful of papers and babbling to myself. And to Randi Kreger, who reached out, flung open the doors to this book, and advised, cajoled, and comforted me along the way: your support has been invaluable.

To Diane and Jim Hall, thank you for your tireless work and for championing all who suffer from BPD. To Dr. Dixieanne Penney, mentor, friend, and colleague, you have been at my side throughout, even keeping the phone under your pillow, just in case. I am so grate-ful for my courageous BPD sisters on the front line: A.J. Mahari, Lisa Dietz, Amanda Wang, and Tami Green. It's been through your friend-ship and example that I've learned to value my own voice and not fear the risk of this exposure. And to Amanda Smith, founder and execu-tive director of the Florida Borderline Personality Disorder Association, you have been my touchstone and companion every step of the way with this book, bringing me back from the edge sometimes on a daily basis. Without your brilliant mind and unwavering love, this book and I would not have survived.

To Shyalpa Rinpoche and the Nyingma Longchen Nyinthig Lineage and to Lama Konchok Sonam Rinpoche, Khenpho Choephel Rinpoche, and the Drikung Kagyu Lineage, my endless gratitude for opening me to the true nature of my mind, and to the Drikung Meditation Center and all those in my Sangha, especially Mary Burke, Tia Harrison, Barbara Creamer, and Dotty Spoor, you have given me a community and a home, and have cradled me in your wisdom and compassion. My deepest thanks to my family, who instilled in me the supreme value of kindness, for your love, care, and courage to grow with me. And to Alexis Tsapatsaris, President of the Drikung Meditation Center, nemesis, Bodhisattva, and heart sister, your talent for opening up a can of whoop ass is only exceeded by your immense compassion.

To Raymond Hartman and Renee Rushnawitz, your generosity and love have provided the means to making this book, and my own recovery, a reality. Even in my dreams, you wait for me with outstretched arms. And finally, to Dr. Saul Rosenthal (who will never take credit for anything but has been with me through this entire journey), I can only repay you by living what you have taught me.

Completed on Losar, Year of the Iron Tiger, 2137. May this book benefit all beings!

Resources

Advocacy and Education Organizations

Behavioral Tech
(dialectical behavior therapy training, referrals, and resources)
2133 Third Ave., Suite 205, Seattle, WA 98121
www.behavioraltech.com; email: information@behavioraltech.org
206-675-8588

National Alliance on Mental Illness (NAMI)
3803 N. Fairfax Dr., Suite 100, Arlington, VA 22203
www.nami.org; email: info@nami.org
Helpline: 1-800-950-6264

**National Education Alliance for Borderline Personality Disorder
(NEABPD)**
P.O. Box 974, Rye, NY 10580
www.borderlinepersonalitydisorder.com; email: neabpd@aol.com
914-835-9011

For a comprehensive list of BPD organizations and resources, go to:
www.BuddhaAndTheBorderline.com

Books on Borderline Personality Disorder

Aguirre, B. 2007. *Borderline Personality Disorder in Adolescents: A Complete Guide to Understanding and Coping When Your Adolescent Has BPD.* Beverly, MA: Fair Winds Press.

Chapman, A. L., and K. L. Gratz. 2007. *The Borderline Personality Disorder Survival Guide: Everything You Need to Know About Living with BPD.* Oakland, CA: New Harbinger.

Friedel, R. O. 2004. *Borderline Personality Disorder Demystified: An Essential Guide for Understanding and Living with BPD.* New York: Marlowe & Company.

Krawitz, R., and W. Jackson. 2008. *Borderline Personality Disorder: The Facts.* Oxford, UK: Oxford University Press.

Kreger, R. 2009. *The Essential Family Guide to Borderline Personality Disorder: New Tools and Techniques to Stop Walking on Eggshells.* Center City, MN: Hazelden.

Porr, V. 2010. *Overcoming Borderline Personality Disorder: A Family Guide for Healing and Change.* Oxford, UK: Oxford University Press.

Books on Dialectical Behavior Therapy

Linehan, M. M. 1993. *Cognitive-Behavioral Treatment of Borderline Personality Disorder.* New York: Guilford.

Linehan, M. M. 1993. *Skills Training Manual for Treating Borderline Personality Disorder.* New York: Guilford.

McKay, M., J. C. Wood, and J. Brantley. 2007. *The Dialectical Behavior Therapy Skills Workbook: Practical DBT Exercises for Learning Mindfulness, Interpersonal Effectiveness, Emotion Regulation, and Distress Tolerance.* Oakland, CA: New Harbinger.

Spradlin, S. E. 2003. *Don't Let Your Emotions Run Your Life: How Dialectical Behavior Therapy Can Put You in Control.* Oakland, CA: New Harbinger.

BPD Memoirs

Cox, V., and L. Robinson (eds.). 2005. *Voices Beyond the Border: Living with Borderline Personality Disorder.* Brentwood, UK: Chipmunkapublishing.

Johnson, M. L. 2010. *Girl in Need of a Tourniquet: Memoir of a Borderline Personality.* Berkeley, CA: Seal Press.

Reiland, R. 2004. *Get Me Out of Here: My Recovery from Borderline Personality Disorder.* Center City, MN: Hazelden.

Walker, A. 2003. *Siren's Dance: My Marriage to a Borderline.* Emmaus, PA: Rodale Books.

Books on Mindfulness and Buddhism

Dzongsar Jamyang Khyentse Rinpoche. 2007. *What Makes You Not a Buddhist.* Boston: Shambhala Publications.

Kabat-Zinn, J. 2005. *Wherever You Go, There You Are: Mindfulness Meditation in Everyday Life.* New York: Hyperion.

Khenchen Konchok Gyaltsen Rinpoche, 2010. *A Complete Guide to the Buddhist Path.* Ithaca, New York: Snow Lion Publications.

Pema Chödrön. 1991. *The Wisdom of No Escape and the Path of Loving-Kindness.* Boston: Shambhala Publications.

Thich Nhat Hanh. 1999. *The Miracle of Mindfulness.* Boston: Beacon Press.

Yongey Mingyur Rinpoche. 2007. *The Joy of Living: Unlocking the Secret and Science of Happiness.* New York: Three Rivers Press.

Multimedia

Back from the Edge: Living with and Recovering from Borderline Personality Disorder. 2005. Produced by Lichtenstein Creative Media (www .lcmedia.com) and the Borderline Personality Disorder Resource Center (www.bpdresourcecenter.org).

> To view: www.LCMedia.com/BPD ·
> To order DVD: www.bpdresourcecenter.org

RethinkBPD: A Documentary on Borderline Personality Disorder. Release date 2012. Produced by Amanda Wang and Jesse Sweet. For more information: www.rethinkbpd.com.

Living with Borderline Personality Disorder: A Guide for Families. 2010. Produced by Dawkins Productions, Inc. To order: www.dawkins.tv.

From Chaos to Freedom: DBT Crisis Survival Skills. 2008. Produced by Behavioral Tech, LLC featuring Dr. Marsha Linehan.

> To order: http://behavioraltech.org/products

References

American Psychiatric Association. 2000. *Diagnostic and Statistical Manual of Mental Disorders.* 4th ed., text revision. Washington, DC: American Psychiatric Association.

Bateman, A, and P. Fonagy. 2004. *Psychotherapy for Borderline Personality Disorder: Mentalization-Based Treatment.* Oxford, UK: Oxford University Press.

Beck, A., D. D. Freeman, D. Davis, and associates. 2004. *Cognitive Therapy of Personality Disorders,* 2nd edition. New York: Guilford Press.

Cook, J. (compiler). 2007. *The Book of Positive Quotations,* 2nd edition. Minneapolis, MN: Fairview Press.

Knowlton, L. 1999. Marsha Linehan: Dialectical behavioral therapy. *Psychiatric Times* 16(7). Available online at www.psychiatrictimes .com/display/article/10168/49651. Accessed February 5, 2008.

Linehan, M. M. 1993a. *Cognitive-Behavioral Treatment of Borderline Personality Disorder.* New York: Guilford Press.

Linehan, M. M. 1993b. *Skills Training Manual for Treating Borderline Personality Disorder.* New York: Guilford Press.

Linehan, M. M., H. E. Armstrong, A. Suarez, D. Allmon, and H. L. Heard. 1991. Cognitive-behavioral treatment of chronically suicidal borderline patients. *Archives of General Psychiatry,* 48(12):1060-1064.

Linehan, M. M., H. Schmidt, L. A. Dimeff, J. W. Kanter, J. C. Craft, K. A. Comtois, and K. L. Recknor. 1999. Dialectical behavior therapy for patients with borderline personality disorder and drug-dependence. *American Journal on Addiction*, 8(4):279-292.

Lis, E., B. Greenfield, M. Henry, J. M. Guilé, and G. Dougherty. 2007. Neuroimaging and genetics of borderline personality disorder: A review. *Journal of Psychiatry and Neuroscience* 32(3):162-173.

Sanderson, C. 2008. DBT at a glance. Handout from Behavioral Tech LLC. Available at http://behavioraltech.org/downloads/DBT_FAQ.pdf. Accessed February 8, 2008.

Schwartz, R. C. 1995. *Internal Family Systems Therapy*. New York: Guilford.

Zanarini, M. C., F. R. Frankenburg, C. J. DeLuca, J. Hennen, G. S. Khera, and J. G. Gunderson. 1998. The pain of being borderline: Dysphoric states specific to borderline personality disorder. *Harvard Review of Psychiatry* 6(4):201-207.

Zanarini, M. C., F. R. Frankenburg, J. Hennen, B. Reich, and K. R. Silk. 2006. Prediction of the 10-year course of borderline personality disorder. *American Journal of Psychiatry* 163(5):827-832.

Kiera Van Gelder, MFA, is an artist, educator, and writer diagnosed with borderline personality disorder. An international speaker and advocate, she is featured in the documentary *Back from the Edge: Living With and Recovering From Borderline Personality Disorder*. She currently lives in Massachusetts at a Buddhist meditation center. For additional information, please visit www.buddhaandborderline.com and www.kiera vangelder.com.

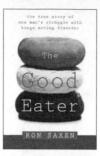

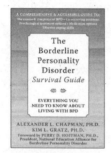

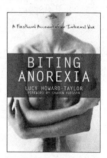